UNTOLD STORIES

Legacies of Authoritarianism among Spanish Labour Migrants in Later Life

Forgetting about Spain's civil war (1936–9) and subsequent dictatorship was long seen as a necessary safeguard for the democracy that emerged after General Francisco Franco's death in 1975. Since the early 2000s, however, public discussion of historical memory has awakened efforts to remember this past through the personal testimonies of Spaniards who experienced it firsthand.

Untold Stories expands accounts of twentieth-century Spain by presenting an ethnography of an ignored population: the impoverished men and women who fled Franco's dictatorship in the 1960s, participating in a wave of labour migration to northern Europe. Now in their eighties, they were born around the time of the civil war and came of age during its repressive aftermath before leaving Spain as young adults. The book features a community of such Spaniards, who gather regularly at a senior centre on the outskirts of Paris.

Drawing on concepts from linguistic anthropology, David Divita analyses conversational encounters recorded among the seniors to demonstrate how a turbulent past shapes mundane moments of social interaction in the present. Documenting what is said as well as what is not, Divita reveals through detailed textual analysis how silence can pervade the creation of social meanings – such as belonging, authority, and legitimacy. *Untold Stories* illuminates the impact of a harrowing historical period on some of Spain's most marginal citizens in the early years of the dictatorship.

(Anthropological Horizons)

DAVID DIVITA is a professor of Romance languages at Pomona College.

ANTHROPOLOGICAL HORIZONS

Editor: Michael Lambek, University of Toronto

This series, begun in 1991, focuses on theoretically informed ethnographic works addressing issues of mind and body, knowledge and power, equality and inequality, the individual and the collective. Interdisciplinary in its perspective, the series makes a unique contribution in several other academic disciplines: women's studies, history, philosophy, psychology, political science, and sociology.

For a list of the books published in this series see page 187.

Untold Stories

Legacies of Authoritarianism among Spanish Labour Migrants in Later Life

DAVID DIVITA

UNIVERSITY OF TORONTO PRESS
Toronto Buffalo London

© University of Toronto Press 2024
Toronto Buffalo London
utorontopress.com
Printed and bound by CPI Group (UK) Ltd, Croydon, CR0 4YY

ISBN 978-1-4875-5427-9 (cloth)   ISBN 978-1-4875-5430-9 (EPUB)
ISBN 978-1-4875-5429-3 (paper)   ISBN 978-1-4875-5431-6 (PDF)

Anthropological Horizons

___

Library and Archives Canada Cataloguing in Publication

Title: Untold stories : legacies of authoritarianism among Spanish labour
   migrants in later life / David Divita.
Names: Divita, David, author.
Series: Anthropological Horizons.
Description: Series statement: Anthropological Horizons | Includes
   bibliographical references and index.
Identifiers: Canadiana (print) 20230539777 | Canadiana (ebook) 20230539882 |
   ISBN 9781487554279 (cloth) | ISBN 9781487554293 (paper) |
   ISBN 9781487554309 (EPUB) | ISBN 9781487554316 (PDF)
Subjects: LCSH: Spaniards – France – History – 20th century. |
   LCSH: Foreign workers – France – History – 20th century. |
   LCSH: Spain – History – Civil War, 1936–1939.
Classification: LCC DC34.5.S65 D58 2024 | DDC 331.6/24604409045 – dc23

___

Cover design: John Beadle
Cover illustration: Clare Luzuriaga

We wish to acknowledge the land on which the University of Toronto Press
operates. This land is the traditional territory of the Wendat, the Anishnaabeg,
the Haudenosaunee, the Métis, and the Mississaugas of the Credit First Nation.

University of Toronto Press acknowledges the financial support of the
Government of Canada, the Canada Council for the Arts, and the Ontario Arts
Council, an agency of the Government of Ontario, for its publishing activities.

*For my parents,
Kathy and Frank*

We speak so much of memory because there is so little of it left.[1]
— Pierre Nora

To understand something human – personal or collective – it is necessary to tell a story.[2]
— José Ortega y Gasset

Contents

List of Illustrations   ix
Acknowledgments   xi
Note on Translation and Transcription   xv

Introduction   3
1 Literacy in Later Life   27
2 Nostalgia for Pueblos Past   45
3 Return Migration on Stage   67
4 History at the Museum   90
5 Search Terms and Sound Bites   114
6 Conclusion   134

Afterword   141
Notes   145
References   157
Index   175

Illustrations

2.1   The first paragraph of Elena's revised composition 62
3.1   World Book Day program (2008) 69
4.1   Brochure from *Bidonvilles: History and Representations, Seine-Saint-Denis (1954–1974)* 92
4.2   At the *Bidonvilles* exhibition 102
4.3   Marville, Rue Rolland, Saint-Denis 103
5.1   Marisol performs her rap on YouTube 130

Acknowledgments

I am above all indebted to the Spaniards who, as Spaniards do so well, absorbed me into their lives and recounted untold stories during the years this book materialized. No words of thanks could ever repay the debt of gratitude I feel for the warmth and generosity that they showed me – especially the late Araceli García Guilvard, who didn't care for pseudonyms but chose one anyway. A bilingual Spanish-French firecracker, Araceli welcomed me into her world in early 2008 and taught me more than I imagined possible over the next twelve years. This book opens and closes with her, but she left a mark on every page.

I thank the scholars in Paris who, also in 2008, helped me understand the particularities of Spanish migration to France: Bruno Tur, Natacha Lillo, and Évelyne Ribert. I am also indebted to the staff and members at the Centre des retraités espagnols à Paris (CERP), the Hogar de los españoles in Saint-Denis, and the Fédération d'associations et centres d'émigrés espagnols en France (FACEEF) – in particular, Josep, Pablo, Inma, Miros, and Gabriel. I am equally grateful to the scholars I met ten years later in Spain, especially Juan Antonio Cutillas Espinosa, Juan Manuel Hernández-Campoy, and Magdalena Díaz Hernández, who provided invaluable insight on questions that emerged during a later stage of this book's evolution.

Two colleagues deserve special mention. Hilary Parsons Dick graciously welcomed my ambush at the Sociolinguistics Symposium in Murcia in 2016 and, hours later over beer on a café terrace, planted a seed that grew into the conviction that I could write this book. Her astute feedback on multiple portions of this manuscript has helped me deepen its arguments considerably. Cécile Evers, my intellectual kin at Pomona College, has helped me grapple with the ideas, organization, and purpose of my scholarship, both within these pages and beyond. I remain grateful for the good fortune that brought us together in Claremont. I also warmly acknowledge vital conversations with other colleagues and/or collaborators in the years since I left grad school, including Kellie Gonçalves, Michele Koven, Netta Avineri, Sandro Duranti, and the late Alexandra Jaffe.

Back in the space-time of U.C. Berkeley, a trio of advisers played crucial roles in my growth as a scholar: Clare Kramsch inspired me to think expansively and defy disciplinary boundaries, always; Mairi McLaughlin introduced rigour when I needed it; and Rick Kern, tireless cheerleader, insisted that I incorporate "at least *some* Spanish" in a dissertation first conceived as a Jocks and Burnouts project *à la française*. I also spent transformative time in the classrooms of Patricia Baquedano-López, William F. Hanks, Mia Fuller, and (at Stanford) Penny Eckert. I must acknowledge as well my undergrad professors at Columbia – Hilary Sachs, Melissa Barden-Dowling, Marina van Zuylen, and the late Edward Tayler – who encouraged a first-gen kid from the Bay Area to believe he had something worthwhile to say. I have tried to emulate their humanity in my own classrooms, from the Alliance Française de Chicago in the late 1990s to Pomona today. I owe more than I can fathom to my students, who never cease to inspire me with their curiosity about, and their openness to, our woefully imperfect world. They also indulge my abiding need to perform all these years after I left the stage.

I treasure my days in Dwinelle Hall with Órlaith Creedon, whose friendship and laughter buoyed me through seven years of grad school. I also thank my Los Angeles family, who emerged later alongside this book – especially Scott Furman, Steve Futterman, Michelle Berenfeld, Nina Berenfeld, and Gina Zupsich. My chosen family elsewhere is too numerous to name, so I mention just some of those folks here: Jane Doherty, Neil Sekhri, Chris Sherrill, Mario Guariso, Brendan Scherer, Jason Mousel, Billette Heidenfeldt, Rich Cooluris, Amy Smoyer, Jaime Muleiro, Edith Muleiro, Eileen Willis, Melissa Lawton, Alex Metzger, Ed Deibert, Jason Poindexter, and the late Ed Tomasiewicz. I also acknowledge the transnational friendships of Aldino Pavone, Hélène Harder, Maite La Roda Pérez, and the late Corinne Cascadès, which evolved during this project and stimulated me during various stints abroad.

In my department at Pomona, Romance Languages and Literatures, I thank my dear friends Peggy Waller and Susana Chávez-Silverman, who comprise my professional home along with these supportive colleagues: Virginie Pouzet-Duzer, Paul Cahill, Jack Abecassis, José Cartagena-Calderón, and Grace Dávila-López. I am also grateful to Colleen Rosenfeld and Mercedes Teixido, without whom Claremont would be inconceivable.

I thank my indefatigable editor, Jodi Lewchuk, and her team of dedicated colleagues at the University of Toronto Press, especially Mary Lui. I am honoured to have this book included alongside the ethnographies that Michael Lambek has shepherded into being since 1991. Jaida Samudra, with her acute editing skills, helped me conceive a structure for this book and hone my arguments throughout. My friend Clare Doherty Luzuriaga gave her time and talent to conjure artwork for this book's cover.

I maintain everlasting appreciation for Pedro Almodóvar and Carmen Maura, who entered my life on a momentous Sunday afternoon during my senior year of high school, the first time ever that I went to a movie alone. My initial encounter with Spain, *Women on the Verge of a Nervous Breakdown* transported me to a world of colourful camp that I wanted desperately to understand. A fine, loose thread tethers that experience to this book, nearly three-and-a-half decades later.

My research for this project was generously supported by various sources of funding: the U.S. Department of Education's Foreign Language and Area Studies Fellowship, which sent me fatefully to Valencia, Spain, twenty years ago; the Dean's Normative Time Fellowship, as well as several summer research and travel grants, at U.C. Berkeley; the Harriet Barnard and Yale Griffith Fellowships at Pomona; the U.S. Department of State's Fulbright Senior Scholar Fellowship, which took me (back) to the Universidad de Murcia. Fortuitously, Mikaela Rogozen-Soltar and Deborah Boehm included me in their Wenner-Gren workshop "Going Back: Toward an Anthropology of Return" in 2019, where I was able to share and refine much of what appears in chapter 3 of this book.

A few portions of *Untold Stories* have appeared in print elsewhere. Some of the data and analysis in chapter 3 were drawn from my article "From Paris to *Pueblo* and Back: (Re)-emigration and the Modernist Chronotope in Cultural Performance," *Journal of Linguistic Anthropology* 24, no. 1 (May 2014): 1–18, https://doi.org/10.1111/jola.12034. Substantial parts of chapter 4 appeared in my article "Recalling the Bidonvilles of Paris: Historicity and Authority among Transnational Migrants in Later Life," *Journal of Linguistic Anthropology* 29, no. 1 (May 2019): 50–68, https://doi.org/10.1111/jola.12211. Some of the data in chapter 5 were included in my article "Online in Later Life: Age as a Chronological Fact and a Dynamic Social Category in an Internet Class for Retirees," *Journal of Sociolinguistics* 16, no. 5 (November 2012): 585–612, https://doi.org/10.1111/josl.12000.

Untold Stories is dedicated to my parents, Kathy and Frank Divita, who cultivated my desire to explore worlds far afield from our

California suburb and who never once wavered in their support of my obsessions: gymnastics, French, New York, and more. I am also grateful to my sister, Tina, and her husband, Jonathan Larson, for their inexhaustible generosity.

My deepest expression of gratitude, however, is reserved for Adam Romero – my heart, my home, my husband – whose intelligence and sensitivity sustain me daily. He appeared like magic during the long labour of this book, and his love gave me fortitude to finish it.

Note on Translation and Transcription

Throughout the book I have translated most of the Spanish- and French-language data into English, and I have used these translations in the body of the text. In cases where the original may provide insight into the personalities or perspectives of my research participants, or it may illuminate some ambiguity, I have included the original in quotation marks, parentheses, or end-notes.

For extended excerpts taken from recordings of conversational interactions and interviews, as well as textual artefacts collected during fieldwork, I give the original language and its English translation side by side. Following Woolard (2016), I have used distinct typefaces in bilingual excerpts to distinguish the more marked language (roman) from the less marked language (*italics*) in each stretch of discourse.

My transcriptions of data throughout the book have been rendered broadly to ensure their accessibility to a wide-ranging readership. They are not intended for fine-grained conversation analysis.

Transcription Key

[roman]	analyst's point of clarification of text
((*italics*))	paralinguistic details, such as gesture or laughter
bold	terms or phrases that are discussed in the analysis
xx	unintelligible
–	interruptions or self-initiated shifts in turns of talk
…	slight pause or brief omission

UNTOLD STORIES

Introduction

On a warm morning in April 2008, I arrived at Amalia's one-bedroom apartment in a suburb north of Paris.[1] Opening the door, she greeted me in French with a trilling *"bonjourrr"* that signalled her provenance of Spain. I responded in kind and slipped off my shoes, certain that a pair of guest slippers were waiting for me just inside. I put them on before following Amalia to the couch in her cramped living room, surrounded by artwork that she had created. "My museum," she declared with a wave of her arm, indicating shelves of terracotta sculptures, colourful doilies, and a life-size papier-mâché replica of Pepita, the protagonist in a popular novella about the Spanish Civil War. As we began chatting, Amalia poured me a glass of sherry and offered me some "little crap" (*petit caca*), referring to the assortment of nuts and pretzels that she had bought for two euros at a discount supermarket nearby.

Eager to share the latest news from the Centro – the centre for Spanish seniors where we had met – Amalia launched into a summary of information gleaned during her visit there the previous day: Amparo and Pedro won the dance contest on Sunday afternoon; Fermín was working on a moody self-portrait in the painting class; and Lina, who led the arts and crafts workshop, claimed to be clairvoyant. After finishing her update, Amalia turned to the familiar topic of her husband, Serge, who had passed away five years earlier. By then I knew that Serge was one of the most cultivated and respectful men whom Amalia had ever encountered. That afternoon she talked about how much he had loved to read.

"Look!" she demanded, reaching under a side table for a worn hardback book, a biography of one of King Louis XV's mistresses.[2] In the early 1980s, she explained, she had worked as a housekeeper for its author, the prestigious Duc de Castries, who offered her this copy in gratitude for her "impeccable service." Amalia opened the cover and showed me an inscription from the duke – "To Serge, with kind respect from the author"[3] – beaming as she awaited my reaction. I told her that I was impressed and remarked with curiosity on the dedication's addressee. Amalia replied that she had given the book to Serge as a means of sharing with him something related to her job – one of several that she held after leaving Spain in 1960. As though triggered by this recollection, she began to recount the many ways that she had capitalized on her talent as a cook and a seamstress over the course of her working life.

Amalia was born in Córdoba in 1938. When we met in 2008, shortly before her seventieth birthday, she had been living in Paris for nearly fifty years. The trajectory that she followed from Spain to France represented a well-worn path among her generational peers, the mostly rural poor who were born around the time of the Spanish Civil War (1936–9) and came of age during its repressive aftermath. Like Amalia, hundreds of thousands of Spaniards migrated to northern Europe in the 1960s, driven by a desire to escape the precarity of their lives under the authoritarian dictatorship of Francisco Franco. Sitting in her living room that afternoon, Amalia retraced her peripatetic past through a sequence of occupations. At the age of thirteen, with just four years of formal education, she became an apprentice in a workshop of seamstresses and developed skills that she would use for the rest of her life. Soon after the regime opened Spain's borders in 1959 to stimulate its stagnant economy, Amalia migrated to Paris in search of work as a domestic servant. For the next ten years she was employed as a live-in maid for a bourgeois family in one of the capital's most affluent neighbourhoods.[4] When she tired of that, she worked as a cook at a presbytery for Catholic priests near Montmartre, then as an usher at a movie theatre on the Champs-Élysées, and later as a housekeeper for an American expatriate in the suburb of Neuilly. I sipped my sherry and listened as Amalia described the various places she had worked and the people she had met, when suddenly she let out a laugh: "I could write a book!"[5]

In late 2007, when I began conducting research on the Spanish diaspora in France, the Centro Manuel Girón where I met Amalia was one of nearly a hundred such organizations throughout the country (Tur and Marmol 2009).[6] Funded almost entirely by the Spanish government, these centres aimed to foster community fellowship among its aging citizens abroad through a variety of organized activities. Like Amalia, almost all of the Centro's members had migrated from Spain as young adults in the 1960s, and they were now retired from the workforce. Their lives had thus been shaped by the extreme vicissitudes of Spain's recent past: civil war, poverty, migration, and diaspora. And yet, dominant accounts of twentieth-century Spanish history have largely overlooked their stories. In most official narratives these migrants are either mentioned briefly in relation to Spain's economic boom during the second half of the dictatorship, or they are eclipsed altogether by more visible expatriates classified as political exiles.[7] As Helen Graham (2012) has observed, the history of this labour migration "remains to be written," just as its social and political repercussions "remain to be reckoned" by Spaniards today (104).

Untold Stories: Legacies of Authoritarianism among Spanish Labour Migrants in Later Life rectifies this lapse, exploring the lives of Spanish labour migrants who have resided in France for decades. Now in their eighties, they form part of Spain's "parenthetical generation" (Richards 2013, 32): Whereas their early lives were marked by the trauma of civil war, their entry into adulthood coincided with a national project of modernization that created a consumer society and offered the possibility of migrating abroad. *Untold Stories* illuminates this precarious history by revealing its legacies in the discursive practices of the individuals who endured it. Through the detailed analysis of their conversational talk, I reveal how Spaniards now in later life espouse communicative values borne out of their experience of social institutions under dictatorship, when they were socialized to keep silent about Spain's turbulent past. The book thus shows how history lives among members of an aging population – not as a static domain of facts and figures, but in the narrative forms that animate or haunt their everyday encounters, in the stories that they recount or leave untold.

Until now, labour migrants in later life have been largely excluded from authoritative historiography, as well as current debates in Spain over how to reckon with a past they know first hand. A subtle paradox thus pulses through these pages: *Untold Stories* presents an ethnography of remembering as it documents a forgotten population. Bringing its experience to light, the book demonstrates how the historical conditions in which individuals come of age inform the communicative practices that they carry across the life course, even across national borders. In the case of twentieth-century Spain, the pervasive repercussions of authoritarianism may be traced in the silences that continue to shape the lives of those born during the war or shortly thereafter – the slowly diminishing generation of Spaniards represented by the people who appear in these chapters.

Aging and Memory in Diaspora

The Spaniards I encountered in Paris embody a demographic trend that has become a "burning topic" among sociologists, historians, anthropologists, and gerontologists in Western Europe: individuals who are entering old age far away from their places of origin (Albert, Ferring, and Lang 2016, 53). As labour migrants from the 1960s and 1970s have reached retirement – not only in France but elsewhere in Europe – scholarship has emerged across disciplines to investigate the experience of aging in settings of migration and diaspora.[8] Much of the research to date has relied on quantitative methods to illuminate the relationships among age, ethnicity, and vulnerability in various countries of residence, identifying the "stressors" that older migrants may face, such as poor health care and housing conditions, along with the risk of social isolation (Horn and Schweppe 2017). Alongside this body of scholarship, however, a more sanguine strand of thinking has emerged around the concept of "transnational aging" – that is, the "process of organizing, shaping, and coping with life in old age in contexts which are no longer limited to a single nation state" or homeland (Horn, Schweppe, and Um 2013, 7). Research from this perspective has focused less on the tribulations of aging migrants than on the many strategies that they use to maintain vital social and economic connections unfettered by distance or borders. To borrow Peggy Levitt and Nina Glick Schiller's (2004) terminology, immigrants aging in host societies might be understood to practise "ways of being" and "ways of belonging" that are shaped by their experience of long-term displacement as well as their position in the life course. Although the practices and relationships that constitute their everyday lives ("ways of being") become restricted as they age, this does not necessarily diminish the affective and national attachments ("ways of belonging") that they have nourished over time.[9]

Barbara Myerhoff's (1978) seminal work on elderly Jewish immigrants to the United States illustrated such complexities long before the concept of transnationalism took hold of the social-scientific imagination (see Vertovec 2009). Her research participants, members of a Jewish senior centre in Los Angeles, engaged regularly in social practices that secured their sense of belonging to a distant homeland, referring with nostalgia to their childhood *shtetls* and the Yiddishkeit that characterized them (284). They also told numerous stories about the past to make sense of the fraught trajectories that had brought them from eastern Europe to California, assembling "charged pieces of personal history" into intelligible narrative forms (108). As Myerhoff (1978) observed, their experience of displacement amplified the desire for a sense of personal coherence often associated with individuals in later life.[10] Although her research participants had not experienced the Holocaust directly, having migrated before its ravages were inflicted, their everyday interactions were very much informed by that horror and its traumatic aftermath. Myerhoff (1984) documented the multiple modes of remembering – not only biographical narratives but also songs, dances, and gestures – through which the seniors assimilated their painful past and fortified feelings of community.

Untold Stories expands the insightful body of scholarship that Myerhoff represents, bringing a discourse-analytic approach to the study of later life in diaspora. The case of twentieth-century Spain, which spans the violent authoritarianism of the regime to the volte-face of democratic transition, offers a rich context for investigating the ways that social and political circumstances shape what and how a community remembers. In the following pages I reveal how the past circulates in mundane moments of social interaction, spotlighting a variety of discursive phenomena in my analysis: narratives governed by long-standing values of revelation or omission; the creation and circulation of texts of various kinds that evoke an idyllic, pre-migratory past; and ideologies about literacy shaped by the experience of social institutions, such as primary school, under dictatorship.[11]

As Paul Connerton (1989) has written, totalitarian regimes attempt to "enslave" their subjects by effacing or revising any memories of the past (14). Franco's Nationalists were no exception, explaining their violent tactics during the war and afterwards as an inevitable crusade against communism and immorality (see Preston 2020, among others). Among Spaniards who fled the dictatorship as young adults in the 1960s, acts of reminiscence in later life reflect the communicative values that they absorbed decades earlier under the repressive conditions of authoritarianism. Throughout the book I illuminate the discursive legacies of political violence by drawing on the imbricated concepts of historicity, chronotope, and silence. Bringing a range of oral and written texts into my analytical purview, I show how aging members of a diasporic community make sense of their place in a life course long shaped by historical contingencies and transnational displacement.

Historicity, Chronotope, and Silence

Anthropological approaches to historical meaning generally focus on the many ways that the past, or ideas about the past, affect social actors in the present. This research aims not to determine what history is but rather to make sense of how it works. Assuming that representations of the past are shaped by personal and political interests in the here and now, scholars have emphasized a conceptual distinction between history and historicity. While history encompasses factual claims about *what happened*, historicity references culturally situated *perceptions* of the past and notions about how to represent it (Cole 2001; Divita 2019; Hirsch and Stewart 2005; Stewart 2016; Wirtz 2016).[12]

Historicity is similar to memory as personal recollection, but the two are not synonymous. That is, most memories of the past might be considered forms of historicity, but not all historicities are forms of memory, given that some of them envelop periods of time broader than that of an individual lifespan. Recent scholarship has illuminated in provocative ways how individuals create historicities given both their present-tense dispositions and orientations towards the future, as well as models for engaging with the past that are available in a particular setting (Stewart 2016, 80).[13] Models of historicity constitute ways of knowing (about) the past that social actors acquire over time as they participate in a range of socio-cultural milieus. As I show throughout this book, such models shape how a community recalls the experience it has shared through the moral frameworks that they entail. Among the Spaniards featured here, for example, nostalgic recollection serves as a valued mode of historicity in discourse designed for the public sphere. Representing past experience through configurations of time and place – chronotopes – that are steeped in sentimentality, the seniors legitimize their claims of belonging to Spain.

First articulated by the literary theorist Mikhail Bakhtin (1981), chronotopes describe the representational ground of time, space, and personhood that governs literary discourse. Defining the neologism simply as "time space," he gave name to "the intrinsic connectedness of temporal and spatial relationships" without which narrative cannot exist (84). Bakhtin analysed a range of literary genres, such as the adventure tale and the romance, to reveal the fundamental purchase of his concept: chronotopes do not privilege time over space, or vice versa, but rather incorporate both into an inseparable whole that provides a frame for novelistic representation. Importantly, he emphasized the "complex interrelationships" through which chronotopes resonate with meaning (252) – that is, through the tension between the time-space of the textual world and that of the listener or reader. It is this final point that most clearly invites consideration of the chronotope, as Bakhtin writes, "in other areas of culture" (84).

Scholars from across disciplines have taken up the concept, demonstrating its use for making sense of various texts and how they function "as X-rays of the forces at work in the culture system from which they spring" (Bakhtin 425–6). Among socio-cultural linguists and linguistic anthropologists, the chronotope has proven fruitful for investigating how social actors create and interpret meaning in everyday interaction through discursive invocations of time and place.[14] The concept is especially germane to the analysis of past recollection, given that acts of remembering draw on spatio-temporal frames in the form of *cultural* chronotopes (the "war" or the "pueblo," for example), as well as in the form of *event* chronotopes – that is, the here and now of an interaction (Agha 2007; see also Perrino 2011).[15] When speakers assemble temporal and spatial points of reference to conjure intelligible realms from before, they relativize and inflect the act of communication itself. As Trouillot (2015) writes, "The past does not exist independently from the present. Indeed, the past is only past because there is a present, just as I can point to something *over there* because I am *here*" (15; italics in the original). Discursive activity that concerns the past thus becomes meaningful through a calibration of chronotopes, as other times and spaces ("over there") are brought to bear on real-time social engagement ("here"). Among Spaniards at the Centro, for example, invocations of one's pre-migratory pueblo often served as chronotopic shorthand for an anodyne representation of rural life in Spain, contrasting sharply with the urban frenzy of the French capital that characterized their present lives.

Untold Stories expands a lively body of linguistic anthropological scholarship that has drawn on the chronotope to analyse semiotic activity in situations of migration and diaspora.[16] Illustrating Bakhtin's understanding of the dialogical nature of chronotopic meaning-making, this research has shown how individuals bring disparate time-spaces into relation with one another to "make sense of and link their lives to global processes" (Dick 2018, 48) – a finding that I highlight here while also addressing the particularities of later life. In a variety of settings, participants at the Centro draw from a shared repertoire of space-time configurations to assimilate not only their experience of migration but also the social position that they occupy as seniors. Such semiotic processes shape their sense of being in relation to time and, thus, to the ongoing project of aging with which they reckon in the present. Evoking acceptable chronotopes – and, crucially, avoiding those that are taboo – they enact ideological mechanisms of differentiation among those who are affiliated with particular historicities within and across generational lines, as well as national borders (see Gal and Irvine 2019). The animation or evasion of such figures among Spaniards in later life points to popular perceptions of moral personhood – that is, perceptions of how people and the world are, as well as how they should be – that have endured since the post-war period (see Dick 2018; Lambek 2010; Robbins 2021).

Given the wide swath of temporal and spatial coordinates within their retrospective gaze, my older research participants engaged avidly in chronotopic meaning-making, activating frameworks of moral evaluation as well as feelings from – and for – the past. As linguistic anthropologists have observed, chronotopic calibration is both referential and affective. While forging relationships among temporal domains, it shapes "our *experience* and thus subjective *feel* for history and place" in the present (Wirtz 2016, 344; italics in the original).[17] Among the seniors, acts of remembering were often accompanied by bald expressions of emotion, as illustrated by the culminating moment in this chapter's opening vignette. The outburst of laughter that precedes Amalia's exclamation – "I could write a book!" – points to a fusion of disparate spatio-temporal realms: the here and now of our interaction, the past of her personal memory, and the future of her speculative remark. It also caps a sequence of recollections mediated by narrative talk.

Narrative in various forms has come to be understood as interactional performance that involves in-the-moment relationships among "narrators, events, speech communities, and cultural contexts" (De Fina and Georgakopoulou 2012, 61).[18] Whether they be monologic turns or conversational interactions, narratives situate social actors in space and time, serving as the discursive fabric through which historicities and chronotopes materialize. Although narratives often concern the past, they necessarily inform social arrangements in the present, providing a collectivity with "textual resources" for the ways of remembering that constitute it (Wertsch 2008, 122; see also Wertsch 2002; French 2012). Narrative thus functions as the linchpin between an individual and the various communities to which she claims membership – a phenomenon that has been well illustrated in studies of migration (Das 2016; De Fina and Tseng 2017; Dick 2018; Piazza 2019). Moreover, as an analytical construct in this ethnography of remembering, narrative obligates a crucial consideration: the silenced, the forgotten, or the otherwise untold.

For the generation of Spaniards featured in this book, there is a tacit and abiding agreement that the most painful aspects of their past – namely, the war and its repressive aftermath – must remain unspoken. As I reveal through the textual analysis of their everyday encounters, such silence operates as an underlying condition of communicative interaction, far more reflexive among my research participants than reflected upon.[19] While other scholars of language have addressed silence as a topical cue in conversational talk (Gumperz 1982; Jaworski 1997; Tannen and Saville-Troike 1985) or a polysemous feature of interactive discourse (Basso 1970), I show how it serves as a conduit of memory and belonging for those whom narrative fails in the wake of trauma (see Kidron 2009). The enduring predisposition to silence among the Spaniards who appear in these pages, almost all of whom migrated from Spain decades ago, attests to the pernicious legacies of a protracted authoritarian regime. Long dislocated from their homeland, they nevertheless uphold communicative values acquired in the early years of the dictatorship and thus preserve indelible yet troubled ties to their generational peers who remained in Spain.

In my examination of the unspoken, I build on insights that Elinor Ochs and Lisa Capps (2001) first articulated in their influential book on conversational storytelling over twenty years ago. After a lengthy discussion of the various dimensions that shape narrative discourse, such as tellability and moral stance, the scholars address "untold stories" in a final chapter, beckoning further exploration of the concept that only partially materialized in subsequent research (252).[20] Drawing on a variety of interactional examples, Ochs and Capps illustrate the psychological, social, and cultural conditions that militate against narrative expression, causing social actors to sublimate the past and preventing significant experiences from becoming audible. I show in similar ways how untold stories shape the content and form of narrative discourse, given enduring notions about what is and is not considered appropriate to discuss. However, I also reveal how the unspoken pervades the creation of social meanings – such as belonging, authority, and legitimacy – and undergirds ideological frameworks for the evaluation of personhood. Heeding what storytellers recount as well as what they omit, I unearth the moral entailments of informal talk that are vital to the sustenance of collectivities at various scales, from a transnational senior centre to a generational cohort (see Hill 1995; Keane 2011; Lambek 2010).

Much of the data presented in these pages was culled from audio recordings of quotidian conversation, both in the Centro's organized spaces and outside them. Alongside my participants' personal recollections, however, I include artefacts that I collected in the field – texts of various kinds that they created, performed, or circulated. My discursive-analytic approach to these poems, compositions, theatrical sketches, and songs reveals how the past circulates in practices of meaning-making that are not necessarily historical in the manner of written (or spoken) accounts of *what happened*, often considered the gold standard of historiography (see Shaw 2002, 4). Instead,

I highlight the temporal and spatial signals that shape conversational encounters, showing the mundane ways that diasporic subjects conjure realms from before to make sense of the "unresolved and still evolving contemporaneity" of their present (Bakhtin 1981, 252). Attending to what is said as well as what is not, I expose pervasive norms among the seniors about how the past shapes and takes shape within narrative discourse, while tracing those norms back to the historical conditions of their emergence. My analysis thus sheds unprecedented light on the communicative practices shared by the last generation of Spaniards for whom a contested history remains within reach of living memory today.

A Brief History of Twentieth-Century Spain

In Spain the term "historical memory" (*memoria histórica*) has become commonplace in political discourse, although it remains something of a floating signifier.[21] The historian Helen Graham (2012) has defined it broadly as a "figure of speech" that references "why, in what context, and with what stakes, certain moments in the past are spoken about in the present" (133). Current debates about the concept encompass a range of conflicting positions, from disparate accounts of the historical record to nuanced claims about its interpretation. As Spaniards have grappled with how to address the legacies of war and Franco's dictatorship, there is scant consensus on what those legacies are or whether discussion is worth having in the first place. In these current disputes over memory, lines are often drawn over which people, groups, or institutions may speak with authority about the past, and to what political ends (see Faber 2018).

Despite a surge of interest in capturing testimonies of personal experience, which began in the late 1990s, labour migrants have been largely ignored by popular and scholarly participants in these debates (Ferrándiz 2008; Labanyi 2008, 2010).[22] Aiming to redress this omission, I include in this introduction a detailed overview of the events and circumstances that have shaped their lives – an overview of what has conventionally been understood as "history." As Michael Richards (2013) has observed, "without exploration of Spain's war and its polarized aftermath it is impossible to explain post-war memories" (6). Thus, I turn to the work of social historians of twentieth-century Spain to lay out the large-scale conditions in which my informants have forged biographical trajectories and upon which they may reflect in the present. Incorporating this historical scholarship into my anthropological project provides a way to make sense of what and how my research participants remember today. Moreover, it enables me to generalize the observations that I make about historical subjectivity and generational experience through my intervention into a relatively small ethnographic field.

What I present is a version of history from the perspective of Spain's labour migrants, including the key events and processes that have shaped the communicative values that they now uphold in later life. This overview thus begins with the period of turmoil and transformation into which my research participants were born: civil war and the imposition of military dictatorship.

1936–59: From Civil War to the End of Autarky

Spain's civil war began in 1936 after a military coup led by General Francisco Franco had failed to overthrow leaders of the democratic Second Republic, whose efforts to modernize the country through social reform were seen by conservatives as a threat to Spain's cultural and religious traditions. The ensuing conflict pitted Franco's Nationalist coalition – including monarchists, religious conservatives, and the Falange Española, a fascist political party – against Republicans, a loose assembly of left-leaning factions aligned with the liberal government that was fighting to hold onto power. For Spaniards on both sides of the struggle, as well as the many citizens who claimed no political affiliation at all, the war marked a tumultuous time during which opponents of Franco's forces were faced with organized forms of terror: persecution, imprisonment, and execution. Although reports on the number of casualties vary, the historian Paul Preston (2012) provides a chilling tally in his prologue to *The Spanish Holocaust*, in which he estimates that approximately 200,000 soldiers were killed in combat overall, and another 200,000 civilians were executed. After the war ended in 1939, some 20,000 Republican sympathizers were shot, and tens of thousands more died in concentration camps and prisons.[23]

After the Nationalist takeover in 1939 the ideological apparatus of Franco's regime soon became known as National Catholicism (nacionalcatolicismo), reflecting the intense pervasion of the Catholic Church into all aspects of social and political life during the first two decades of the dictatorship. As the historian Julián Casanova (2010) remarks, "in no other authoritarian regime in the twentieth century did the Church assume such political responsibility and play such a central role in policing the country's citizens as Spain" (108). The Francoist state essentially "outsourced" many of its primary functions, such as the provision of education, to strict religious authorities (Encarnación 2014, 206). In the early post-war years, then, the regime exerted control over Spanish society by conflating notions of national loyalty with moral rectitude, squelching any impulse to resistance through the looming threat of visible manifestations of power, such as extrajudicial executions.

The anguish inflicted by the war and these phenomena left indelible traces in the lives of Spaniards born during this stretch of time. As my conversations with seniors attest, the conflict was not a distant political event but rather a phenomenological reality that affected them "as bodily and psychological hardship, hunger and illness, and loss" (Richards 2010, 128). During the first years of dictatorship the elders surrounding these youth preferred not to talk about the war and its painful consequences, enacting a practice of keeping silent about the past that had come to govern all sectors of Spanish society. As the anthropologist David Kneas (2018) has written, such reticence epitomizes the experience of many individuals in the aftermath of traumatic events, as they attempt to formulate fragile subjectivities "out of the contested fabric of prior violence" and the uncertain "peace of the present" (753; see also Coutin 2016).

During this first stretch of the post-war period, Franco's regime insisted on political and economic autarky to ensure Spain's freedom from foreign influences. Such a resolute turning inward, coupled with the rapid adaptation of Spanish society to the ways of life under dictatorship, was meant to preclude the possibility of ideological contamination from outside. It also enabled Franco to present a "gentler" face to his people, no longer the "enforcer of the law, but … a leader who inaugurated public projects and rewarded the hard work of Spaniards" (Casanova 2010, 107). This shift in strategies of self-presentation may go some way towards explaining positive representations of Franco's legacy today. Nevertheless, the regime's isolationist policies caused nearly twenty years of economic stagnation, while post-war economies elsewhere in Europe experienced an unprecedented boom. More concerned with maintaining docile citizens than anything else, Franco did little to address the needs of impoverished Spaniards. Denied adequate and sustained schooling, they scrambled for work in early adolescence without any chance of engineering social or economic mobility – a hardship shared by almost everyone I encountered at the Centro. As Spain's "economic winter" extended well into the 1950s, the Nationalist ideal of autonomy gradually dissolved, and the regime began to realize that the outside world had left it far behind (Grugel and Rees 1997). The time for modernization had come.

1959–75: From Migration to the Death of Franco

In 1959, Franco's government implemented a National Economic Stabilization Plan to prevent a socio-economic meltdown, introducing forms of industrial development in Spain that had benefited its European counterparts in the years following the Second World War: an open market; a focus on services, such as banking and tourism; and an open-border policy. The regime thus officially sanctioned transnational migration for the first time, triggering a wave of departures by Spaniards searching for a way out of poverty. According to Spain's National Institute of Emigration, nearly 1.8 million Spaniards left the country between 1959 and 1973, and 700,000 of them never returned (Vincent 2007, 183).[24]

Most of these migrants headed to developed countries in the north, such as France, Germany, and Switzerland, where their labour was needed to maintain the rapid economic growth that had begun there in the early 1950s. For my research participants, Paris and its environs served as an especially attractive destination because of the ease with which work could be found in the automotive and construction industries (for men) and domestic service (for women). Earlier waves of Spanish migration – at the turn of the twentieth century and, again, during the civil war – had created an extensive network of Spanish expatriates in and around the French capital, a demographic reality reflected in the many local ethnic associations that had been created to serve them. Like their predecessors, the majority of "third-wave" Spanish migrants after 1959 came from rural towns and had little formal education. Nevertheless, once they began working in France, they were able to save large sums of money due to the discrepancy in wages relative to those in Spain. This improved financial situation enabled them to make annual return visits to their pueblos, where they were often admired for the social and economic capital that they seemed to have accrued abroad. The impression of success belied their vulnerability in Paris, however; they struggled to adapt to an unfamiliar culture and to communicate in a second language, working extensive hours for employers who were sometimes eager to exploit their inexpensive labour.

Throughout the 1960s, French and Spanish authorities emphasized the temporariness of labour migration – a strategy that benefited both sending and receiving societies. The rapid economic growth that occurred during France's so-called Trente glorieuses (Glorious Thirty), from 1945 to 1975, had created a temporary need for manual workers that its own citizens could not fulfil; the country thus welcomed foreign workers until a sharp economic downturn in the mid-1970s. For Spain, the mentality of impermanence among its expatriate citizens meant continued financial and personal investments in their home country. Indeed, many Spanish migrants opened savings accounts, sent remittances, and often bought apartments in their pueblos after just three or four years of working in France. Such was the case among most of the Spaniards whom I encountered at the Centro. Living abroad, they found themselves "with their asses between two seats" (Oso Casas 2004, 115), encouraged by the French administration to prolong their stay indefinitely, while the regime in Spain ensured that they maintain ties to the homeland. The temporariness of their migratory project meant that Spaniards in France were unlikely to generate much affinity for their new surroundings. In most cases they had minimal social contact with French people and, at least in their initial years abroad, they learned to speak just enough French to navigate mundane interactions, but little more.

Up until the early 1970s, Spanish migrants actively participated in Spain's modernization, pumping its economy with money sent back from abroad. The rapid development caused by these financial infusions became known in Spain as the *milagro español* (Spanish miracle), which lasted for over a decade before stopping short due to an international oil crisis in 1973. By that time, the boom had introduced new practices of consumption into the lives of those living across all sectors of Spanish society, upsetting the Church's stranglehold on the shape of everyday life. The geographical mobility that drove this development – from pueblo to city in Spain, and from Spain to countries in northern Europe – made it impossible for the regime to continue enforcing its rigid principles of conduct. The dramatic social change experienced by those who remained in Spain created a rupture between two different ways of life under dictatorship, enabling them to distance themselves further from painful aspects of the past. The stark contrast between the suffering of the early post-war years and the consumerism of the 1960s spurred a deferral of any form of historical reckoning. Moreover, on a personal level there remained "good psychological reasons for trying to forget" the brutality of war and its aftermath (Richards 2006, 88). And yet, the government remained dictatorial. The Law of Political Responsibilities, for example, which had been created by Franco in the final months of the war to legalize various forms of cultural and political control, was repealed in 1945. Cases against citizens remained in process, however, until 1966, thereby sustaining "repressive effects" throughout Spanish society that lasted until Franco's death nearly a decade later (Graham 2005, 134).

As Spain became less dependent on its migrants abroad to fend off financial collapse, it began to forget about them (Oso Casas 2004, 96).

The move by Spanish politicians and economists to frame this period of time as a miracle effectively erased the nature of its cause, at least in part, by mortal – and migrant – agents. Meanwhile, for Spaniards who remained in France, their migration story was absorbed into a dominant narrative of French citizenship as a project of assimilation into the body politic. Nevertheless, as Europe suffered from the oil crisis and the economic slump that it precipitated, the French parliament created a law in 1974 that effectively closed its borders. To encourage the departure of those who had arrived during the preceding decade, it offered ten thousand francs to anyone who would willingly return to their country of origin. In the following year Franco died. Many Spanish migrants took advantage of these circumstances to realize the dream of return that had thus far sustained them in France. In 1968 the French census reported that 607,000 Spaniards were living in France, constituting 25 per cent of the total foreign-born population at the time. This figure was cut nearly in half over the next fourteen years; by 1982, only 321,000 Spaniards remained, approximately 9 per cent of France's total foreign residents (Lillo 2007, 17).

1975–2007: From the Pact of Forgetting to the Law of Historical Memory

After Franco's death in 1975, Spain's transition to democracy found its ballast in an amnesty law that enshrined what became popularly known as the *pacto del olvido* (pact of forgetting), a blanket pardon of any illegal acts or human rights violations, on either side, in the interest of protecting the fledgling democratic state. The pact came to be seen as a necessary component of Spain's democratic transition and eager pursuit of "outrageous hypermodernity," obscuring the avid promotion of forgetting by former members of the Francoist state (Labanyi 2007, 95). Nevertheless, the investment in amnesty on both sides effectively ensured a complicit oblivion, foreclosing all forms of transitional justice, such as truth commissions and human rights prosecutions, like those later generated by civil and judicial bodies in Argentina and Chile. As Omar Encarnación (2014) writes, the pact of forgetting "succeeded in turning the past into a taboo among ordinary Spaniards, by making discussions of the violence of the Civil War ... inappropriate and unwelcome in almost any social context" (3). For those who had come of age during the war's repressive aftermath, such as the Spaniards who populate these pages, this political manoeuvre only reinforced their socialization into the discursive practice of remaining silent about the past.[25] And yet, Spain's past was not as easily forgotten as the pact's proponents desired. Instead, it remained the "very 'ghost' or driving force that determined the emphasis on consensus politics in Spain," even long after the transition (Ribeiro de Menezes 2010, 11). In other words, the new democracy was haunted by the spectre of what amnesty had absolved. The absence of any reckoning in the wake of Franco's death fed multiple and conflicting interpretations of the historical record, all of which were sublimated into silence by the state so that Spain could look with confidence towards the future.

It was not until 1999, with the publication of *Víctimas de la guerra civil* (Victims of the civil war), a volume of essays edited by the historian Santos Juliá Díaz, that public talk about Spain's past became framed, first and foremost, in terms of victimhood as opposed to fraternal conflict (Labanyi 2008).[26] This mode of recollection drove grassroots efforts to bring to light the traumas inflicted by the Franco regime. Most notably, the Association for the Recovery of Historical Memory (Asociación para la recuperación de la memoria histórica), or ARMH, has since its inception in 2000 lobbied for the exhumation and identification of remains found in mass graves created by Francoist forces throughout Spain during the war and the ensuing years of terror (Ferrándiz 2008, 2013, 2014, 2018; Rubin 2018, 2020). The ARMH formed part of a burgeoning number of citizen groups intent on illuminating all aspects of the war and its painful consequences – an intergenerational movement driven largely by the progeny of those who had experienced these traumatic phenomena directly, such as my research participants in France and their generational peers in Spain (see Faber 2018; Golob 2008; Labanyi 2007). These civilian movements towards restitution in the early 2000s eventually sparked legislative action. Between 2005 and 2007 the social democratic party then in power drafted three statutes that officially acknowledged victims of the dictatorship for the first time in Spain's history: the 2005 Law of Children of the War, the 2006 Statute of Spanish Citizenry Abroad, and the 2007 Law of Historical Memory.[27] Put forth thirty years after Franco's death, these statutes, and the historical reckoning they were meant to compel, stoked widespread debate. For some critics on the left, they were perceived as toothless symbolism, while some on the right saw them as an unnecessary and politicized reopening of wounds.[28]

Of the three, the 2006 Statute of Spanish Citizenry Abroad most directly concerns the population featured in this book. Among other provisions, it made clear the Spanish government's intention to promote the well-being of its older citizens abroad – migrants who had left Spain for whatever reason – through guaranteed health care, social security, and financial assistance (Boletín Oficial del Estado 2006). Although the law did not introduce any new rights or benefits, it marked the state's first explicit recognition of a cause-and-effect relationship between the dictatorship and economic migration. It thus upset an established hierarchy by which exile, primarily perceived as political, overshadowed labour migration in dominant narratives about recent Spanish history. Indeed, previous efforts at addressing the "institutionalized amnesia" enshrined in the pact of forgetting had focused almost exclusively on recording accounts of and by the political refugees who had fled Spain during the war or shortly thereafter (Davis 2005, 863). With the statute from 2006, however, the "millions of anonymous emigrants" who left Spain for economic reasons in the 1960s had finally and officially been acknowledged by the state (Tur 2015, 71; see also Chaput 2015).

The 2006 statute also addresses the vast network of Spanish cultural associations abroad, supporting their creation and maintenance through particular attention to the services that they provide (Boletín Oficial del Estado 2006, 44160).[29] Such associations, which first became popular at the time my research participants arrived in Paris, recall the mutual-aid societies established in 1920s France to respond to a wave of Spanish migration between the two world wars. In the 1960s these sites responded to the uncertainty of what it meant to be a Spaniard in diaspora during a time of radical social and political transformation in Spain. Today they function as community centres where older participants can congregate and speak Spanish with their peers. They often contain a bar or restaurant, facilitate cultural events and weekly activities, such as Spanish language or dance lessons, and serve as community resources, where members can help one another with the administrative tasks associated with living transnationally.

When they were formed more than fifty years ago, such centres both fed and deferred the desire to return permanently to Spain. Since that time they have helped Spaniards maintain social and symbolic ties to their place of origin, whether national or regional, while remaining abroad. Similar to the associations featured in Paul Silverstein's (2004) work on Algerians in France, these Spanish institutions have "underwri[tten] forms of group belonging at a distance," in large part by facilitating the re-creation of popular cultural phenomena, such as music and food (11). Patrons of the Centro's café, for example, can pay a few euros for a plate of serrano ham and a Spanish beer in a room decorated with red-and-yellow bunting that evokes the national flag. Such centres thus provide their members a sense of belonging through ethnic and aged fellowship, though in some cases their funding has become less reliable given its dependence on a politically unstable Spanish administration.[30]

Ethnographic Research at the Centro

The Centro Manuel Girón, a modest, two-storey brick building, sits in a suburban neighbourhood of Paris once called la Petite Espagne (Little Spain) for the wave of Spaniards who settled there in the 1920s. Established in 2003 with funds largely supplied by Spain's Ministry of Labour and Social Affairs, the Centro, as its members refer to it, serves a sizeable population of Spanish migrants who arrived in the 1960s and are now retired from the workforce.[31] According to a report from the Federation of Associations and Centres for Spanish Emigrants in France, the organization that oversaw its construction, aging Spaniards in France find themselves at risk of social and economic exclusion (Martínez Veiga 2000, 4). The Centro aims to redress these precarious circumstances, admitting anyone who meets the following three criteria: they must be at least sixty years old, Spanish citizens, and legal residents of France.

When I began conducting fieldwork at the Centro in late 2007, it had a roster of over two thousand registered members, of which approximately one-quarter had visited in the previous twelve months. They hailed from various regions in Spain, although a majority came from pueblos in the central and southern parts of the peninsula: Andalucía, Extremadura, and Castilla la Nueva.[32] Occasional light-hearted jokes based on regional stereotypes revealed members' underlying affinities. Nevertheless, the Centro's mobilization of generic forms of Spanish culture, such as flamenco and football, muted possible tensions arising from territorial differences and created a prevailing sense of national belonging.[33] As Susan Gal and Judith Irvine (2019) have observed, "when people move to diasporan locales, their changed vantage point is likely to reduce the salience of internal variation" with regard to linguistic and cultural differences (229). When I asked Elena, a seventy-six-year-old woman from Santander, why she winced upon hearing French at the Centro, she exclaimed, "Because here *we're in Spain!*"[34]

From 2007 throughout 2008, and again in 2013, I attended the Centro on a daily basis, participating alongside its members in a variety of activities: theatre, internet, and Spanish literacy courses; an arts and crafts workshop; cultural excursions to museums in and near Paris; and weekly dances on Sunday afternoons. I also spent hours in the Centro's café, chatting with people over coffee or beer about the trajectories that had brought them to France. Before long I came to recognize the Centro's core members – approximately eighty people who attended multiple days a week, either to take part in its activities or to fraternize in its common spaces. I spent time with some of them outside the Centro as well, eating lunch or watching television in their homes or accompanying them on errands around the city.

Participation at the Centro was pointedly gendered, reflecting the traditional socio-cultural milieus in which its members had come of age in post-war Spain. Most men preferred to gather independently in the café, playing cards and socializing, while women often took part in scheduled events and classes (cf. Robbins 2021). Over time I came to focus my ethnographic attention on settings of collaborative recreation that touched on historical matters, such as museum visits, or that stimulated narratives about the past, such as the literacy workshop. Because women were more likely than men to participate in such organized activities, the people who appear in the following pages are predominantly female.[35] During my time in the field I came to know twenty-five of these women closely, many of whom participated in more than one workshop on a weekly basis. Whereas their male counterparts tended to refrain from extended discussion about their personal experience, these women seemed to appreciate my curiosity about their lives, responding to it more often than not by engaging in spirited conversation. Many of them began with frank inquiries about my age, associating me with offspring upon hearing my response. (I had just turned thirty-five when I began conducting fieldwork, while they ranged in age from sixty-four to seventy-eight.) Moreover, they were accustomed to interacting with people like me at the Centro, where two of its main staff members were also younger and male: Pablo, the twenty-eight-year-old theatre and language instructor from Mexico City; and Josep, the thirty-eight-year-old activities director from Barcelona. These men appear throughout this book, underscoring the rich historicities that emerge in conversations among mixed-aged participants.

My educational background also reinforced a significant axis of distinction between me and my research participants. Many of the seniors had a limited amount of formal schooling and actively sought to improve basic literacy skills, as I discuss in detail in chapter 1. In our initial interactions the mention of my affiliation with an American university, along with a description of my objectives, elicited little more than blank stares from my interlocutors – which was not surprising given their unfamiliarity with the exigencies of higher education. They associated my interest in the Centro in broad terms with the future production of a book, affiliating me with another scholar, Natacha Lillo, who had published *La Petite Espagne* in 2004, or with the smattering of news reporters who had visited the Centro in the years since it had opened. Such perceptions conferred authority on my presence in the field; they also pointed to the local value of written artefacts, such as the weathered book that Amalia brandished while we drank sherry in her apartment, integral to practices of remembering among the seniors. When I handed out and explained the written consent forms required by my university's institutional review board, for example, many agreed enthusiastically to sign them, excited by the prospect of taking copies home as "souvenirs" (*recuerdos*) of my time at the Centro.[36]

Revelations of my place of origin were most often met with amicable questions about life in California that served as a gateway to informal conversation. More than anything else, though, my pronunciation of Spanish signalled my status as foreign, and it sometimes triggered code switches into French by those who assumed that I felt more comfortable in that language. For the most part, I followed the linguistic lead of my interlocutors, using whichever code they seemed to prefer given that I am equally proficient in both. Almost all of the women opted for Spanish, the default language of social interaction at the Centro. A few of them, though, had developed a predisposition towards French, either because, like Amalia, they had married Frenchmen, or, in one case, the woman had arrived in France as the child of political exiles.[37] Nevertheless, having lived and worked in France for forty years at the time I met them, everyone demonstrated at least colloquial proficiency in the language and used it with some regularity in their daily lives. They often accommodated French-speaking visitors to the Centro, including their grandchildren or neighbours, and some of them code-switched into French with regularity in conversational exchanges that were otherwise conducted in Spanish. In the textual data that appear throughout *Untold Stories* I have attempted to illustrate the rich multilingualism that characterized their experience by including the original languages – Spanish or French – alongside English translations.

Life Stories

The bulk of my fieldwork entailed participant observation, which I documented in eight hundred pages of field notes, and extensive audio recordings of conversational interaction, over two hundred hours of which I transcribed and analysed. In addition, I conducted life-story interviews with my core group of consultants, a common practice among ethnographers of older populations (see Danely 2014; Degnen 2012; Hazan 1980; Myerhoff 1978; among others). These comprised loosely structured, informal conversations, sometimes occurring over the course of several meetings, in which I asked seniors to tell me about the primary events, experiences, and turning points of their lives (see McAdams 2001). Given the vital role of storytelling among those in later life, most of the seniors welcomed these encounters as opportunities for personal reflection – what Cathrine Degnen (2012) has referred to as "memory talk." Much like Barbara Myerhoff's (1978) research participants in southern California, Spaniards at the Centro "narrated themselves perpetually," keeping journals, writing poems, and recounting their experience to willing interlocutors (33). My life-story interviews thus proved instructive for their referential content as well as their discursive form.[38] Not only did these conversations help me discern meaningful commonalities across a heterogeneous corpus of biographical narratives, but they also illuminated the communicative values that governed talk about the past among the seniors. As Paul Connerton (1989) has written, a life story "is part of an interconnecting set of narratives; it is embedded in the story of those groups from which individuals derive their identity" (21).[39] Life-story interviews thus helped illuminate how my research participants made sense of their affiliation with social collectivities formed in relation to time, from the Centro to the Spanish diaspora to a broader generational cohort.[40]

"Later Life"

The term "later life," which I use throughout this book, does not denote a fixed analytical category but rather a temporal envelope that begins at the end of one's working years; in Spain and France this moment generally falls between the ages of sixty-two and sixty-seven.[41] Popular Western notions about this stage of life, epitomized by Peter Laslett's (1991) concept of the "third age," include the personal enrichment that it promises through an individual's renewed participation in social and creative activity. Drawing on the psychologist Bernice Neugarten's (1974) differentiation of the "young-old" from the "old-old," Laslett contrasted the "third age" with the "fourth age," a period in the final years of life characterized by frailty, dependence, and a preoccupation with mortality. Although Laslett and his adherents have been criticized for the socio-economic assumptions underlying their image of healthy, productive aging, their ideas have nevertheless captivated the popular and political imagination (Lamb 2014, 2017; Robbins 2021; Twigg and Martin 2015). By the early twenty-first century the concept of the third age had come to characterize public discourses all over Europe, where it continues to be "mobilized not just by older activists, but by policy makers and European Union (EU) bureaucrats, politicians from all spectrums, and the popular and scholarly press" (Greenberg and Muehlebach 2007, 190). Indeed, many of my research participants seemed to have absorbed these discourses as well. On multiple occasions they referred to themselves in Spanish as belonging to *"la tercera edad"* (the third age) – a stretch of time in the early years of retirement envisioned as an opportunity to participate in social institutions such as the Centro and to perform activities, such as caring for grandchildren, associated with being seniors. I espouse the term "later life" as a neutral equivalent to "the third age," eschewing the ideological entanglements around what it means to grow older "successfully" (see Corwin 2021; Lamb 2017; Robbins 2021).

Across Space, Over Time: A Road Map of Remembering

Untold Stories traces the movement of my research participants across space and over time. Each chapter features a different social setting or organized activity at the Centro, playing on themes that recreate a slack chronology of their life trajectories: from their childhood and adolescent experiences in Spanish pueblos to transnational migration and growing old in France.

Chapter 1 presents participants in the Escuela, the Centro's Spanish literacy workshop. They comprise a group of women whose elementary education in the 1940s entailed no more than three or four years of religious indoctrination. I analyse texts that they produced in the workshop, along with related conversational interactions, to delineate the deep-rooted moral frameworks about language and literacy that colour their practices of remembering today. I argue that their participation in the workshop serves as an act of return and redress, enabling them to "go back" to school and develop the skills of literacy that they understand themselves to lack in later life, given the state of public education in the early years of the dictatorship.

Chapter 2 shifts focus from the legacies of early childhood to recollections of the pre-migratory pueblo in the 1950s. The chapter turns on a modest assignment from Pablo, the Escuela's instructor, for which he asked participants to draft compositions describing their pueblos in preparation for a community performance at the Centro. The women's texts, along with the conversational interaction that they provoked, shed light on the communicative values, such as silence, that shape public discourse about the past among this diasporic population. Moving across discursive realms variously perceived as public or private, formal or informal, the seniors reveal the balance of revelation and omission that they calculate to produce felicitous representations of historical content and to enact moral agency.

In chapter 3, I conduct discourse analysis on a different kind of text altogether: a one-act play that was written and performed by participants in the Centro's theatre workshop. The play recounts a Spanish migrant's decision to leave Paris and return to her pueblo, where she encounters an altered landscape that no longer feels like home. This ethnographic material highlights a later phase in the Spaniards' life trajectories – the stretch of time in the 1970s before their temporary migration became permanent, during which they wrestled with the possibility of returning definitively to Spain. Juxtaposing interactions from rehearsals with evidence of audience reception, I reveal the remarkable polyvocality in a collectivity with respect to the representation of its members' past experience. The cultural performance featured in this chapter enables multiple vectors of reflexivity among the seniors, exposing the boundaries of tellability and the moral entailments of their narrative practices.

Chapter 4 advances slightly in the sequence of migration experience, presenting a series of exchanges occasioned by a Centro-sponsored excursion to a local museum. Led by Josep, the activities director, a small group of seniors visited an exhibition on the bidonvilles, or shantytowns, that had existed nearby until the mid-1970s. Indeed, some of the seniors had lived there before settling into more permanent housing. During their visit they engaged with official representations of a past that they had experienced first hand, illuminating how different modes of knowing – here, the scholarly-historical and the personal-biographical – may be marshalled to underwrite claims of authority and belonging in a diasporic present.

In chapter 5, I examine discursive data from the weekly internet class designed and taught by Josep. Thematically the chapter pivots into the present, as seniors learned to use computers for the first time, searching for content, such as news and recipes, associated with Spain. My analysis of interactions in the class underscores the Spaniards' desire to calibrate chronotopes of a past lived elsewhere with their here and now; it also reveals the vital role of music in this enterprise. One woman in the course created and uploaded a rap song to YouTube, the video-sharing website, realizing the internet's potential for imaginative self-transformation. I analyse this process in close detail to illustrate further the local value of text production in practices of remembering that extend both back to the past and forward to the future.

A concluding chapter summarizes the principal themes of the book and discusses their repercussions in ongoing debates about historical memory in Spain.

"I Could Write a Book!"

Texts of various kinds – poems, plays, compositions, songs – appear in each of these chapters, vital to the aging population featured in this book. Their circulation marks the bounds of a community that are drawn through its everyday acts of remembering the past. But these texts also project their authors into the future, serving the impulse towards memorialization epitomized by Amalia's remark in this chapter's opening vignette, "I could write a book!" Her exclamation, punctuating a string of recollections, signalled a pivot from narrative discourse about her personal history to an indirect evaluation of its merit. This imagined book would both confer authority on Amalia and promise her preservation for posterity.

"I could write a book!" pops up in different settings throughout these pages, an informal remark among older individuals eager to communicate the legitimacy of their biographical trajectories. But the playfulness of this platitude belies an underlying urgency. Sidelined by official historiographies, Spanish labour migrants in later life are now members of a generation that grows smaller with each passing year. *Untold Stories* thus serves as a material proxy for their speculative tome, a modest intervention into the timely and terminal project of their remembering.

1 Literacy in Later Life

On Tuesday afternoons at the Centro, a group of ten women would file into a small room next to the café to attend Lengua castellana (Spanish Language), a weekly workshop in which they developed reading and writing skills in their native tongue. The students referred to the class affectionately as the Escuela, or primary school, reflecting their perception of its fundamental pedagogical goals and the modesty with which they pursued them. For ninety minutes every week they sat around a large oval table and engaged in rudimentary exercises that included dictation, composition, and oral recitation. The class was a lively affair, as its participants navigated their way through these activities with a mix of enthusiasm and shared frustration, projecting their voices above the din coming from café patrons nearby. They readily applauded when a peer performed with precision or pluck, identifying the stressed vowel in a polysyllabic word, for example, or reading haltingly out loud to the end of a handwritten composition. They also commiserated about the challenges they faced as students in later life, interjecting comments about memory and forgetfulness, for example, which elicited knowing nods from classmates.

One participant in the course, Marisol, was a short, energetic sixty-five-year-old who attended the Centro on a regular basis. Born in 1943, she migrated from her pueblo in central Spain at the age of twenty-five to join an older sister who had settled in Paris a few years earlier. After an especially confusing lesson on verb forms, Marisol sighed, turned to Pablo, the serious twenty-seven-year-old graduate student who was teaching the Escuela, and said, matter of factly, "It's difficult at our age, son." Her remark provoked a familiar surge of commentary among her peers on the limits of their capacity to learn given their situation in "old age" (*la vejez*). Pablo interrupted with a click of his tongue and words of reassurance, pointing out that the women already *knew* Spanish; they just needed to learn the names and functions of grammatical concepts. As the women shook their heads and grumbled playfully in protest, Marisol responded with a shrug, "We don't have the basics because we never went to school."

Indeed, few of the women who attended the Escuela had ever mastered "the basics," having come of age between the violence of civil war and Spain's protracted efforts at modernization, which began in the mid-1950s. Most of them had attended school for only three or four years during the most repressive period of Franco's dictatorship in the 1940s. At the time, Spain's fledgling education system was overseen by the Catholic Church, which infused its pedagogy with religious principles that aimed to create docile citizens rather than literate subjects. In the early years of Francoism, public school failed to impart essential technical skills, seeking instead to ensure students' absorption of the social values of the regime and their eventual participation in an unqualified workforce (Grugel and Rees 1997).

Although the initial education policies of the dictatorship targeted Spain's poorest citizens indiscriminately, different notions about the relationship between literacy and gender informed how those policies were enacted. Men with poor literacy skills were often considered developmentally "delayed," while women, a "large, silent, and silenced majority," were seen as "self-sacrificing servants" who avoided displaying intelligence around men for fear of losing their femininity (Llavador and Llavador 1996, 139).[1] Traces of this ideological distinction endure among members at the Centro today, where the Escuela's students are exclusively female, and men prefer to play cards with one another rather than take part in its organized activities (cf. Robbins 2021). In private conversations Pablo surmised that men at the Centro perceived participation in the literacy workshop as an admission of deficiency; their avoidance of the classroom thus constituted a vestige of peninsular machismo. For women, the Escuela provided a setting in which they could openly acknowledge their inadequate education and its enduring legacies in their current lives.

A few weeks after the exchange with Marisol, Pablo asked participants to reflect on their experience in the class since he had begun teaching it a few months earlier. Many of the women commented that they found it worthwhile because, even if ninety minutes a week did not amount to much time, their lack of knowledge was so extensive that any practice would help. Rosario, a stylish seventy-three-year-old woman with auburn-dyed hair and large tinted reading glasses, had migrated from a pueblo outside of Granada in the mid-1960s. She now attended the Centro solely on Tuesdays to compensate, as she said, for "what we never learned well." Before she began to take the class, she suffered from "a sort of complex, from fear" of reading and writing, along with a sinking conviction that it was too late for her to acquire the knowledge that she lacked. Echoing the remarks of many of her classmates, she went on to reveal that she had carried this sense of inadequacy throughout her adult life:

| Lo único que me ha faltado en la vida es haber ido a la escuela, haber aprendido a estudiar, leer. Eso me ha faltado mucho, mucho. Es una cosa que – por las circunstancias que has tenido en tu vida – no lo podías hacer. | The only thing that I've missed in my life is having gone to school, having learned to study, to read. I missed that a lot, a lot. It's something that – because of the circumstances that you've had in your life – you weren't able to do. |

When Rosario identified an aching sense of lack – "the only thing that I've missed in my life" – many of her classmates nodded. This feeling of something missing impelled them to attend the class week after week, pursuing the basic knowledge that had been denied them because of the unnamed "circumstances" of their lives: poverty, dictatorship, labour, migration. Their voluntary return to the Escuela as adults constituted an educational project that had eluded them – a project that for many was personally motivated and imbued with uncertainty about their capacity to succeed at it.

On the heels of her remark Rosario shook her head and added, "You know, we have so many problems," referring at once to the affective challenges that she had just mentioned and the mundane mechanics of writing that they had yet to master, "like the comma." Such abiding "problems" with literacy often generated shame among the Escuela's participants, associated as they were with the technical skills that had long been mastered by individuals among other populations at their stage in the life course. Indeed, Josep, the Centro's activities director, had first considered calling the course a literacy workshop, but was concerned that the term "literacy" (*alfabetización*) bore too much stigma. He settled on "Spanish Language" for what he perceived as its neutrality and the legitimacy that it lent to the enterprise of learning.[2] In class at the Centro the women could openly express abashment among generational peers who had received the same inadequate education due to the political epoch into which they had been born.

In this chapter I explore how this feeling of lack from the past motivates the pursuit of literacy in the present. Performing discourse analysis on classroom interactions, along with texts of various kinds that the women produced and circulated, I reveal a shared value of the literate subjectivity that knowledge of reading and writing makes possible. Participants in Lengua castellana were driven by a desire to cultivate literacy skills that would mediate their relationships (to people, things, and ideas) and confer cultural capital. Moreover, I show how the women's perception of their scholastic enterprise makes visible the link between literacy and time. Learning how to read and write "well" not only serves the project of historical redress but also provides a means for projecting oneself into the future through authoritative modes of self-presentation meant to outlast the present.

The Escuela: Student Participants and Conceptions of Literacy

Most of the women who attended the Escuela had arrived in later life with a similarly limited repertoire of technical skills and the language-related ideologies that endowed those skills with value. At opposite extremes on a scale of proficiency, Carmen and Benita stood out from their peers due to the particularities of their biographical circumstances, which had affected their access to education. As a child growing up in Andalucía, Carmen had never attended school. Her father died suddenly when she was five years old, forcing her into agricultural labour to help support her family. She recalled the difficulty that she experienced after migrating to Paris, trying to navigate the public transportation system without knowing how to read, which she did for thirty-seven years while cleaning apartments in neighbourhoods throughout the city:

Me tenía que poner en el metro una cosa para hacer el trasbordo, para que no me equivocara. No sabía nada. Lo he pasado muy mal, ¿eh?	I used to have to locate something specific in the metro station to do the transfer so that I wouldn't make a mistake. I didn't know anything. It was really awful, eh?

As soon as she retired at the age of sixty, Carmen participated in a French literacy program sponsored by the municipal government. Although she could not write anything other than her name when I met her at the Centro ten years later, she spoke with pride about her ability to decipher signs in the metro and magazine covers at the supermarket.

Benita, who was sixty-eight years of age and had a very different educational background, was the only participant in the class (and indeed at the Centro) who did not identify as an economic migrant or a political refugee. Her father had been a successful farmer, and her mother had been a schoolteacher. During her adolescence she became romantically involved with a childhood sweetheart from her pueblo, whose parents had migrated to France shortly after the war. They eventually married, and she moved to Paris to join him. Benita thus occupied a unique social position at the Centro, which she invoked with regularity. Able to read and write with ease in both Spanish and French, she considered the Escuela a "review" of information that she already knew, and she often assumed the role of unofficial assistant to Pablo. But Benita, like Carmen, was something of an outlier. All of the other women in the class had only received a few years of formal schooling in Spain, during which they managed to develop rudimentary abilities to read and write. They could now decode written texts without a guarantee of comprehension; they could also communicate a range of ideas in functional and sometimes creative writing that often defied standard form.

When Pablo asked them what they hoped to gain from the course, the women identified practical and formal "problems," as Rosario had that included difficulties with spelling and punctuation common to many Spanish speakers learning how to write. During a dictation exercise one afternoon Paquita, a sixty-nine-year-old woman from a pueblo near Albacete, blurted out her frustration with an orthographic distinction that often confounds students of Spanish: "The *v*, there's no way I can get it. For me they're all *b*'s!"[3] Similarly, Marisol struggled with word boundaries – that is, as she said, "how to write words together and apart." One afternoon in the arts and crafts workshop, for example, she showed me a text in which she had written *"con vosotros"* (with you) as *"combo sotros,"* a collocation that proved challenging both for its word boundary *and* the *b/v* distinction.

Such remarks from participants in the Escuela reflected what they meant by "the basics" of literacy. They also indicated the extent to which Pablo's pedagogical tactics, especially when he began to teach the class, did not correspond to their needs and abilities. Pablo had come from Mexico City to Paris in pursuit of a master's degree in theatre. As he mentioned to me privately, he had accepted the job for practical reasons: he needed money, and it was convenient. Pablo rented a studio in a building nearby that was owned by María, an avid member of the Centro. Soon after he moved in, she suggested that he apply for a part-time position as the Centro's acting and language instructor. Although he had extensive experience with theatre performance and direction, he had never taught Spanish or literacy, a lacuna reflected in his methodology. For the first few weeks that I attended the Escuela, for example, Pablo spent most of the class time reading aloud grammar rules from a textbook, which the students were meant to transcribe into spiral notebooks: "We use the letter *j* in the verb tenses called 'strong preterits': 'I said'; 'I drove'; 'I brought.'"[4] At one point he read aloud a lengthy lesson from a chapter titled "Greek Prefixes and Homophones." Given the arcane nature of such vocabulary and concepts, which participants in the Escuela had never before encountered, these exercises failed to impart applicable knowledge about spelling and grammar. And yet, the women performed the dictations in earnest. They struggled to focus on the orthographic accuracy of their transcriptions, frequently asking Pablo to repeat himself and sometimes mumbling that they had no understanding of what they were writing down. They seemed at times to ignore how these exercises failed to teach them what they wanted to learn in any meaningful way, such as the distinction between *b* from *v* or the placement of word boundaries. Respecting Pablo's authority as instructor, an institutional role that he often performed with dramatic seriousness, they were prone to misrecognizing their bewilderment as a symptom of biographical circumstance – "because we never went to school," as Marisol said – rather than a consequence of inadequate pedagogy. The state of confusion induced by Pablo's methods thus seemed to resonate with their experience and expectations around institutional learning and the acquisition of scholarly knowledge in general.

The variation in abilities among the women rendered literacy a meaningful point of reference in processes of social differentiation, as they oriented towards a shared language-ideological framework that valued the ability to read and write elementary texts, rather than one that privileged a particular social register of Spanish or a geographical variety of the language perceived to be standard. This is a likely explanation for the absence of any sense of superiority towards Pablo with respect to his Mexican variety of Spanish, which was phonologically distinct from that of the Escuela's members. When Carmen first revealed to the class that she had never gone to school, Carolina, a participant from Valencia, wanted to know which part of Spain she had come from. Her answer, "Andalucía," came as little surprise, given its status as one of the most poverty-stricken, retrograde areas of Spain and the place of origin of many migrants who travelled north of the Pyrenees.[5] It thus confirmed a pervasive hierarchy of geographic values that situated regions of Spain in relation to one another based on shared perceptions of their relative backwardness or modernity (see Rogozen-Soltar 2017).

Paquita, another woman in the course, responded to Carmen's revelation by applauding the "crazy merit" (*mérito loco*) that she demonstrated by attending school for the first time as an adult. Although Paquita also struggled to read out loud and had difficulty assembling sentences into coherent paragraphs, she hailed from a pueblo in what is now Castilla–La Mancha and had attended school for a handful of years. Her warm-hearted praise for Carmen thus not only served as encouragement but also signalled the slight position of moral superiority from which she uttered it. Carolina, for her part, just sighed and shook her head, alluding to the shared circumstances of the historical epoch into which they had all been born: "Our generation, eh?" Such interactions among participants in the Escuela revealed a potent ideological framework through which members of the community often situated themselves and one another. The women generated meaningful social distinctions according not only to regional provenance but also to degrees of literate subjectivity, measured in part by each individual's ability to read out loud and to use correct spelling and punctuation in their written texts. As Carolina's comment suggests, this ideological framework tethered them to their generational counterparts in Spain, who had shared experiences of a painful past – as stunted schoolchildren, as young adults who struggled to read and write with ease – and bore its affective legacies in the present, often manifested in shame.

"There's No Shame in Going to School at Our Age!": Literacy in Later Life

One afternoon as the Escuela drew to a close, the women gathered their belongings and commiserated over the confusion generated by the complicated spelling rules that Pablo had dictated earlier that day. After a few moments, Lina, one of the more advanced students in the Escuela, cleared her throat to interrupt. Like the others, she had attended school for only four years, leaving at the age of eleven to sell eggs in a market near her pueblo in Galicia. Her interest in writing as a pastime, however, drove her to develop the skill through practice over the course of her adult life. Recently retired from her career as a seamstress, she led the Centro's weekly arts and crafts workshop and spent much of her free time engaged in artistic projects, such as collage, sewing, and creative writing. Once she had summoned her classmates' attention, Lina registered exasperation with an exaggerated eye roll and a shake of her head: "Because you say 'at our age this and that,' I'm going to read you a poem that I wrote about our class, 'The school for the third age.'" When the women fell silent, she began to recite the following:

"La Escuela de la tercera edad"	The school for the third age
1 Dicen que "a nuestra edad, ir a la escuela, ¿para qué?"	1 They say, "Why go to school at our age?"
2 Es un decir por decir.	2 Those are just empty words.

3 En el Centro tenemos un maestro que nos enseña a leer y escribir.
4 Tiene una sonrisa linda y muy simpática, pero sobre todo mucha paciencia con todos nosotros,
5 Que de tanto trabajar, el tiempo hemos dejado pasar y borrar lo poco en España que hemos aprendido.
6 Sé que tengo cierta edad, hace tiempo que no cuento los años.
7 Pero cuando voy a esas clases me siento joven,
8 Se hacen nuevas amistades.
9 Descubres que no eres la única a olvidar, o que olvidó lo poco aprendido.
10 No es una vergüenza a nuestra edad ir a la escuela.
11 Es un honor, un placer,
12 El honor de sentirse joven por adentro,
13 El placer de decir que nunca he estado para aprender a leer y a escribir.
14 Si te sientes incómodo con lo poco que sabes, no es difícil, ni lo pienses,
15 ¡Reúnete con nosotros en el Centro!

3 At the Centro we have an instructor who teaches us how to read and write.
4 He has a beautiful and very nice smile, but especially a lot of patience with us,
5 Who, from working so much, let time pass and erase the little that we learned in Spain.
6 I know that I am of a certain age, I haven't counted years for a while.
7 But when I go to those classes I feel young,
8 We make new friendships.
9 You discover that you're not the only one to forget, or who forgot the little that was learned.
10 There is no shame in going to school at our age.
11 It is an honour, a pleasure,
12 The honour of feeling oneself young on the inside,
13 The pleasure of saying that you're finally about to learn to read and write.
14 If you feel uncomfortable with the little that you know, it's not hard, don't think twice about it,
15 Come join us at the Centro!

After Lina had uttered the final verse – an invitation to anyone who might feel shame about their lack of knowledge to come join them at the Centro – the other women erupted into applause with cries of ¡*Olé!* and ¡*Bravo!* Even Pablo cracked a smile, telling Lina that she was going to make him cry.

In her modest paean to the classroom where they had come to learn "how to read and write" (line 3), Lina evokes dominant discourses about "the third age" – a population that has forgotten lessons learned long ago (line 9) and requires a surfeit of patience from an instructor, especially with regard to matters of literacy (line 4). She also alludes to the particularities of the experience of those who are present, highlighting the "little that [they] learned in Spain" (lines 5 and 9) and the extent to which they laboured later on, as she implies, after their migration to France (line 5). Such biographical facts explain their participation in the Escuela today, answering the question voiced by an unspecified, general "they" in the opening verse (line 1): "Why go to school at our age?" Lina's text thus points towards perceived violations of educational values that continue to imbue the everyday lives of the workshop's participants: it evokes the lamentable education policies of post-war Spain; it also reflects broad expectations about what individuals in later life should be able to *do* – that is, read and write with ease. The women in the Escuela, and a majority of the Spanish migrants I encountered in Paris, lack what they perceive to be foundational forms of knowledge – "the basics," as Marisol said – due to the social and political conditions into which they came of age.

In the poem Lina acknowledges the familiar feeling of shame through its negation, stating outright that "there is no shame in going to school" in later life (line 10) as a means of encouraging the poem's addressees, imagined peers whose educational lives were similarly conditioned by post-war Spain, to join them in their class. Such a remark belies the embarrassment among their community of Spanish migrants, exposed far more frequently in the Escuela (and elsewhere at the Centro) through subtle comments and gestures rather than direct expression: diffident disclaimers about one's halting recitation or illegible penmanship, for example, or amplified praise for a peer's "merit" merely for complying with Pablo's directions. Lina's declaration reveals the prevalence of what it disavows, the feeling of discomfort generated by a lack of knowledge, but she presents a possibility for its alleviation: the reminder that one is not alone. In the Escuela, she writes, any shame about reading and writing dissolves in shared efforts to recall the little knowledge that may have been lost. As I observed over the months that I attended the class, the social dimension of such an enterprise was paramount to its efficacy. In a classroom among peers with similar limitations and desires, the seniors seemed open to learning the material at hand as their affective hurdles diminished.

Lina's poem thus illuminates the intersecting ideologies about age and literacy that circulate at the Centro, and perhaps among those in later life in general who lack reading and writing abilities that they feel should have been acquired at an earlier age. "It's not hard," she states (line 14), addressing their concerns, not only about the challenges of being a student but also about the decision to attend school in the first place and the admission of ignorance that such a decision implies. Throughout the poem she illuminates the age-related tension of those who, through biographical circumstances, find themselves in old age returning to a place – school – associated with a much earlier period of the life course. The poem's title, "La escuela de la tercera edad," encapsulates the chronotopic friction that animates the text: the Escuela bears connotations of childhood and, in this context, the past in Spain (line 5); the "third age" references a phase of life presumably saturated with accumulated experience and the wisdom that it engenders, the here and now of France. But the literacy skills that these women have carried into later life trouble a hegemonic chronotope associated with being old: they have lost, or have yet to acquire, rudimentary forms of knowledge. Their presence in a classroom provokes doubtful queries from an imagined interlocutor who presumes their shame (line 1) and to whom the poem serves as a kind of response. Lina's text argues for a calibration of chronotopes that plays on non-dominant notions of age – the *there-then* of primary school with the *here-now* of the "third age" – a calibration so unorthodox that it may cause self-consciousness or discomfort among those with whom it resonates. Lina thus appeals to people aligned with the figures of personhood that these chronotopes evoke, generational peers who understand through their experience the untold stories behind the term "Spain" (line 5): post-war poverty, a flagrantly deficient education system, exile.

The geographical corollary of France, however, does not appear in the poem. Instead, Lina mentions the slow-burning erasure of whatever knowledge had been acquired before migration (line 5). From "working so much" over time, she suggests, the women have arrived in later life with less proficiency in reading and writing than they had in their youth. She situates labour in ideological opposition to learning by suggesting that only now, in retirement, can she and her audience at last (re)turn to the classroom. The Centro, where Spanish migrants of a similar age congregate, accommodates whatever chronotopic tension may be created through the pursuit of knowledge associated with schoolchildren. Moreover, the act of learning as an older adult produces the valued effect of feeling young (lines 7 and 12), a disjuncture that generates positive affect. Lina describes it here as an "honour" for those courageous enough to acknowledge that they do not know how to read and write as well as they would like.

Collecting Paper and Books: Material Artefacts and Memorialization

"Photocopies for Everyone!"

After Lina had finished reciting her poem, Carolina insisted that it be circulated among everyone present, a high form of praise for women in the Escuela, who valued material manifestations of literate activity: "That should be photocopied for everyone!" Throughout the course I observed them collect paper avidly, whether it be sheets from notebooks on which they had taken dictation, their own compositions, or photocopies of literary excerpts that Pablo gave them to practise reading at home. For the first month or so that I attended the Escuela, for example, he handed out chapters from a turgid, descriptive tome that had been published in 1917 – Azorín's *El paisaje de España visto por los españoles* (Spain's countryside as seen by Spaniards). With each chapter of the book dedicated to a different region in Spain, Pablo hoped that the texts would inspire the women for an upcoming writing assignment about the pueblos where they had grown up, as I discuss in chapter 2. Judging by their frequent complaints, however, Azorín's arcane language and tangled syntax proved too difficult for them to understand. As María said with a shrug upon receiving the chapter on Murcia, a region in southeastern Spain, "I don't understand anything. Nothin'!"[6] And yet, the women insisted on collecting whatever photocopy Pablo or their peers passed around, dutifully filing them in protective plastic sheaths that they brought regularly to class. After Marisol realized that her collection of chapters was incomplete because she had been absent when Pablo assigned one of them, she ran up to him after class to say, "I don't have Cataluña! Can you make me a photocopy of Cataluña?" Later that week in the arts and crafts workshop, though, she admitted to me that she found the texts "boring" (*aburridos*) and failed to see their practical value.[7]

Following Pablo's directions, the women also carried Spanish-language dictionaries to class, although it was clear that these resources served no practical purpose. As one of the students asked, "How can we look up words when we don't know how to spell?" Nevertheless, they brought their dictionaries to class without fail, a gesture that reflected not only their deference to Pablo and recognition of his authority but also the symbolic value of books and what they were thought to embody. In this setting in particular, where participants focused on developing basic literacy skills, books were prized not for their content – indeed, the students in the class often had difficulty engaging with them in any conventional way – so much as for the forms of knowledge that they represented and the claim to moral personhood that their possession made possible. The women often mentioned with pride that a French historian, Natacha Lillo, had published a manuscript about Spanish immigrants in Paris in 2004; some of them welcomed my presence in the field with the understanding that it was related to a similar objective. Books were seen as material artefacts that embodied legitimate forms of discourse and conferred authority on those who claimed to value them, just as Amalia did in the vignette with which *Untold Stories* opens. Books indexed the literate subjectivity that participants in the Escuela seemed so eager to acquire.

In other settings as well, the workshop's members demonstrated an interest in collecting and circulating written material. One afternoon in the arts and crafts workshop, for example, Marisol unexpectedly pulled from her purse a faded, dog-eared paperback in French titled *Elles sont raides, celles-là!* (Those ones are naughty!), a collection of bawdy jokes that had been published in 1980. She opened it and attempted to read an excerpt out loud, faltering as she sounded out the words. Given such difficulties, her possession of the book seemed to demonstrate her value of literacy and printed texts as much as it did her appreciation for ribald humour. She then handed the volume to me and asked if I would read the joke to Amalia, who was knitting nearby. After I had done so, Amalia laughed heartily and asked Marisol where the book had come from:[8]

1 AMALIA ((*smiling voice*)): où tu as trouvé ce livre si cochon?
2 DAVID ((*reading the title of the book*)): Elles sont raides, celles-là!
3 MARISOL: je l'ai trouvé dans une poubelle
4 AMALIA: c'est pas mal, eh?
5 DAVID: c'est marrant, oui
6 AMALIA: où tu as trouvé ça?
7 Marisol: bah, dans une poubelle
8 AMALIA: dans une poubelle ah!
9 MARISOL: non mais quand je fais – quand j'étais en – quand j'étais gardienne
10 AMALIA: ah *sí*
11 MARISOL ((*to me*)): j'étais gardienne d'immeuble

1 AMALIA ((*smiling voice*)): where did you find such a filthy book?
2 DAVID ((*reading the title of the book*)): *Those ones are naughty!*
3 MARISOL: I found it in a trash can
4 AMALIA: it's not bad, eh?
5 DAVID: it's funny, yes
6 AMALIA: where did you find it?
7 MARISOL: bah, in a trash can
8 AMALIA: in a trash can, ah!
9 MARISOL: no but, when I was doing – when I was in – when I was a concierge
10 AMALIA: ah *yes*
11 MARISOL ((*to me*)): I was an apartment building concierge

12 AMALIA ((*to me*)): tu vois? on a fait des poubelles
13 DAVID: ah oui
14 MARISOL: donc euh je sortais les poubelles et des fois il y avait des livres
15 AMALIA: on a fait – on a fait les poubelles des –
16 DAVID: ouais
17 AMALIA: ouais des fois, eh? pas mal, moi j'en ai récupéré un qui – qui – vieux! – vieux! – mais ça valait le coup celui-là

12 AMALIA **((*to me*))**: you see? we used to deal with the trash
13 DAVID: ah yes
14 MARISOL: so um I used to take out the trash and sometimes there were books
15 AMALIA: we dealt – we dealt with the trash of –
16 DAVID: yea
17 AMALIA: yea and sometimes, eh? not bad, I found one that – that – old! – old! – but that one was really worth it

Recovering from a burst of laughter, Amalia does not at first catch Marisol's response to her question and thus repeats it (lines 1 and 6). When Marisol explains that she retrieved the book from a trash can in the building where she worked as a concierge thirty years earlier, she conjures for Amalia a chronotope of their past that is instantly recognizable, evoking as it does familiar workplaces from a period of time shortly after their migration. Unfazed by the revelation, Amalia offers a matter-of-fact "ah yes" without looking up from her knitting. The women then address their turns at talk to me, suggesting their awareness that I might find the book's provenance remarkable. "You see?" asks Amalia in line 12, "We used to deal with the trash." Corroborating Marisol's disclosure, she uses the first-person plural pronoun in her remark – "*on*" (we) – and recalls a few turns later that she once found a valuable old book in similar circumstances (line 17). The artefact's origins thus illuminate some of the labour conditions experienced by Spanish migrants in Paris and their inextricable entanglement with gender and class. Women rather than men worked as concierges, exchanging their management services for stipends and housing in the city's bourgeois neighbourhoods. Their responsibilities included taking out the trash – a dirty, undesirable task that at the very least provided an occasion for retrieving objects of interest. Amalia's recollection of once finding a book that was "really worth it" because it was "old! old!" (line 17) points to a similar ideological framework for evaluating written material. Books found in the trash may have held little value for the middle-class French people who had discarded them, but they constituted objects of desire for Marisol and Amalia. Even a tawdry tome could evidence their esteem for knowledge and their yearning for literate subjectivity.

Claims to Literate Subjectivity

The women in the Escuela also asserted their value of literacy through explicit claims about the acts of reading and writing in which they engaged. They often detailed the quantity or types of texts that they consumed, further revealing an understanding of linguistic proficiency to be a vital aspect of moral personhood. During a class discussion in which Marisol voiced a familiar complaint about the struggle of learning how to spell at her age, Benita interrupted impatiently to suggest that a more disciplined practice of reading would help her learn word boundaries: "But isn't it useful for you to read, read, read?!" Marisol shot back that she read regularly: "I read, I read, I read, I read! But I read in French!" The problem, she explained, was that it was too difficult to find Spanish books in Paris, and so she was forced to wait until her annual return visit to her pueblo near Toledo to buy them. Marisol's charged response to Benita included somewhat exaggerated claims about the trouble of finding Spanish material in France and the frequency with which she read in French. A few weeks earlier she had mentioned in the Escuela that she had bought a Spanish dictionary in a bookstore near the Place Saint-Michel in central Paris; moreover, her laboured efforts at reading aloud a brief excerpt from a book of French jokes suggested that she would have difficulty doing so at length.

Marisol's retort to Benita, who read and wrote with ease and saw her role in the Escuela as a resource for the other participants, served as a telling face-saving gambit. At the Centro, participants valued first and foremost the ability to read and write with confidence. However, *claims* of making the effort to master these skills served as an adequate proxy to the skills themselves, pointing to entangled associations among literacy, agency, and moral rectitude. Even among individuals in similar circumstances, it was often difficult for the women to overcome a deep and enduring sense of shame over their lack of education. Nevertheless, participants in the Escuela could index their "merit" by actively engaging with texts of various kinds, thereby displaying their investment in self-improvement through the pursuit of knowledge that they lacked. Thus, with regard to matters of language and learning, they prized any evidence of self-determination. Avowals of literate activity also diverted attention from what seniors saw as their limitations, enabling them to skirt revelations of their deficient abilities or of their insufficient attempts at ameliorating them.

Similar to assertions about reading practices, claims of authorship – who wrote what and for whom – were also not uncommon. After the women had heartily applauded Lina's poem and we had filed out of the classroom, for example, Benita pulled me aside to tell me under her breath that Lina had read the exact same text a year earlier, but it had been dedicated to Ana, their instructor at the time. Although it had not been intended for Pablo, at least originally, Lina's written offering to the class, which included explicit words of praise for its instructor, worked to display her as a certain kind of student, one who could marshal literacy skills towards the authorship of creative work. She thereby established herself as an authority vis-à-vis the process and her peers, a position that both facilitated and was reinforced by the encouragement that she often gave them.

On other occasions the women recited or presented copies of texts that they claimed to have written, or they ascribed authorship to people whom they knew. A week before I left Paris after my first stretch of fieldwork, Carolina handed me a poem that she had transcribed from memory and attributed to her brother; it was a gift, she explained in a note, *"para que te a cuerdes de mi"* (so that you remember me).[9] In another instance, Josep, who wanted to include work from the seniors in a photocopied program for an upcoming public performance, showed me a couple of texts from participants in the Escuela, pointing out complex turns of phrase and vocabulary that suggested at the very least the women had not written these poems and paragraphs without assistance. Whatever motivated their claims – a mistaken or misleading notion of a text's provenance or perhaps a different sense altogether of what is meant by authorship – they all suggest the local value of written texts and the authority that they confer on the individuals who produce them. Claims to authorship – whether direct ("*I* wrote this") or indirect ("I know who did") – legitimized a person's social position as a literate subject. They also revealed something of particular importance to members of this group of women and perhaps their generational peers more broadly, who came of age in deprived social and economic conditions, the legacies of which they continue to reckon with today. Such assertions worked to establish the women's alignment with desirable social types and assuaged their apprehensions about engaging in literary practices of any kind.[10]

"I Would Write a Book ... If I Could"

The Escuela provided a welcoming space for participants who felt shame about not being able to read and write with ease. The women made sense of their activity in the classroom through ideologies about reading and writing that were entangled with dominant notions about what it meant to acquire certain forms of knowledge in later life. In this chapter I have linked these ideologies to their experience of the inadequate school system created during the early years of Franco's regime, examining their shared value of literate subjectivity as revealed through the circulation of texts of various kinds – original works, such as Lina's poem, and literary excerpts introduced by Pablo in exercises on dictation.

Among individuals in later life an investment in the refinement of literacy practices amplifies their temporal dimension. Written texts, once created, can circulate across space and over time; they provide a means of documentation that can be carried into the future as they represent the past. "One of the most important roles of literacy is the transcendence of time," Tusting, Ivanic, and Wilson (2000, 211) write, highlighting the value of preserving something "locally present in order that it may be reconstructed/remembered/drawn on in the future when the event itself will be absent." With regard to personal recollection, the very act of writing entails an abstract projection of self and story into an unknown future, a recording of historicity to be reckoned with later on. Such texts anticipate a calibration of chronotopes in which the present becomes recognized as the past. Through literate activity, people may thus transform themselves into agents of historicity, producing authoritative representations of their experience. This is a particularly valuable social position when regimes of historical knowledge ignore the lives that they have led, which, in the case of participants in the Escuela, have been shaped by intersecting forms of marginality that they have experienced as poor, migrant women. Any underlying shame about "going to school at our age," as Lina writes in her poem (line 10), may be attenuated by the authority that derives from the ability to inscribe personal history into material artefacts.

For the women who attend the Escuela, the issues left in the wake of their deficient education in post-war Spain took on a different meaning in later life. The metaphor that I often heard during fieldwork – "I could write a book!" – points simultaneously towards their awareness of the historical meaningfulness of their lives and the local value of written texts for the authority that they conferred upon the individuals who created them. The remark evokes a dominant understanding of the value of books as objects that record lived experience, thereby preserving it for posterity. A book not only embodies scholarly knowledge but also provides a means of projecting oneself into the future. Whether it comprises academic historiography, personal recollection, or perhaps some combination thereof, a book is produced through the fundamental literacy practices that the women in the Escuela felt they lacked and wanted so keenly to acquire. The common refrain "I could write a book!" thus dissimulates a poignant tension. Haunting this hypothetical metaphor is the condition that stipulates its possibility: "I could write a book ... *if I had the skills to do so.*"

The sense of lack that they had carried since childhood ached a bit differently as they confronted the discordant limitations and desires that they associated with their age: the capacity of their memory in the present (*la memoria*) and the impulse to carry their memories into the future (*los recuerdos*). Pablo once asked about the women's yearning for what he described as "well-spoken and well-written Spanish" (*un español bien hablado y bien escrito*), and Nuria replied:

Mismo que llevamos muchos años aquí [en Francia], dentro de nuestro corazón siempre es España. Y cómo hemos tenido la mala suerte – yo, por ejemplo, que no he tenido tiempo de aprender en la escuela allí [en España] – pues el poco tiempo que estamos aquí [en la Escuela] es una satisfacción. Pero ahora hay muchos recuerdos. Pienso que vamos siendo mayores, y pensamos en la vida que hemos tenido en España y en las cosas que nos han faltado. Hoy día, por ejemplo, si estuviéramos allí, también estaríamos muy bien. Estamos más perdidas nosotras que las que se han quedado allí, que no han salido al extranjero. Viven feliz. Tienen su familia, que a nosotras nos falta eso – nuestra familia que nos hemos dejado allí. Hay algo que nos falta al interior nuestro.	Even though we've been here [in France] for many years, Spain is always in our hearts. And because we had the bad luck – me, for example, who didn't have time to learn in school there [in Spain] – the little bit of time that we're here [in the Escuela] is satisfying. But now there are many memories. I think that we're getting older, and we think about the life that we had in Spain and about the things that we missed. Today, for example, if we were there, we would also be fine. We're more lost than the ones who stayed there, who didn't go abroad. They live happily. They have their family, which we lack – our family that we left behind there. There's something that's missing from within us.

Nuria's answer to Pablo's question provoked vigorous nods among her classmates, as Paquita volunteered a remark on their behalf: "I think you've answered for many of us."[11] Explaining why she attends the Escuela, Nuria gives voice to what are by now familiar tropes among this population. She notes that they could not attend school when they were younger because of their "bad luck" of having been born during a difficult historical epoch. Without recounting them explicitly, she alludes to the consequences of dictatorship on the domestic lives of Spaniards, whose families were often fractured ideologically by political differences or separated geographically through the distance imposed by transnational migration. Conjuring a chronotope of kinship (Agha 2015), Nuria imagines that the lives of those who remained in Spain are full of what she and her peers have lacked in France: family and the happiness that derives from their proximity. She also brings up the prevalence of memories – "many memories" – that she associates with "getting older" and her participation in the Escuela. Thoughts about the past in Spain generate a familiar sense of displacement, as Nuria and her peers "abroad" find themselves "more lost" than members of their generation who did not emigrate. "Well-spoken and well-written Spanish" serves them as a means of fortifying ties to the place that they left behind, where their national affiliation is sometimes questioned because of their long-term absence and the traces of elsewhere that inflect their speech when they return.

Literate subjectivity, the sense that one has of oneself as educated and the forms of agency that it enables, not only compensates for what was missing from a childhood conditioned by the policies of an authoritarian regime but also sanctions claims of national belonging through the learned use of language with which a homeland is associated. Literacy promises a legitimate and durative form of remembering through the act of writing and the material artefacts that it generates. For participants in the Escuela and at the Centro generally, the exclamation "I could write a book!" thus bares a disjuncture between the desire for an authoritative form of memorialization and the lack of knowledge that such a project requires. This predicament goes some way towards explaining their dedication to the class despite Pablo's inadequate pedagogy, as well as their avid attachment to texts of various kinds, including poems, books, and, as I discuss in the next chapter, narrative compositions about their pueblos.

2 Nostalgia for Pueblos Past

In early 2008 the Centro's members and staff buzzed with anticipation of its upcoming celebration of World Book Day, an international event dedicated to the promotion of reading that takes place annually on 23 April, the date that Miguel de Cervantes and William Shakespeare died in 1616. The Centro commemorates the occasion with public performances of songs and scenes prepared by participants in its music and theatre workshops; students from the Escuela often recite original texts that they have produced in class. Shortly after I began attending the literacy workshop in January, Pablo asked the women to draft compositions about their pueblos – the villages or towns in Spain where they had been born and raised – with World Book Day in mind. As he revealed to the students when presenting the assignment, he hoped that some of them would be willing to read these texts aloud during the event.

Pablo anticipated that the project would prove both engaging and manageable for the Escuela's participants, given the intimate knowledge and affective pull that talk of their pueblos involved. For Spaniards at the Centro, "pueblo" conjured a place and time from the past imbued with the simplicity of family and the natural world – not unlike *shtetl* for the Jewish migrants from Eastern Europe in Barbara Myerhoff's (1978) research in Los Angeles. The expression "mi pueblo" resonated with a polysemous charge, at once referencing a geographical location ("my village" or "my town") and a group of people bound together through their affiliation with a particular place ("my people"). For those living in diaspora an invocation of one's pueblo communicated attachment to Spain; it also fortified claims of belonging that were often perceived as tenuous by the Spaniards whom they encountered upon return visits from France.

During the weeks leading up to World Book Day the women practised reading their compositions out loud in class. Based on feedback from Pablo and their peers, they would then make revisions at home, bring them back the following week, and begin the process again. The awareness that their texts would be presented and evaluated in public seemed to shape their discursive form. Many students embedded fragments of sentimental language into their descriptions, drawing on a familiar representational frame for talk about the past: nostalgia. In this chapter I analyse "literacy events" in the classroom – that is, "occasion[s] in which a piece of writing is integral to the nature of the participants' interactions and interpretive processes" (Heath 1983, 93) – to reveal how nostalgia operates as a dominant regime of historicity (Hartog 2016) among a diasporic population. Crucially, I attend to concomitant and sometimes conflicting modes of engagement with the past to show how notions about the untold – what can (and cannot) be said by whom and under which circumstances – shape conversational interactions and underwrite claims to moral personhood.

Nostalgia, a Dominant Mode of Engagement with the Past

Nostalgia is commonly understood as a longing for what no longer exists, "a yearning for what is now unattainable, simply because of the irreversibility of time" (Pickering and Keightley 2006, 920). Across areas of study – including history, literary criticism, psychoanalysis, and postcolonial studies – scholars have interrogated the paradox by which nostalgia functions. Although it is tied to estrangement, it also operates as a means of "cultivating intimacy through shared expression" among those who claim a common past (Boyer 2012, 20). Recent scholarship has traced the evolution of nostalgia from its origins as a medical condition in seventeenth-century Switzerland to its commonplace use today as a "household term" across languages and cultures, having "colonized the most remote corners of our globalized world" and spawned "a commercially successful aesthetic branded as 'retro' or 'vintage'" (Dodman 2018, 6; see also Fritzsche 2001; Starobinski 1966). Current anthropological investigations of the phenomenon have emphasized how its emergence in particular moments reveals more about social configurations in the here and now than about the past itself (see Angé and Berliner 2015, 5). In her research on Bergamasco in northern Italy, for example, Jillian Cavanaugh (2004, 2009) has shown how social actors mobilize nostalgia to make sense of present-day language shift and its socio-economic entanglements. Within communities formed through the experience of spatial and temporal displacement, such as the Spaniards who are featured in this book, the evocation of nostalgia for the past may help them negotiate forms of diasporic belonging in the present.

Associated with the experience of rupture – then from now, there from here – nostalgia has been tied to modernity and the dispositions that it enables, a symptom of living in an epoch defined by increased fragmentation and uncertainty. As Boym (2007) writes, nostalgia "appears to be a longing for a place, but it is actually a yearning for a different time" (8). Such yearning generates social meaning through a relation of contrast with the spatio-temporal coordinates – the here and now – in which this act takes place, as well as with other, non-sentimental modes of engaging with the past that are intelligible in a given socio-cultural milieu, which I likewise explore throughout this chapter. The chronotope is thus ripe for recruitment in the analysis of nostalgic discourse, given its conflation of past times and places into a unified object of longing. For many participants in the Escuela, mere mention of the word "pueblo" activated a cultural chronotopic frame through which they conjured now-distant places saturated with a familiar temporality: the simpler, slower pace of rural life "back then."

In what follows I perform detailed textual analysis on one of the pueblo compositions to demonstrate the formal characteristics of nostalgic discourse that materialized among women in the Escuela. I also refer to commonalities in the broad corpus of their texts that suggest a prevalent understanding among students about how a pueblo, and the past with which it is associated, should be represented for public display. Among my research participants, nostalgic discourse, with its entailment of the unsaid, conforms to the regime of anodyne communication that tends to shape quotidian interactions at the Centro. As I show in this chapter, the seniors sustain a sense of institutional cohesion in part by engaging in narrative modes that constrain their talk about the past and its enduring legacies in the present.

Nostalgia for the Pueblo

Although women at the Centro generally hailed from municipalities with populations ranging from a few hundred to a few thousand inhabitants in various regions across Spain, they represented small-town life in similar ways. Despite the difficult conditions of their childhoods during the early post-war period, their compositions largely comprised idyllic depictions of rural landscapes that included details about animals and vegetation, as well as fond recollections of the activities that these settings allowed. Most of the texts comprised sequences of simple sentences and narrative fragments of personal experience. Such features coalesced into largely descriptive compositions that reflected the students' limited exposure to the mechanics of writing.

Marisol's account of her pueblo illustrates many of the formal and thematic characteristics that appeared throughout the eleven compositions produced. I present it here in its entirety:[1]

Composition 1: "The Best Paradise I Have Ever Known"

(1) Yo nací en Navalcán, en la provinica de Toledo. (2) Entonces **mi pueblo** era pequeño, y todos nos conocíamos. (3) Hoy todo es diferente. (4) Ahora es más grande. (5) Me siento un poco perdida. (6) Cuando yo era pequeña, siempre estaba en la calle. (7) Entonces las calles estaban llenas de barro. (8) Y cuando llovía, bajaban los regueros por todo **el pueblo**. (9) Yo recogía suelas de alpargatas y hierros, y a cambio, me daban teveos, que me gustaban mucho leer. (10) También me gustaba mucho ir al campo, a recoger cosas de la temporada, sobre todo en primavera, que todo es más bonito. (11) **Mi pueblo** no tiene museos ni catedrales, pero para mí, cuando en él estoy, me siento en el mejor paraíso que mis pies hayan pisado.

(1) I was born in Navalcán, in the province of Toledo. (2) Back then **my pueblo** was small, and we all knew one another. (3) Today everything is different. (4) Now it is bigger. (5) I feel a bit lost. (6) When I was small, I was always in the street. (7) Back then the streets were full of mud. (8) And when it rained, trails of water would form all around **the pueblo**. (9) I used to collect espadrilles and iron, and in exchange, they would give me comic strips, which I liked to read a lot. (10) I also used to like to go out to the meadow to collect seasonal things, especially in spring, when everything is prettier. (11) **My pueblo** doesn't have museums or cathedrals, but for me, when I'm in it, I feel as though I'm in the best paradise I've ever set foot in.

Marisol begins her composition as many of her classmates did, naming the town in which she was born and locating it within Spain's regional geography: Navalcán, in the province of Toledo, is about one hundred miles southwest of Madrid. In this brief paragraph Marisol repeats the word "pueblo" three times (lines 2, 8, and 11), modifying it twice with the possessive adjective "my." This collocation appeared throughout the seniors' texts, as well as in conversations with other members at the Centro, reflecting the deeply personal affiliation that they feel with their places of origin.

From the outset of her composition Marisol activates a chronotopic contrast through the use of temporal deictics that situate her pueblo as it used to be in relation to how it is now. As she writes in lines 2 through 5, "**Back then**, my pueblo was small, and we all knew one another. **Today** everything is different. **Now** it is bigger. I feel a bit lost." Marisol thus juxtaposes "back then" with "today," associating the former with the pueblo's small size, which facilitated a provincial kind of familiarity among its inhabitants – "we all knew one another" – that she seems to appreciate. She invokes an explicit disjuncture between that moment and now: Navalcán has grown bigger and become unfamiliar to Marisol, who describes herself as feeling "a bit lost" when she returns (line 5). This description of her pueblo today corresponds to other urban centres – namely Paris, where she now resides – that repel any impulse towards nostalgic longing because of their cold modernity. Bringing these chronotopes into relation with one another, Marisol articulates a stance on the differences that this juxtaposition highlights: the pueblo that she recollects from the past was a more hospitable place than it is now.

Throughout the compositions the temporality of the pueblo was often represented rhythmically through a recurrence of seasons or activities. By associating spring with a surge of prettiness (line 10), for example, Marisol refers to changes wrought upon the pueblo's landscape by cyclical time. Such recollections appeared elsewhere, as the women underscored the countryside's natural beauty by naming its specific elements – wheat, almond trees, chestnut trees (*trigo, almendros, castaños*) – in relation to seasonal cycles. The women also made ample use of the imperfective aspect, denoting actions or states of mind that were habitual, continuous, or recurring in the past and thus lacking precise temporal boundaries. Marisol's brief paragraph illustrates the prevalence of this verbal form: "*era*" and "*estaba*" (was); "*llovía*" (used to rain); "*recogía*" (used to collect); "*me gustaba*" (I used to like). Given its articulation of meaning from within an action or state, and thus, possibly, from a more subjective stance, the imperfective aspect works to produce the generalized feeling of longing that characterizes nostalgic discourse (Fleischmann 1995).

In the last sentence of her composition, however, Marisol shifts to the present tense, invoking once again a description of her pueblo today: "My pueblo doesn't have museums or cathedrals, but for me, when I'm in it, I feel as though I'm in the best paradise that I've ever set foot in" (line 11). Most likely alluding here to Paris, Marisol puts forth a contrast between her pueblo as it is now and larger cosmopolitan centres, which are often associated with grandiose architectural structures and cultural institutions. Bringing village and city into the same interpretive frame, Marisol activates an ideological framework that sets these places in hierarchical relation to one another – and the pueblo prevails.

Even though she acknowledges that Navalcán has changed and that she sometimes feels lost there when she returns, Marisol punctuates her composition with a starkly positive evaluation of it as the "best paradise" that she has ever known, casting the preceding mundane descriptions in a nostalgic light.[2]

Many of Marisol's classmates described their past lives in Spain in equally rosy terms. Remembering her pueblo in Andalucía, for example, Rosario wrote the following:

| No éramos ricos, pero qué felices éramos – toda la familia, mis abuelas, mis abuelos, mis hermanos, tíos y vecinos. | We weren't rich, but we were so happy – the whole family, my grandmothers, my grandfathers, my siblings, my aunts and uncles, and my neighbours. |

Rosario suggests that material wealth mattered little in the pueblo of yore, given its tightly knit structures of kinship. Such "chronotopic formulations of affinity" appeared throughout the texts, revealing the commonplace conflation of recollected village life with wholesome familial intimacy (Agha 2015, 414). Marisol's use of pronouns in the first two sentences of her paragraph reverberates with a similar sentiment. The switch from the first to third person points towards her perception of a fused relationship with the pueblo community at the time that she lived there: "**I** was born in Navalcán, in the province of Toledo. Back then … **we** all knew one another" (lines 1 and 2). This comforting familiarity contrasts with the social fragmentation that Marisol and her peers experience when they make return visits to their pueblos from France. And yet the pueblo remains an object of nostalgic longing. The yearning for a place enfolds a recollection of the social relationships that once sustained it; nostalgia for the pueblo entangles space, time, and personhood within a familiar chronotopic frame.

Marisol's text articulates a particular representation of the past – one that softens, excludes, or simply ignores its negative or painful dimensions. As I learned through conversations with her, Marisol was born into an impoverished family with five children, and her mother died when she was three years old. She attended school until the age of twelve, at which point she left in search of work to help support her family. Thirteen years later, in 1968, without possibilities of social mobility in Spain, she decided to migrate to France, where she lived with her sister's family for two years in a bidonville north of Paris (see chapter 4). Mobilizing a chronotope of nostalgia, Marisol's composition comprises a selective engagement with the past that includes certain details and omits others.

Such remembering dominated her classmates' texts as well. Most of the other women displayed similar sentimental stances on the facts of their biographical trajectories and the historical circumstances in which they had unfolded – at least within the bounds of the written assignment. In conversations about the assignment, however, they revealed other modes of engagement with the past, manifesting non-nostalgic – sometimes even "anti-nostalgic" (Bissell 2015, 218) – dispositions that complicated certain social relationships at the Centro.[3]

Anti-nostalgia and Social Distinction

Nostalgia not only functions as a unifying frame for a community formed through historical circumstances but also may be summoned by individuals who wish to differentiate themselves within it. For Paula and Benita, who were affiliated with the Centro but claimed marginal status with respect to its core members, assuming an oppositional stance on nostalgia bolstered claims of social distinction. Their biographical circumstances, which, for different reasons, positioned them outside the category of "labour migrant," fostered alternative historicities that displaced nostalgic longing with a kind of present-day pragmatism.

At seventy-eight years of age, Paula was the oldest woman in the Escuela. Born in 1930, she migrated to France nine years later at the end of the war, accompanying her parents into political exile. She had thus spent half of her childhood outside of Spain. Paula's identification as a Spaniard was primarily tethered to her experience of war and displacement, both of which, as far as she was concerned, militated against any form of wistful reminiscence. Moreover, she preferred to speak French. Even in class, where code-switching was often disparaged as an impediment to improving one's literacy skills in Spanish, she readily alternated between the two languages. Paula's promiscuous use of the codes that comprise her linguistic repertoire, including a variety of Catalan spoken in her pueblo in Aragón, reflected her lack of investment in the ideology of monolingual purity that motivated many of her classmates to participate in the Escuela. Through various semiotic means, then, she signalled her distinction from the other women in the class and the community of Spaniards whom they represented.

Paula's composition comprised a matter-of-fact description of the landscape and livestock of her pueblo near Teruel. One day after class I ran into her on the platform at the train stop near the Centro as we were both heading back into Paris. During the brief ride we sat together and chatted. Paula revealed to me her frustration with some of her peers for their inclination towards nostalgic recollection, commenting, "I don't understand them. If Spain is so much better, then why don't they just go live there?" Paula thus assumed an explicitly oppositional stance on the practice of nostalgic remembering that she observed in the Escuela. Along with her adherence to language ideologies that challenged monolingual norms, she recruited such anti-nostalgia as part of an ongoing project of self-differentiation. Paula's rejection of nostalgia also helped amplify the meaningful distinction between labour migrants and political refugees – a distinction entangled with variegated claims of belonging to Spain. Given their association with poverty and illiteracy, the former have long been considered inferior to the latter, when they have been considered at all (see Tur 2007). Indeed, their absence from most official historiographies of twentieth-century Spain reflects their lower status.

Like Paula, Benita distinguished herself from the other women in the Escuela by explicitly dissociating herself from what she perceived as their habitual expressions of nostalgia. Because of her family's socio-economic position, she had experienced a different life trajectory than her peers. As I stated in the previous chapter, Benita's father had been a successful farmer, and her mother had been a schoolteacher. In her adolescence Benita fell in love with a man who had immigrated to France with his parents during the war but returned to her pueblo every summer. After they married in 1968, Benita joined him in Paris, where he was employed as a manager in a factory.

Unlike her classmates, Benita had never worked outside of the home. Although she was strongly affiliated with the Centro and the diasporic community that it represents, she regularly invoked the particularities of her experience to distinguish herself from her peers. Benita's critique of nostalgic discourse served this very purpose. One afternoon in the Escuela after listening to some of her classmates' compositions, she said:

Yo no tengo ninguna nostalgia de España. Cuando voy, voy y me la gozo. Y cuando vengo aquí, vengo y me la gozo. Y no tengo ningún problema de – pero el caso es que no he trabajado. No tengo la misma situación. Siempre me ha gustado ir al cine, al teatro, a los museos. Y a todo lo he seguido haciendo.	I don't have any nostalgia for Spain. When I go, I go and I enjoy it. And when I come back here, I come back and I enjoy it. I don't have any problem with – but the thing is I never worked. I don't have the same situation. I've always liked to go to the movies, the theatre, and the museums. And I've kept doing that all along.

Claiming that she does not have the "problem" of her peers, Benita describes her transnational mobility in matter-of-fact terms: she comes and goes without any stirrings of sentimental longing. Her situation is different, she explains, precisely because she has never worked. She thus embodies a different kind of migrant than her peers.

Benita goes on to associate the expression of nostalgia with a lack of the cultural interests that she has cultivated due to the good fortune of her upbringing. Romanticized recollections of the past, she suggests, remain the preserve of the relatively uneducated expatriates who fled conditions of poverty. Benita summons a figure of personhood – that is, a poor rural Spaniard – and projects this onto her peers, thereby assuming a counterpoint stance that affirms her modernity and sophistication. According to the ideological framework that Benita evinces, the expression of nostalgia functions as a marker of social class and education. Owing to their limited schooling and lack of exposure to the arts, labour migrants are prone to talk about the past with facile sentimentality. Distinguishing herself thus from the others present, Benita lays claim to the literate subjectivity that her peers in the Escuela desire, while foreclosing the possibility that they might engage in a similar act of identification (see chapter 1).

Carolina, a stout seventy-one-year-old with a booming voice and a ready smile, took issue with Benita's remark. Brusquely cutting her off, she made a gesture with her thumb and forefinger to indicate "money":

Toma – a todas nos ha gustado. Pero hacía falta tener *esto* para ir [al cine, al teatro, a los museos].	Wow – we all liked that. But you needed to have *this* to go [to the movies, to the theatre, to museums].

Carolina invokes what this group of migrants shares with Benita, as well as what renders them distinct. It is not that they are uninterested in cultural institutions and experiences, but rather that they have never had the financial means to enjoy them. Riled by Benita's remarks, Carolina pointedly alludes to the poverty that provoked their migration and explains their lack of cultural capital today; without money they were not able to go to theatres and museums. It is easy to understand her annoyance: Benita has invoked a hierarchy of migrants structured around labour and literacy, thereby implying her peers' moral inferiority and the difficulty of their transformation through a course such as the Escuela.

Most economic migrants to France retained the conviction that they would eventually return to Spain, which may partly explain their predisposition towards nostalgic recollection. The deferral of this return – which, as I discuss in the next chapter, continues to haunt the diasporic present long after the decision to remain – may have generated chronotopes of nostalgia to sustain an imagined future in their place of origin. Spaniards like Paula and Benita, who migrated under different circumstances, assimilated their settlement in France untroubled by the pull of the past. The pueblo may draw them back every summer, but Paris has become home. Their anti-nostalgic discourse illustrates how concomitant modes of engagement with the past provide a collectivity the means of producing social-semiotic effects in the present. As I show in the next section, individual social actors may exploit multiple and sometimes conflicting historicities in a similar way to make sense of painful personal memories.

Discrepant Historicities

Surges of Sorrow

Carolina was an avid participant in the Centro's many activities and spoke with pride about her enduring ties to Spain. One afternoon in the Escuela she shared her composition about her pueblo near Valencia, explicitly invoking nostalgia in her concluding sentence:

Sus madreselvas floridas a la orilla de los caminos eran un gozo verlas y yo recuerdo todo con un poco de nostalgia.	Its flowering honeysuckles along the pathway's edge were a pleasure to see, and I remember everything with a bit of nostalgia.

During our conversations outside of class I often heard Carolina talk affectionately about Valencia and how she and her husband returned there regularly from Paris. And yet, outside of the parameters of the written assignment, she accessed other chronotopic frames for representing the past. Towards the end of the session in which she read her composition out loud, for example, Pablo left momentarily to retrieve some photocopies from the main office. While he was out of the room, Carolina began to declaim a lengthy poem that the students had studied in class – "El hada azul" (The blue fairy). Known for her memorization skills, Carolina often performed such recitations to the enjoyment of her classmates, explaining that she practised them at home to keep her mind sharp. After her performance, which triggered hearty applause, Carolina boasted that she could easily recite from memory another poem, which she ascribed to her father: "My father had one, too, because he was in prison for so many years." Without any prodding, she began to deliver the following text:

"Vuela ... vuela ... golondrina"	Fly ... fly ... swallow:
Golondrina, ¿estás cansada,	Swallow, are you tired,
que te has posado en la reja,	because you're resting on the prison bars
y no vuelas alborozada	and you aren't flying overjoyed
en busca de tu pareja,	in search of your partner,
que estará desconsolada?	who is probably inconsolable?
¿O es que quieres endulzar	Or is it that you want to sweeten
con tu armonioso trinar	with your harmonious warble
las tristes horas del preso?	the sad hours of a prisoner?
No te marches, golondrina,	Don't go, swallow,
aun hay sol en la montaña;	there's still sun above the mountain;
mientras la tarde declina	while the afternoon grows late
trina, golondrina, trina	chirp, swallow, chirp
y al pobre preso acompaña.	and keep the poor prisoner company.
Oye, golondrina hermosa:	Listen, beautiful swallow:
Tú que estás libre con brío,	You who are free with spirit,
¿quieres volar presurosa	Would you like to fly quickly
a una viejecita llorosa	to a tearful old woman
entregarle un beso mío?	to give her a kiss from me?

Here, Carolina stopped herself, overcome with emotion. Her classmates waited a beat before calling out, "*¡Muy bien!*" (Very good!), and "*¡Es precioso!*" (It's lovely!). After a moment Carolina continued her recitation:

Cruzarás en raudo vuelo	In your swift flight you will cross
montañas, ríos, y valles –	mountains, rivers, and valleys –

At this point Carolina's voice broke, and she began to cry. After a brief pause Elena, another student in the course, spoke softly: "Bad memories. *Of course*. Calm down, calm down. Don't recite any more, and you can say it another day."[4] Carolina took a deep breath and went on:

Y en el valenciano suelo,	And on Valencian land,
quizás a mi madre halles.	perhaps you will find my mother.
No le digas que estoy triste,	Don't tell her that I'm sad,
no le digas que he llorado.	don't tell her that I've cried.
Dile que aunque encarcelado,	Tell her that even though I'm imprisoned
sonreía esperanzado	I was smiling, hopeful
la tarde en que tú me viste.	on the afternoon that you saw me.
Cuelga en su balcón tu nido,	Hang your nest on her balcony,
y con tu dulce cantar,	and with your sweet song,
recuerde al hijo querido,	remind her of her beloved son,
no la dejarás llorar.	you won't make her cry.
Ya no hay sol en la montaña,	There is no longer sun over the hills,
el campo pierde color;	the field is losing colour;
mientras la tarde declina,	While the afternoon grows late,
vuela, golondrina, vuela.	fly, swallow, fly.
Déjame con mi dolor.	Leave me with my pain.

As soon as Carolina finished, her classmates applauded enthusiastically and told her that it was lovely. María then asked if the poem had indeed come from Carolina's father, to which she responded affirmatively:

Esa es de mi padre. Yo tenía el papel, y la ha escrito para sus bisnietos ... Es raro que me pase esto, ¿sabes?	It's from my father. I used to have the paper, and he wrote it down for his great-grandchildren ... It's weird that this is happening to me, you know?

There is ambiguity here with respect to Carolina's understanding of the poem's provenance. When she says, "It's from my father," it is unclear if she is claiming that her father wrote it or if she is merely stating that he passed it on to his progeny.[5] Regardless, the women's eagerness to verify the origin of the text and Carolina's assertion of proximity to its author (either through creation or transmission) point again towards the capital that accrues to members of this population through claims of authorship. Carolina then comments on her peculiar surge of feeling: "It's weird that this is happening to me, you know?" Reciting "Fly ... fly ... swallow" to her peers, she evokes her childhood and its painful associations – including the war and her father's imprisonment – memories that cannot be resuscitated through a chronotope of nostalgia. And yet the same coordinates of place and time animate the sentimental, written description of her pueblo. The poem thus mediates an engagement with the past that generates a different kind of affect: sorrow rather than nostalgic longing. Delivering a poem that summons painful aspects of her past in the same setting in which she recalls the pleasant flowering honeysuckle of Valencia, Carolina exposes a repertoire of historicities among her discursive resources – concomitant modes of engagement with the past that entail various forms of knowledge and affect and that are differentially valued in relation to the setting and mode of their activation.

In this classroom and at the Centro generally, appropriate representations of the past – that is, those worthy of written documentation and performance – tend to be grounded in anodyne chronotopes, of which nostalgia serves as paradigmatic token. The institution and its members thus uphold the culture of silence that took root in the aftermath of war and continued to govern talk about the past into the present. When Carolina breaks this silence, pivoting from recollections of flowering honeysuckle to the loneliness of imprisonment, Elena, a seventy-six-year-old woman from Santander and a regular member at the Centro, intervenes to offer solace and a gentle reminder that some topics are perhaps best left unspoken. She refers to these as "bad memories." Her evaluative remark evokes an economy of memory in which recollections of the past may be good or bad, but the latter provoke an invitation to silence or, at the very least, to indefinite postponement: "You can say it another day."

Elena thus enacts the discursive practice featured in the poem. She mirrors the prisoner, who entreats the swallow not to reveal what it has witnessed – the hopelessness evidenced by his crying. Instead, the bird must bear a positive message that belies the despair of imprisonment: "Tell her that ... I was smiling, hopeful on the afternoon that you saw me." Such emotional dissimulation exemplifies the effects of the war and its aftermath on the intimate lives of Spaniards at the time, which the women attending the Escuela understood first hand. Their emotional reactions to Carolina's recitation, which included hearty applause as well as tearful eyes and averted gazes, suggested that it resonated with aspects of their own experience. Talk of trauma generated by political circumstances beyond one's control may be muted in public discourse as a strategy to avoid social discord and the pain of personal revelation. Some stories might be better left untold. Pablo's pointed interventions into the writing process, by which he encouraged students to elaborate their compositions with intimate details about their lives in post-war Spain, revealed the obstinate silence that shaped expressions of historicity among the Escuela's participants and members of the Centro more generally.

Obstinate Silence

During the second week of the assignment Elena read the following composition in her distinct, raspy voice. Instead of featuring her pueblo exclusively, the relatively lengthy text charted a biographical trajectory from her birth in Santander in northern Spain to her retirement in Paris. She composed the text as one solid paragraph, switching from third-person to first-person verb forms, an inconsistency that Pablo and some of the others noted once she had finished reading. It began as follows:

Composition 2: "Elena Was Born in Santander on the Sixteenth of July in 1932"

(1) Elena nació en Santander 16-07-32. (2) Vivió allí hasta la edad de 9 años. (3) Después se fue a vivir con sus padres a un pequeño pueblo de la provincia de Salamanca donde eran mis padres. (4) Y allí fui al colegio hasta los catorce años. (5) A veces ayudaba a mis padres con ciertas tareas, como ir al campo a buscar hierba para los animales que tenían. (6) En el verano iba a espigar, hacía mucho calor. (7) No teníamos agua en casa, y tenía que buscarla a dos kilómetros ...

(1) Elena was born in Santander on 16-07-32. (2) She lived there until the age of 9. (3) Afterwards she went with her parents to live in a small pueblo in the province of Salamanca where my parents were. (4) And there I went to school until the age of fourteen. (5) Sometimes I helped my parents with certain tasks, such as going to the fields to look for grass for the animals that they had. (6) In the summer I used to collect grain, it was really hot. (7) We didn't have water in our house, and I needed to go get it two kilometres away ...

Elena read her composition rapidly from beginning to end, eschewing vocal inflection and pauses between sentences. After

Nostalgia for Pueblos Past   59

suggesting that such a presentational style might make it difficult for an audience to follow the text, Pablo illustrated how to break up a composition more clearly into small paragraphs. Taking a large easel pad that served as the classroom's blackboard, he asked Elena to help him make an outline of her composition, divided up according to each of its main ideas. To make the text more coherent and engaging, he explained, Elena should expand upon each of these ideas with personal details. Focusing on the first two sentences, which concerned Elena's childhood, he encouraged her to imagine how to do so:

1 PABLO: no lo vas a dejar así en un solo párrafo, lo vas a redondear

2 ELENA: de acuerdo
3 PABLO: te falta decir más sobre eso
4 ELENA: sí sí, porque hay pocas cosas
5 PABLO ((*to another student*)): paciencia –
6 ELENA: te cuento de cuando tenía cuatro años – fíjate – que empezó la guerra de España
7 PABLO: sería muy bonito que dijeras eso
8 ELENA: *oh là là*, teníamos que correr cuando venían a bombardear los aviones, que eran los alemanes, teníamos que correr a escondernos en los refugios
9 PABLO: ahh sería muy interesante que hablaras de eso
10 ELENA: me acuerdo de eso – fíjate – cuando ya entró Franco y todo eso, que me acuerdo que me hacía mi madre una

1 PABLO: you're not going to leave this in just one paragraph, you're going to fill it out

2 ELENA: okay
3 PABLO: you need to say more about this
4 ELENA: yes yes, because there isn't much there
5 PABLO ((*to another student*)): patience –
6 ELENA: I could tell you about when I was four – listen – the Spanish war started –
7 PABLO: it would be really nice if you said that
8 ELENA: *oh là là* we had to run when planes came to bomb, the Germans, we had to run and hide in a shelter
9 PABLO: ahh it would be really interesting if you talked about that
10 ELENA: I remember that – listen – when Franco had arrived and all that. I remember that my mother used to give me

peina con un chinchorro con un lazo rojo, y vinieron los de – los falangistas – y a mi madre la –	a hairstyle with a net with a red bow, and they came – the *falangistas* – and said to my mother –
11 CARMEN: yo me lo acuerdo también –	11 CARMEN: I remember it, too –
12 ELENA: la dijeron, "oiga, al favor de quitarle ese lazo a la niña"	12 ELENA: they said to her, "hey, please take that bow out of the girl's hair"
13 BENITA: porque era rojo –	13 BENITA: because it was red –
14 ELENA: porque era rojo, sí, señora	14 ELENA: because it was red, yes, ma'am
15 NURIA: ay pues eso sería muy bonito –	15 NURIA: oh well it would be really nice –
16 ELENA: y luego después mi padre fue – bueno si le cuento todo tengo un libro	16 ELENA: and then later my father was – well, if I tell you everything, I'd have a book

Before this exchange begins, Pablo advises Elena on how to revise her draft – that is, by identifying the sequence of ideas that she has included and then "filling [them] out" in separate paragraphs (line 1). After acknowledging that "there isn't much there" in what she has written (line 4), Elena goes on to provide the kind of personal details that Pablo has been encouraging women to include in their compositions throughout the class.

Born in 1932, Elena was slightly older than most of the other women in the Escuela. She was four years old when the war broke out and remembers its disquieting effects on her quotidian world. Before recounting a narrative from that period, she establishes a chronotopic ground that evokes a particular time and place in the past: "the Spanish war started" (line 6). She goes on to sketch some of her family's distressing actions during the time frame that this event provoked: "We had to run when planes came to bomb" (line 8). Uttering the imperative "listen!" (line 6), she both entreats her interlocutors to pay attention and signals the interest of her forthcoming recollection: On one occasion a member of the Falange, the fascist political party aligned with Franco, asked her mother to remove a red bow from her hair (lines 10 and 12). As the historian Julián Casanova (2010) explains, that colour was associated with the dictator's communist and Republican rivals during the war and its immediate aftermath (98). The exchange that Elena describes between her mother and a soldier provokes reactions from her classmates, who index membership in their generational cohort by demonstrating knowledge of such historical phenomena. Carmen interrupts Elena to claim that she harbours similar memories of that past – "I remember it, too" (line 11) – while Benita anticipates the anecdote's punchline: "Because [the bow] was red" (line 13). In the final line Elena voices a version of the refrain discussed in chapters 1 and 2 – "if I tell you everything, I'd have book!" This both suggests an awareness of the performative dimension of her interaction with Pablo and legitimizes the content of what she has recounted. Her declaration also points towards the local value of written discourse as an authoritative medium of personal recollection.

Elena's brief narrative illustrates the fraught time period in which it is set: bombs fall, and families must run for cover; a girl's bow becomes a sign of sedition. Although she recounts the memory rather matter of factly, Elena seems aware of its affective resonance, imploring her classmates twice to listen (lines 6 and 10) and uttering an evaluative discourse marker in French – "*oh là là!*" (line 8) – that calls attention to the impressive details about to be revealed. The mere mention of the war sparks Pablo's enthusiasm, and he encourages her to write more about it (line 7); he even repeats the remark after she reveals details about German bombardments (line 9). Such interventions are meant to challenge Elena and her classmates to disclose stories that typically remain unspoken, engaging in a form of reflexivity that articulates a collision of the personal and the historical based on their intimate experience of transformative political events in the past. Elena begins to do so by invoking Franco and the Falangists before offering a brief narrative in which her innocent, four-year-old self was subjected to the intimidation and fear with which the regime was associated. Bringing these figures into relation with one another – a girl and a fascist soldier – Elena elicits an animated response from her interlocutors. She also indirectly indexes a political position that she came to hold in later life, critical of the authoritarian dictatorship that the Falangists, in part, made possible.

Despite Pablo's encouragement to include such recollections in her composition, Elena returned the following week with a simple revision, extending the paragraph about her childhood with only one additional sentence (see figure 2.1):

Miercoles 16-04-2008
Elena nació en Santander el dia 16-07-32. Vivio alli hasta la edad de 9 años, **paso su niñez con mucha dificultad a causa de la guerra.**

Wednesday 16-04-2008
Elena was born in Santander on 16-07-32. She lived there until the age of 9, **she had a very difficult childhood because of the war.**

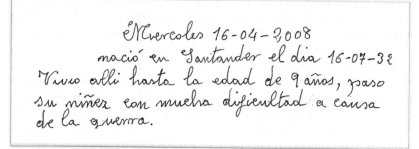

Figure 2.1. The first paragraph of Elena's revised composition
Source: Image courtesy of the author.

In her understated revision Elena alludes to the experience of trauma but excludes the extraordinary details that excited Pablo and her classmates. Her omission points to a disjuncture between what an individual recollects and what she deems appropriate for public expression, to the communicative value of silence among her peers with regard to talk about their painful past.

A week after Elena had read this version in class, I ran into her in the cafeteria and asked about the changes she had made to her composition. She shrugged and explained that she preferred not to add the details that Pablo recommended because she did not want to talk about "those negative things" (*esas cosas negativas*), which often "stir people up" (*agitan a la gente*) and create tension. Elena's withholding of details about her wartime experience was thus motivated by an interest in safeguarding social cohesion at the Centro. It also manifested the norms for discourse about the past that typically organized talk among the Spaniards, whether in Spain or abroad, who had lived through this period of time (see Aguilar 2002; Faber 2018; Graham 2012; Richards 2013). In the conversation with Pablo earlier, which occurred outside the bounds of the written assignment, Elena evoked the past without any sentimental longing, bringing up the war and its deleterious effects on her family's everyday life – but this openness was only momentary. Ultimately she resisted Pablo's suggestion to include such details in writing, illustrating the extent to which deliberate gestures of silence govern public representations of the past within this social realm.

Insight from the Generational Sidelines

To make sense of the practices of remembering that I observed at the Centro, I asked the activities director, Josep, one evening over drinks near his apartment why he thought the seniors seemed inclined to recall the past in nostalgic terms. He shook his head and replied that any negative narrative about the past is "forbidden" (*prohibida*), alluding to dominant notions among Spaniards in later life about how the dictatorship should be discussed, if at all. Josep went on to describe how such communicative norms operate today within his own family in Barcelona:

Mi padre no habla de la guerra. Mis abuelos tampoco. En España fue muy duro, ¿eh? La gente no quiere hablar … Se habla mucho del pasado como si fuera algo nostálgico, idealizado, y tal y cual, cuando tuvieron una juventud de mierda. Que hablan del pasado no me extraña. Que hablan del pasado idealizándolo me deja alucinado.	My father doesn't talk about the war. My grandparents either. It was really hard in Spain, eh? People don't want to talk about it … [Those at the Centro] talk a lot about the past as though it were something idealized and nostalgic and everything, when they had a really shitty youth. It doesn't surprise me that they talk about the past. But the fact they idealize it amazes me.

Josep's age and his institutional role afforded him a unique perspective on social practices among participants at the Centro and the much broader cohort of older Spaniards that they represented. As the historian Helen Graham (2012) has written, the offspring of Spain's elderly have been more open to discussing contentious aspects of Spain's past in pursuit of the historical reckoning that had never materialized after the transition to democracy. As a member of these younger generations, Josep was flummoxed by the act of representing the past in "idealized and nostalgic" terms – consternation that he shared with some of the Centro's more marginal members, such as Paula and Benita. Nevertheless, he *did* understand the deliberate turn to silence regarding past experiences perceived as "really hard." His own socialization through Spanish institutions, such as family and school, had endowed him with a sensitivity to the legacies of Spain's recent history and an awareness that, for many older Spaniards, the past was a discursive minefield of "forbidden" topics best avoided or, at the very least, broached with discretion. This principle guided his interactions with seniors at the Centro. He deferred to them delicately when discussing historical matters, intent on acknowledging their expertise on the past acquired through biographical experience (see chapters 4 and 5). Pablo, for his part, seemed to have been less familiar with these historical-interactional norms. In the Escuela and the theatre workshop (discussed in chapter 3) he was a tireless advocate of personal reflection and disclosure as ways of dealing directly with painful memories. His upbringing in Mexico and his affinity for dramatic theatre may go some way towards explaining the discrepancy between his interactional tactics and Josep's.

Impossible Talk

Ideologies about the past and how it should operate as a topic of discourse in the present shape the modes of remembering that circulate in a socio-cultural milieu. Notions about a memory's appropriateness, its aesthetic qualities, or its affective potency can render political the historicities by which individuals and communities are constituted. For the most part, Spaniards at the Centro avoided such complications, deeming chronotopes of nostalgia to be appropriate frames of recollection for animating public depictions of past experience. To be sure, such benign spatio-temporal figures obfuscated their political stances with respect to historical matters.

At social institutions such as the Centro, nostalgic discourse displaces talk about the past that might provoke discord among members, thereby facilitating a kind of "institutional coexistence" (*convivencia asociativa*) through a felicitous balance of avoidance and revelation (Ribert 2015b, 34).[6] Benita, whose unique status gave her insight into the Centro's social dynamics, echoed this thought to me one afternoon in private:

Tout le monde veut s'entendre bien. Personne ne parle de la politique. Mais presque tout le monde est d'accord pour parler de la dictature. Tous les gens qui sont venus ici [en France], ils ont souffert parce qu'il n'y avait pas de liberté [en Espagne]. Tu ne peux pas imaginer la faim qu'ils ont eue. Comment ils vont parler ces gens de Franco? C'est pas possible.	Everyone wants to get along. No one talks about politics. But here almost everyone agrees as far as the dictatorship goes. Everyone who came here [to France] suffered because there was no freedom [in Spain]. You can't imagine the hunger that they experienced. How are these people going to talk about Franco? It's not possible.

Despite the probability of their shared contempt for the dictatorship, Spaniards at the Centro do not discuss political matters in the interest of maintaining social harmony. According to Benita, talk about Franco is simply "not possible" because it conjures the traumatic conditions that precipitated their migration to France and explains, in a sense, their indefinite presence in Paris. Benita alludes to the silence around political matters that is associated with the generation of Spaniards who were born at the time of the war. As the social historian Michael Richards (2013) has remarked, they came of age during an epoch in which their elders preferred to leave their painful past behind, a decision with pervasive emotional consequences: "The silence which surrounded children's lives in the 1940s was both stubborn and intangible, producing an unfathomable sense of instability and pervasive feelings of stigma, frustration, and anguish" (133). The values that shape talk about the past among Spaniards in later life seem to constitute a protracted outgrowth of the discursive silencing that emerged in the wake of war, only to be reaffirmed later on by the state during its transition to democracy in the 1970s, when it called for blanket amnesty.

But, as Elena revealed, silence is not the same as forgetting. In the final version of her composition she mentioned unspecified "difficulties" caused by the war before resuming an anodyne narrative of mundane events. To avoid the discomfort of self-disclosure and the public agitation of traumatic recollection, she withheld details from her written text but exposed painful aspects of her past in an off-record moment of interaction. If Elena were to recount the sweeping entanglement of experience and emotion that constituted her early life, she, too, would "have a book." Here the metaphorical tome serves as an alibi for silence, as she invokes the impossibility of including – or rather, the necessity of omitting – all the "bad memories" that make up her harrowing history.

Among transnational migrants whose pathways have been shaped by distressing historical events, chronotopes of nostalgia serve benign acts of recollection, casting the past in the warm glow of reminiscence. But this should not be dismissed as facile sentimentality. As Debbora Battaglia (1995) writes, nostalgia can function as a "vehicle of knowledge" through which social actors articulate "appropriate feelings toward their own histories" and "their detachment from – and active resistance to" whatever disempowering conditions have shaped them (77). Moreover, alongside this prevalent mode of remembering, other historicities circulate within a community's discursive repertoire. At the Centro these include expressions of anti-nostalgia that disavow rose-coloured chronotopes of the past in favour of a more pragmatic amplification of the present. Occasionally they encompass raw expressions of sorrow. Such variation may obscure an important commonality: how individuals engage with the past is informed by their histories of migration as well as their social situation in later life. Felicitous representations of the past depend in part on perceptions of the communicative event in which they are put forth, whether they are public or private, official or unofficial. Remembering itself becomes a means of creating social meaning in the present, helping individuals make sense of their place within the socio-cultural realms with which particular memories are associated. This becomes even more apparent in the next chapter, in which participants in the Centro's theatre workshop negotiate the staged representation of a powerful narrative trope in their diasporic milieu: return migration.

3 Return Migration on Stage

After nearly nine years of working as a live-in nanny for an affluent family in Paris, Amalia returned to Spain. By then the two children in her care had become young adults, and she was tired of the civil unrest that affected life in the French capital during the events of 1968.[1] Moreover, she had achieved the financial objectives that motivated her to leave home in the first place: she had bought an apartment in Córdoba for her mother and grandmother, and she had saved a large sum of money. But, as she revealed to me one afternoon over lunch in her apartment, her resettlement in Spain was short lived:

J'avais le mal du pays, donc je suis rentrée [en Espagne] en '69 pour ne plus revenir. Mais je ne suis même pas restée un an. Je m'étouffais là-bas! Tout avait changé.	I was homesick, so I went back [to Spain] in '69 permanently. But I didn't even last a year. I was suffocating there! Everything had changed.

Although she was content to be reunited with her family, Amalia missed the independence that she had come to appreciate in France. She had been driven back by homesickness, but Córdoba had changed so much since her departure that it no longer felt like home. After just nine months in Spain, she migrated again to Paris, where she decided to remain permanently.

Most of the Centro's participants did not attempt such a return to Spain, even though they, too, initially conceived their migration as temporary. Like Amalia, they had left for Paris in the 1960s with the intention of accumulating enough wealth to elevate their social status back home – a mentality shaped in part through calculated efforts by Franco's regime, which created policy to ensure their abiding attachment to the homeland and thus a steady stream of remittances that would fuel Spain's fledgling economy. Lured by high interest rates, they also opened savings accounts in Spanish banks, and many of them bought real estate in their pueblos after just three or four years of working abroad.[2] Thanks in part to such contributions from hundreds of thousands of migrants, Spain experienced an economic "miracle" that foretold the emergence of new forms of consumerism across all segments of Spanish society in the years leading up to Franco's death in 1975.

Amalia, along with many of her peers at the Centro, believed that her role in the enterprise of modernization had not been adequately recognized by the Spanish state. As she told me emphatically over lunch, "*We* are the ones who lifted up that country! And *they* forget!"[3] As Spain caught up to its northern European counterparts in socioeconomic ways that would soon be consolidated politically in the transition to democracy, the status that Spanish migrants had acquired in France gradually dissipated. While many migrants returned to Spain during this period of time, encouraged in part by French authorities eager to reduce a bloated workforce, others did not. Taking into consideration employment opportunities, their children, who had been born in France, and access to valued French institutions such as education and health care, they began to imagine extending their transnational trajectories indefinitely. Over time the probability of return dissolved into the resignation to remain.

Nevertheless, among the Spaniards whom I encountered in Paris – that is, migrants who stayed in their host country – return migration endures as a meaningful trope. In late 2007 when I began attending the Centro's weekly theatre workshop, which was led by Pablo, its participants were in the midst of rehearsing an original one-act play about the topic that would be performed at the upcoming World Book Day event: *¿Volver a España?* (Back to Spain?) (see figure 3.1). The play's title both asked the question that dogged their initial years in Paris and alluded to the ambivalence with which they answered it. Its story was immediately familiar to those at the Centro: A Spanish migrant in Paris, after living there for a number of years, decides to return to Spain; when she arrives in her pueblo, she is disappointed by what she discovers; realizing that she was better off in France, she leaves for Paris once again. The play thus stages the complexities of return migration – both the promise of its possibility and the consequences of its enactment – illuminating its enduring significance as a narrative frame for migrants who never went back permanently to Spain.

In this chapter, I explore the abiding resonance of return for the population of diasporic Spaniards that the Centro represents, analysing

Celebración
del Día
Internacional
del Libro

La Plaine, 23 de abril 2008

Figure 3.1. World Book Day program (2008)
Source: Courtesy of CERP – Maison d'Espagne de la Région Parisienne.

their representation of the phenomenon as a reflexive practice that sheds light on the experience of long-term transnationalism. Theatrical performance activates in pronounced ways the chronotopic calibration through which texts generate meaning; in the *here and now* of the performance event, the spectator evaluates the *there and then* of the story on stage. In what follows, I conduct detailed discourse analysis on the text of *Back to Spain?*, as well as on interactions that it instigated in rehearsal and reactions that it generated in performance. These conversations show how discrepant manifestations of a common narrative about the past may drive processes of social differentiation for diasporic subjects negotiating their place in the present.

Cultural Performance, Reflexivity, and the Modernist Chronotope

As a scheduled, temporally and spatially bounded event meant to occasion collective participation, *Back to Spain?* could be considered what Richard Bauman (2011) has termed a cultural performance, a form of culture about culture that reveals its values as they are "embodied, enacted, and placed on display before an audience" (715). Such performances function through a mechanism of reflexivity by which the self, or an aspect of the self, is presented as an object of consideration. Cultural performance, as Bauman (1992) writes, is an "especially potent and heightened means of taking the role of the other and of looking back at oneself from that perspective"; it enables a kind of "consciousness of consciousness" among performers and audience alike, who reflect on shared experience in the process of enactment and the evaluation of representation (48).[4] Crucially such acts of reflexivity are often shaped – or, in the case of theatrical performance, *directed* – by intervening social actors with personal or political interests in how remembering and representation occur.

Performative events call attention to the semiotic forms through which people reflect on and make sense of their experience, activating the processes of stancetaking and (dis)affiliation through which members of a collectivity situate themselves within it (see Jaffe 2009). Such forms include narrative structures, as well as the cultural chronotopes that ground those narratives in particular times and places, circumscribing the figures of personhood that inhabit them. These "invokable histories," as Jan Blommaert (2015, 110) has referred to them, may be accessed by members of a collectivity who are familiar with the narrative in question. Chronotopes, in other words, constitute forms of cultural knowledge that enable the production of intelligible discourse and claims of belonging to social collectivities. As I reveal through my analysis, *Back to Spain?* makes sense to its audience members in large part because it trades on a recognizable spatio-temporal frame in their semiotic repertoire: the modernist chronotope.

Within this particular chronotope, time is mapped onto space in such a way that places of origin are associated with backwardness and provincialism, while places of settlement evoke forwardness and progress. The modernist chronotope has proven to be a productive analytic among linguistic anthropologists who investigate situations of migration and diaspora (see, among others, Dick 2010, 2018; Divita 2014; Karimzad 2016; Karmizad and Catedral 2021; Koven 2013a; Paz 2018). As this scholarship has shown, the modernist chronotope enables individuals to make sense of their migrant lives, present or past, real or imagined (Dick 2010, 2018). The performance and reception of *Back to Spain?* reveal how this chronotope circulates among participants at the Centro as an accessible resource for representing a time in the past when return was still possible, serving as an official "picture" of the way things were – or at least a picture deemed non-polemical by a director eager to placate actors and audience (Agha 2007, 322). In the play's culminating monologue, however, temporalities shift as the modernist rendition of the return narrative is suddenly suffused with regret. The juxtaposition of such conflicting historicities illustrates not only the enduring potency of the return narrative for Spaniards in diaspora but also the value of chronotopic variation in social processes that sustain formations of community.

The Making of *Back to Spain?* Collaboration and Collective Reflexivity

The play begins with an opening monologue by Luisa, a Spanish migrant in Paris and the play's protagonist, in which she decides to return to her pueblo; a companion then enters to escort her back to Spain, reciting an excerpt from a nineteenth-century Spanish novel as she does so. The following sketches are comedic, including three successive conversations between Luisa and the women she encounters in her village. In the final scene Luisa recites a melancholic poem in which she describes her disappointment with what she has found upon her return and decides to migrate once again to Paris. Through this somewhat disjointed sequence of scenes, *Back to Spain?* traces a familiar arc of return migration, from Paris to pueblo and back again.

The play emerged from a collaboration between Pablo and Lina, who, as an active member of the Centro and leader of its arts and crafts workshop, was known for her artistic proclivities. When Pablo first arrived at the Centro, he had an ambitious vision for what the workshop participants might accomplish. A number of times in our private conversations he used the French expression *"aller plus loin"* (go further) to describe what he intended the seniors to do, invoking the possibilities of self-discovery inherent in his understanding of theatrical representation. Indeed, he exhibited a similar interest in his role as the instructor of the Escuela. The term "go further," he explained, was often deployed by teachers of the acting courses that he was taking in his master's program at a nearby university. He fashioned his serious pedagogical style partly in imitation of them, wanting to ensure that the workshop's participants acknowledged his authority and took his craft seriously. Because of his earnest demeanour and insistence on discipline, some of them playfully referred to him outside of class as *el dictador* (the dictator), alluding to Franco and the early years of his regime.

When Pablo asked workshop participants what they wanted to perform for the upcoming World Book Day celebration, Lina offered some unrelated sketches and a poem about small-town life in Spain. Although he was disappointed by the simplicity of her texts, as he expressed to me privately, members of the theatre workshop seemed to appreciate them, laughing heartily when they were read in rehearsal. Despite his sense that they were not likely to push seniors to "go further," Pablo ended up using them to appease the workshop's participants, as well as the Centro's director, who had encouraged him to find material that was politically neutral. Nevertheless, throughout rehearsals he encouraged the student actors to draw on their histories of experience as transnational migrants for whom the possibility of permanent return shaped their lives abroad during their initial years in Paris. With the exception of Benita, who had migrated because of marriage, and Manuel, whose family had fled Spain as political refugees shortly after the war, all of the students in the theatre workshop – eleven women and two men – arrived in Paris as labour migrants in the 1960s, intending to return to Spain within a few years. Thus, they had experienced first hand the events that the play depicted, which primed them to engage in the process of reflexivity advocated by Pablo.

Onstage: Representation and Reflexivity in Rehearsal and Performance

Act I: The Ambivalence of Return

Pablo crafted a narrative arc out of Lina's sketches by arranging them sequentially and devising two opening scenes that established a preliminary context. The first of these began with an empty stage. After a few moments of silence a worn leather suitcase slides to the centre from behind a screen. The audience is thus compelled to consider this object and what it represents even before Luisa, the play's protagonist, walks onstage. In rehearsal one afternoon Pablo explained that the suitcase had both practical and symbolic functions. Given that the number of participants in the workshop was greater than the number of roles available in the play, he had asked four different actresses to share the principal part; during each of their scenes they would hold the suitcase to establish continuity of character. More importantly, he added, the suitcase was meant to represent the difficult decision that Luisa faced: should she return to Spain or shouldn't she? The following interaction, which took place during the second week that I began observing rehearsals, illustrates Pablo's dramatic intentions and his style of directing. Here he models for Rosa, the senior who would play Luisa first, how to interact with the prop in order to communicate the character's emotional state:

1 PABLO ((*bending over and then recoiling*)): "¿Lo haré? No lo haré."	1 PABLO ((*bending over and then recoiling*)): "Will I do it? I won't do it."
2 ROSA: ¿no lo he hecho así?	2 ROSA: isn't that how I did it?
3 PABLO: no es el movimento, es la decisión, ¿yea? ... la importancia de la maleta – no es sólo una maleta, es tu vida ¿yea? ... son tus recuerdos y tus ganas de ir o de volver ¿yea? ... mucho más pausado y mucho más que te toque la decisión ¿yea? ... aquí piensa que está toda tu vida que estuvo en España	3 PABLO: it's not the movement, it's the decision yea? ... the importance of the suitcase – it's not just a suitcase, it's your life yea? ... it's your memories and your desires to go or to come back yea? ... much more of a pause and let yourself be moved by the decision yea? ... think that all of your life that was in Spain is in here
4 ROSA: hago que – eso ... hago así ... entonces la cojo ... "Me voy a España."	4 ROSA: I do – this ... I go like this ... and then I take it ... "I'm going to Spain."
5 PABLO: exacto ... la maleta te espera ... ((*He reaches for the suitcase, which is in the middle of the stage.*)) la vas a tomar y vas a imaginar que la vas a tomar ((*He narrows his eyes and leans toward the suitcase.*)) y te vas a ir sin decir nada – ¡y no! ((*He pulls back his arm quickly and stands upright.*)) algo te detiene... yo no sé ... tú sabes mejor que yo qué te detiene a quedarte en un lugar que no es tu patria	5 PABLO: exactly ... the suitcase is waiting for you ... ((*He reaches for the suitcase, which is in the middle of the stage.*)) you're going to take it and you're going to imagine that you're going to take it ((*He narrows his eyes and leans towards the suitcase.*)) and you're going to leave without saying anything – and no! ((*He pulls back his arm quickly and stands upright.*)) something holds you back ... I don't know ... you know better than I do what keeps you staying in a place that isn't your homeland

As Pablo describes it, the suitcase represents the life that Luisa knew before her migration to France, encapsulating her memories of Spain and motivating her desire to return. The brief opening scene thus establishes the temporal and spatial coordinates that dominate the ensuing narrative: it must be the 1970s, when such decisions were generally made, and if Luisa is leaving for Spain, then she must now be in Paris. The suitcase reflects a potent collision of chronotopes within the narrative world that *Back to Spain?* stages – a desire to leave Paris in the present, a recollection of Spain from the past – that drives Luisa to make her decision once she enters the stage to retrieve it.

For her part, Rosa seems to focus on the physical mechanics of the scene – "the movement" (line 3) – in lieu of its emotional stakes. Pablo thus encourages her to express the character's ambivalence about her decision, alluding to the emotional charge that it carries: "Let yourself be moved" (line 3). After re-enacting the physical movements that he wants Rosa to imitate, he offers an abstract motivation for them – "something holds you back" (line 5) – before suggesting indirectly that she mine her migratory past in order to imagine what it might be. His subsequent remark that this experience has endowed her with knowledge he cannot access – "you know better than I do" (line 5) – invokes the phenomenological expertise associated with her age and biographical trajectory, even as it reaffirms the authority conferred by his institutional role as instructor. In other words, Pablo pushes Rosa to approach her performance reflexively, recollecting her own decision with respect to return as a means of representing it truthfully on stage. Rosa, for her part, seems reluctant to engage in such personal reflection, much like her peers featured throughout this chapter.

This opening scene is distinct from those that follow by a virtual absence of dialogue, with the exception of the brief remarks that Luisa asks the audience directly, looking them in the eye: "Will I do it?" "I won't do it." "I'm going to Spain!" When Luisa turns to exit the stage, a traveller (*viajero*), played by Benita, enters and takes her by the arm. As she guides Luisa slowly across the stage, Benita recites an excerpt from *El señor de Bembibre*, a novel published in 1844 by the Romantic writer Gil y Carrasco. In private conversations Pablo explained to me that he wanted to include such an excerpt in the play as a means of varying its content and elevating its register. Given Benita's position as the most educated member of the Centro – her mother had been a schoolteacher while Benita was growing up in Valladolid – he asked her to read it. The excerpt, which describes the landscape of Galicia, was titled "De camino a España" (On the way to Spain) in the program:

Estaba poniéndose el sol detrás de las montañas que parten	The sun was setting behind the mountains that split the territory

| términos entre el Bierzo y Galicia, y las revestía de una especie de aureola luminosa que contrastaba peregrinamente con sus puntos oscuros. Algunas nubes de formas caprichosas y mudables sembradas acá y acullá por un cielo hermoso y purísimo, se teñían de diversos colores según las herían los rayos de sol … y era difícil imaginar una tarde más deliciosa. | between el Bierzo and Galicia, and it was covering them with a kind of luminous aura that contrasted strangely with their dark peaks. Some clouds of capricious and mutable shapes sown here and there in a beautiful and pure sky were stained in various colours, depending on how they were pierced by the sun's rays … and it was difficult to imagine a more delicious afternoon. |

The florid language of this excerpt stands in sharp contrast to Luisa's laconic opening scene, marking a shift in geographical setting from France to Spain as she leaves behind an urban setting to enter a pastoral idyll. A confluence of features distinguishes this text and its performance from the dialogue that makes up the remainder of the play: its large quantity of adjectives and adverbs; its arcane lexical items, like *"aureola"* (aura) and *"capriciosa"* (capricious); Benita's slow and meticulous enunciation of it; and the fact that she reads it. All these elements work to highlight the mythic quality of Gil y Carrasco's description of Spanish countryside as Luisa makes her way back to the pueblo that she left behind, driven by the idealized representation of Spain that the traveller describes. Although Luisa does not respond verbally to the description, Pablo wanted Julieta, the senior who was now playing her, to react to the countryside that was depicted around her. He told her one afternoon in rehearsal:

| Empiezas a entrar en el paisaje español. Entonces te estás viendo lo que extrañabas a ti … Estás viendo – como si estuviera el paisaje – todo lo que querías ver. | You begin to enter the Spanish countryside. So, you're seeing what you were missing … You're seeing – as though the countryside were there – everything that you wanted to see. |

As Pablo interprets the scene, nostalgia for the place of origin breeds an idealized image of it – one sees exactly what one *wants* to see – that will be revealed as a delusion upon return. Julieta, after receiving his direction in rehearsal, slowed her gait, looked around in all directions, and sighed with a subtle smile – all as a means of communicating non-verbally the soothing effect of seeing her homeland. The traveller animates a voice within the chronotopic frame that is established in the first scene. Using literary language, she both constructs an image of Spain and gestures iconically towards the romanticized nature of that image. It is not tied to any specific pueblo but rather a general, idyllic countryside (*paisaje*) that provokes nostalgic longing and draws Luisa back to Spain. When the traveller finishes reading the excerpt, she escorts Luisa offstage to her village.

Act II: The Moment of Arrival and the Modernist Chronotope

At this point Lina's sequence of comedic sketches begins. During rehearsals Pablo focused on the actors' physicality and textual accuracy rather than their characters' internal motivations, as he had done with Rosa for the opening scene. The first of the three sketches begins when Luisa enters the stage again with the suitcase, but the part is now portrayed by Verónica. She has arrived in her pueblo at last and is about to encounter three of its inhabitants – Juana, Matilde, and Maruja – who surprise her with their backward ways. Juana, the first villager, walks on-stage in striped leg warmers and a denim miniskirt, and she has a colourful headscarf tied under her chin – a costume that Concepción, the woman portraying her, first revealed to her peers with eager anticipation. The character's exaggerated and comedic appearance announces a shift in chronotopic frames; nostalgia has given way to the humorous charge of the modernist contrast. Throughout the scene Juana's mouth is scrunched to one side so that she is difficult to understand when she speaks. The conversation begins when Luisa inquires after her physical appearance:

LUISA: ¿Qué te ha pasado que tienes la cara hinchada de un lado?	LUISA: What happened to you that your face is swollen on one side?

Juana explains that she has a new boyfriend, and so she wanted to buy anti-aging cream that she saw advertised on French television. Shocked by its price, she decided instead to make her own using "a base of snail slime" (*una base de caracole*) after seeing a similar product offered in Spain. Juana explains that she hunted down some snails and then applied them directly to her skin:

JUANA: Me puse los caracoles en la cara; uno me entró en la nariz, el otro pasó al oído. ¡Y menos mal que no me los puse en el culo!

JUANA: I put snails on my face; one went up my nose, another went in my ear. And thank goodness that I didn't put any on my ass!

Upon hearing this, Luisa's eyes widen before she apologizes and tells Juana that she must leave to catch a bus. The discursive structure of their interaction, in which Luisa asks a series of direct questions and Juana responds at length, often repeating herself, establishes the protagonist as a kind of "straight" counterpart to the eccentric villager. In contrast to Luisa's even-tempered manner, Juana recounts her anecdote with agitated excitement, speaking quickly and waving her arms: she wants to look younger because of a new romantic partner; she foolishly uses snail slime to do so, which culminates in the physical deformity that the actress exploits to incite the audience's laughter. Their interaction is thus animated by the modernist contrast by which France is associated with expensive cosmetics that succeed in making women look younger, and Spain is associated with crude homemade remedies that result in disfigurement. A cluster of semiotic features – clothing, physical gesture, vulgarity ("on my ass!"), and the content of her improbable narrative – all work to establish Juana as a characterological type: an eccentric Spanish villager whose desperate measures to combat aging leave her in a ridiculous predicament.

The following two scenes display similar representations of rural Spaniards constructed through an assemblage of linguistic features and other semiotic forms. Like Juana, the characters of Matilde and Maruja embody simple-minded, old-fashioned types familiar to actors and audience alike. Throughout the scenes the women portraying these villagers engaged in physical activity that they thought would evoke rural eccentricity: the actress playing Matilde chose to lick a lollipop absent-mindedly, while the actress playing Maruja, sporting a black velvet hat with a red plastic carnation, knit with rapt attention. Meeting these villagers, Luisa inquires after their well-being. When their responses reveal ignorance of common health issues (Matilde) and modern technology (Maruja), she intervenes matter of factly to offer advice that she has most likely gleaned from her experience in France. In her second encounter with a villager Luisa offers a diagnosis to Matilde, who states that she has not been feeling well:

MATILDE: Desde que he vuelto de vacaciones me pasan cosas muy raras. Unos dicen que es la tercera edad; otros dicen que son los sofocos. Pero yo no sé.
LUISA: Pero Matilde – ¡eso es la menopausia!
MATILDE: ¿Pero qué menopausia ni qué narices? Yo no conozco a esa persona.

MATILDE: Since I got back from vacation, strange things have been happening to me. Some people say it's my age; others say it's hot flashes. But I don't know.
LUISA: But Matilde – that's menopause!
MATILDE: But what the heck is menopause? I don't know that person.

After Matilde has described her symptoms, Luisa suggests that she is experiencing menopause; Matilde, however, interprets Luisa's diagnosis as a proper noun. The villager is ignorant of the term for a medical condition associated with women at her life stage. Dumbfounded, Lusia tells her that she must leave for an appointment. As she walks away, she expresses exasperation by throwing her arms in the air and uttering to herself, "Oh, what a day!" (*Ay, ¡qué día!*). For the Spaniard upon return, interactions with retrograde villagers lay bare a disjuncture in temporalities. Luisa's migration to France has carried her into the future, while the people she left behind in Spain remain stuck in the past.

Such time-related humour informs Luisa's subsequent encounter with Maruja, who begins their scene seated on a bench (*un banco*).[5] When Luisa tells her that she is headed to the bank (*el banco*) to deposit money, Maruja misinterprets the homophone, warning Luisa that leaving money beneath a bench would be imprudent. Taken aback, Luisa explains to her that a bank "is like an office, where they keep money and have chequing accounts." Maruja responds by recommending an alternative:

MARUJA: Haz como yo. Los meto debajo del colchón, y cuando salgo los meto en una bolsa y los escondo entre las tetas.
LUISA: Mujer, ahora todo es moderno.
MARUJA: Sí, sí, modernísimo. Mi vecina contó que tiene una tarjeta que la mete en un agujero, y sale todo el dinero que quiere.
LUISA: No, Maruja – ¡eso es una tarjeta bancaria!

MARUJA: Do like I do. I put it underneath the mattress, and when I go out, I put it in a bag and hide it between my tits.
LUISA: But, woman, now everything is modern.
MARUJA: Yes, yes, very modern. My neighbour told me that she has a card that she puts into a hole and out comes all the money that she wants.
LUISA: No, Maruja – that's a bank card!

Maruja purports to understand the ways in which financial transactions have become "very modern," but, like Matilde, she reveals her misunderstanding of how such conveniences function. The rural, ignorant characters are thus summoned as counterpoints to Luisa, underscoring by contrast her modernity and the breadth of the knowledge that she has acquired in France. The lack of sophistication is indexed by particular traits: the women who stayed behind in the pueblo are obtuse, stubborn, and old, impervious to the ways in which their ignorance confines them to an outmoded temporal frame.

Before she ends her conversation with Maruja, and thus the series of comedic sketches, Luisa steps forward towards the audience and whispers, "They're all crazy!" (¡Son todas locas!), articulating for the first time an explicit evaluation of what she has found upon return. Although the line was not part of Lina's original sketch, Pablo added it as a way of inviting the audience's complicity in her assessment, as he explained to Verónica in rehearsal. The comment reaffirms the modernist narrative frame, revealing Luisa's awareness of difference between her and the individuals she left behind in Spain – difference established according to values that she has acquired while abroad. Living and working in France, she has learned ways of being modern, while they have remained in the past. From Luisa's new-found perspective, they now seem "crazy" or abnormal rather than simply unchanged.

Act III: The Expression of Sorrow and Chronotopic Variation

The comedic sketches do not prepare the audience for the final scene that follows, however: "What remains of all that?" (¿Qué queda de todo aquello?), an autobiographical poem that was written and performed by Lina. A sombre, nostalgic monologue, the scene restores the initial tone of the play, functioning as a sort of bookend to the opening. In the poem Luisa describes the disappointment that she feels upon returning to her pueblo because the Spain that she remembers no longer exists:

"¿Qué queda de todo aquello?"	What remains of all that?
1 En un pueblecito de España que yo no puedo olvidar	1 In a *pueblecito* in Spain that I cannot forget[6]
2 Había una linda casita donde yo nací ...	2 There was a pretty little house where I was born ...
3 Guardo en mí tantos bellos recuerdos ...	3 I have kept so many beautiful memories with me ...
4 Cogí un día el tren y fui al pueblo ...	4 One day I took the train and went to the pueblo ...

5	¡Qué tristeza! ¡Qué desilusión!	5	What sadness! What disappointment!
6	Los vecinos no eran los mismos,	6	The neighbours weren't the same,
7	No había flores en el jardín,	7	There weren't any flowers in the garden,
8	Todo era diferente.	8	Everything was different.
9	El tiempo pasado había borrado las huellas de mis pasos.	9	Passing time had erased the footprints of my steps.
10	Ya no se oían las risas de los niños jugando en la calle.	10	You no longer heard the laughter of children playing in the street.
11	Ya no se veían las mamas sentadas en el banco bordando.	11	You no longer saw mothers seated on benches embroidering.
12	Todo estaba vacío.	12	Everything was empty.
13	Ya no paseaban los jóvenes con sus novias alrededor de la plaza ...	13	Young men no longer walked around the square with their girlfriends ...
14	Cuanta tristeza sentí, cuanta soledad.	14	I felt so much sadness, so much loneliness.
15	Cada uno va a lo suyo, cerrando así la puerta de la amistad.	15	Everyone goes his own way, thus closing the door to friendship.
16	Tan sola me sentí.	16	I felt so alone.
17	Es triste de pensarlo, pero es la realidad.	17	It's sad to think about it, but it's reality.
18	Mi pueblo querido –	18	My dear pueblo –
19	Me voy para la ciudad.	19	I'm leaving for the city.
20	Sí – me voy para la ciudad.	20	Yes – I'm leaving for the city.

The tone of Luisa's monologue in this final scene differs from those that precede it; here the return to her pueblo evokes sadness (lines 5, 14, 17), disappointment (line 5), and loneliness (lines 14, 16). The Spaniards she encounters are different than she remembers them (line 6). Unlike Juana, Matilde, and Maruja, the villagers described in the poem take no interest in her or her return. The friendliness that she has associated with her pueblo indeed no longer exists, and its inhabitants, whose simplicity and eccentricity are highlighted in earlier scenes, are represented here as distant and self-involved (line 15). Luisa's poem thus offers an alternative perspective on return to that displayed before this moment. Her "beautiful memories" still drive her home, but her arrival there evokes a dispiriting realization: the people from her pueblo are not stuck in the past; rather, they have moved on to a present from which she is excluded, all traces of her earlier existence among them having been erased by time (line 8). The square and streets of the pueblo are empty, and there is thus no way of accentuating her modernity through contrast. The poem alters the modernist chronotope that structures earlier scenes: the place remains the same, but its temporal coordinates have shifted. Luisa's poem describes a moment later in time, when the modernist distinction between France and Spain has become obsolete. Unable to return to the place that she remembers so clearly, she sees no other option but to migrate once again to Paris. Holding her suitcase to her chest, she studies her surroundings before uttering, "I'm leaving for the city," and exiting the stage.

Lina's monologue instantiates a convergence of perspectives – subject (the "I" of the poem), author, and performer – in a single voice. As he did with Rosa and the opening scene, Pablo encouraged her throughout rehearsals to summon her own experience of migration in order to envision what she describes. Lina took this exercise very seriously, performing the text multiple times in rehearsal while holding the suitcase in different ways; she even solicited Amalia's help one Saturday afternoon to practise the recitation on their own. Lina's poem invokes nostalgic correlates of the modernist chronotope as she speaks about what her pueblo has lost, conjuring images of village life – women embroidering, children playing, lovers walking – that prove to be a chimera. In Lina's sombre account the modernist contrast that organized the depiction of a generic Spanish pueblo dissolves. Places – pueblo and Paris – then coincide, enveloped within the homogenous temporal frame of the present.

Reflections on Return and Its Representation

During a private conversation that Lina and I had after the performance, she explained that her poem's narrative was inspired by her own attempt at return:

Es verdad que fue así. Llevé a mi hijo para que sepa donde yo he vivido de niña, y no había nadie en el patio. Ahora no juega ni nadie ni nada. Es cierto que se va volviendo como aquí en Francia, que nadie da "buenos días" a nadie.	It's true that it was like that. I took my son so that he'd know where I lived as a girl, and there was no one in the courtyard. Now there's no one playing anything. It's certain that it's becoming like here in France, that no one says "hello" to anyone.

Just as in the poem, Lina's nostalgia for her pueblo transformed into disappointment once she arrived. What she found in Spain was indeed familiar but not for the reasons that she had anticipated; instead her pueblo had come to resemble France, or more specifically Paris, where children do not play outside and people do not greet one another in the street. In other words, the village had come to resemble the city. During rehearsal Lina described this discovery as "the sad moment" (*el momento triste*) of the play, when Luisa realizes that the contrast between city and village is no longer meaningful. The coordinates of the modernist chronotope that had sustained Spaniards during the first years of migration had been erased by time. This realization triggers a second – and permanent – migration to Paris.

As Lina explained, the narrative of her poem was based largely on personal experience. During our conversation she revealed an additional reason that motivated her decision to migrate a second time:

Mi sueño – mi sueño – *mon dieu* – esperaba *la retraite* para poder irme para España, y mi hijo no se adaptó allí. Sacrifiqué toda mi vida, y mi marido murió, el pobre, de un cáncer. Y mira, no puedo realizar ese sueño. Pero es así. No se adaptó [mi hijo]. Ahora le pesa porque allí hubiéramos tenido un piso maravilloso con tres habitaciones, cuarto de baño, una cocina enorme, y lo que compré aquí [en París] es pequeñito. Yo duermo en el comedor.	My dream – my dream – *my God* – I was waiting for retirement to be able to go to Spain, and my son didn't adapt there. I sacrificed my whole life, and my husband died, the poor man, from cancer. And look, I can't realize that dream. But that's the way it goes. He [my son] didn't adapt. Now he regrets it a little because there we would have had a marvellous apartment with three bedrooms, a bathroom, an enormous kitchen, and what I bought here [in Paris] is tiny. I sleep in the dining room.

As I learned from our conversations offstage, Lina's attempt to return was unsuccessful in part because of a personal reason: her son, who was born and raised in Paris, was unable to adapt to life in Spain. Nevertheless, she continues to harbour the dream that motivated this attempt, as her use of the present tense in reference to it suggests – "I *can't* realize that dream" – even if she has resigned herself to its unattainability. She readily conjures the life that they could be leading in Spain through recourse to very concrete images – the size and layout of the apartment that she imagines they would have. Lina omits these details in her performance of return, highlighting instead her narrative's forlorn dimensions, dolefully evoked through descriptions of change and an implied admission of failure. There are no traces here of the modernist distinction animated earlier in *Back to Spain?* even if she alludes to it in her poem. Instead Lina evokes other contrasts that suggest how she makes sense of her experience of migration in the present: her pueblo as she remembers it and her pueblo as it is now; the life that she has now in Paris and the life that she imagines she could be living in Spain. Luisa's final monologue thus articulates Lina's personal, sorrowful version of the familiar narrative of return – one that was not appreciated by all audience members, as reports from some of her peers suggested.

Audience Reception and Regimes of Reflexivity

Nearly one hundred people attended the performance – far more than anticipated by the Centro's staff, who had printed only sixty programs. A few of the performers' family members came, but the audience mostly comprised older individuals whom I recognized as participants at the Centro. Excited to see their friends on stage, many of them brought cameras to shoot pictures or record video of the performance. Although they applauded enthusiastically after each scene, the comedic sketches evoked the most vociferous responses. People laughed heartily at the villagers' eccentric outfits and the vulgar remarks that some of them made – snails "on her ass" and money "between her tits," for example. Although it was clear that the audience appreciated these sketches, I had more difficulty evaluating their interpretation of the serious scenes that opened and closed the play. At the beginning of *Back to Spain?* when Luisa declares that she has decided to go to Spain, a couple of audience members shouted out *voilà* and ¡*olé!* as she left the stage. At the end of the play, when she decides to return to Paris, a few men in the audience called out *bravo*, and the woman seated next to me leaned over and whispered in French, "That's true. I lived it."[7] On the day of the performance I asked a few audience members what they had thought of it; all of them responded with benign remarks, describing it as "entertaining" (*divertido*) and complimenting the actors on their memorization skills.

During the theatre workshop that occurred a week later, Pablo asked students to sit in a circle and discuss their experiences at the World Book Day event. In response most of them stated that they had been nervous, but that they were pleased with their performances. A number of them recalled the audience's laughter as evidence of the amusement generated by the production. A couple of participants, however, were more critical, claiming to have heard negative reactions from some audience members about the narrative represented onstage. Manuel, who performed in a sketch unrelated to *Back to Spain?*, explained that he had spoken with two or three individuals who said that they had been confused by its sequence of scenes. Concepción, who played the role of Juana, spoke in more general terms about the play's serious moments:

La gente ha dicho que esa historia la tiene todo el mundo, y no les hacía falta escucharla aquí.	People said that everyone has that story, so they didn't need to listen to it here.

Some of the other actors nodded in agreement. Such comments suggested a wider scope of responses to the performance than amusement alone – or, perhaps, of perceptions of those responses among the performers, as I was unable to verify what Manuel and Concepción had reported. Nevertheless, it echoed similar remarks expressed in the Escuela by students who found it tedious to listen to classmates' compositions that described painful memories of the past, and who preferred instead to leave such narratives untold. This prevalent disposition among members at the Centro complicates ideas about what constitutes a "tellable" account – that is, stories of significant personal experience – in scholarship on narrative (Ochs and Capps 2001; see also Labov and Waletzky 1967). As Concepción remarked, the audience was already familiar with the plot of return migration and its challenges, even if, as Manuel suggested, some of its members had difficulty following the storyline from beginning to end. And yet, this familiarity, at least with the experiences represented in the earnest moments with which the play opened and closed, seemed to foster resistance among audience members towards the performance's reflexive potential as Pablo understood it. Indeed, in rehearsals his attempts to coax naturalistic performances out of the seniors had been directed almost exclusively at the women portraying Luisa in serious moments of decision-making. As with Jillian Cavanaugh's (2009) research participants, who took pleasure in watching nostalgic representations of their "Bergamasco past" staged in northern Italy, "it was enough to feel close to the scenes depicted, perhaps have a laugh or two," but any efforts to foster critical or reflexive engagement were "reviewed suspiciously and resisted" (119).

During the feedback session Pablo acknowledged the criticism expressed by some of its participants before pressing students to consider what they thought audience members had expected from their performances and, more generally, their participation in a cultural institution such as the Centro:

Cuando dicen que la gente está contenta o no, ¿qué es lo que le gusta a esta gente cuando viene al Centro? ¿Cómo nombrarían lo que trae [nuestro espectáculo] a esa gente? ¿Qué es lo que ellos vienen a buscar aquí?	When you say that people are happy or not, what is it that these people like when they come to the Centro? How would you name what it is that [our show] brings to these people? What is it that they come to look for here?

As Pablo explained to me later, he meant to encourage students in the theatre class to think critically about their performance as well as the social function of places like the Centro. But in response they offered observations that he considered facile: people came to see the performance because they were "curious" (*curioso*); people came to the Centro "to have a good time" (*pasar un buen rato*). Participants in the workshop seemed disinclined to engage in the kind of transformative reflexivity that Pablo meant his questions to incite – for, indeed, he had asked the seniors to "go further" in their understanding of the Centro's function. Instead, they discussed their performance as a diversion for those who attended it, unaware of, or uninterested in, its reflexive potential as a mirror of their experience. And yet, as audience reactions and Concepción's reported comments suggest, performers and audience members alike *did* see themselves in the narrative presented onstage – even if there were elements of the story that they preferred to leave unspoken.

The actors' comments illustrate how the reflexivity that cultural performances make possible – that is, as Richard Bauman (1992, 48) writes, the act of "taking the role of the other and of looking back at oneself from that perspective" – may entail various modes of engagement with the narrative represented onstage. The merit of such performances may not necessarily lie in the degree to which they succeed at generating reflexive engagement as scholars and theatre professionals understand it, but rather in the process of evaluation, whether conscious or not, that performance and spectatorship involve. Notions of authenticity may thus rely less on a narrative's situation in space and time – indeed, *Back to Spain?* encompasses more than one spatio-temporal frame – than on the "communicative norms and commensurability of experience" according to which it is performed (Graber 2015, 356). What is reflected back to an audience is only part of a collectivity's experience or a particular representation of that experience. As such, it may evoke varied reactions among the individuals who comprise it, both onstage and offstage, depending on their experience of the past and the historicities that they produce in the present. Such reactions serve processes of social differentiation in part through the stances and the claims to moral personhood that they make possible.

Encore, Five Years Later: The Modernist Chronotope over Time

In 2013 I returned to Paris for a few months to revisit the Centro. During that time I sat in on the theatre class again – but now it was led by Ana, an animated young woman from Granada who taught middle school in Paris. (I discovered that Pablo had left the Centro four years earlier, shortly after my departure from the field.) At the sessions that I attended, students did improvised scenes in preparation for an upcoming performance: excerpts from ¡Bienvenido, Mister Marshall! (Welcome, Mister Marshall!), a well-known comedic film directed by Luís García Berlanga that was released in 1953. A satire, the film recounts a few frenzied days in the life of a small pueblo in what is now the northern province of Castilla y León. The plot follows a cast of villagers as they prepare for the arrival of three American diplomats whom they hope to impress with stereotypical representations of Spain in order to receive financial aid under the aegis of the Marshall Plan. (Mr Marshall refers to George C. Marshall, the American secretary of state who oversaw the design and implementation of the Marshall Plan following the Second World War.) At the end of the film, despite all the villager's preparations, the caravan of American diplomats drives through the town without stopping. Once again, the pueblo is left behind.

Ana's pedagogical style contrasted markedly with Pablo's. She laughed readily along with her students and praised them enthusiastically when they completed an improvisation; she also often arrived late, inciting the chagrin of some participants. There was thus little trace of the discipline that had preoccupied her predecessor. And yet, similar to Pablo, Ana seemed compelled to encourage her workshop's participants to engage reflexively with theatrical material. Her choice of this particular film, a commentary on early Francoism through its tongue-in-cheek portrait of a typical pueblo, provided an opportunity to engage with the past from a critical perspective. But the amateur actors seemed uninterested in this possibility, focusing instead on the humour that derived from a modernist contrast anchored in the representation of backward villagers, just as they had five years earlier.

¡Bienvenido, Mister Marshall! is an ambiguous text. Its political critique had been indirect enough to pass through censors in 1950s Spain, whose attention had most likely been diverted by humorous stereotypes immediately familiar at the time and no less potent over fifty years later. As with *Back to Spain?*, the film fell within the bounds of acceptable narrative forms at the Centro – that is, it obligated nothing more than a light-hearted engagement with its content and themes. In the theatre workshop it did not seem to occur to anyone to "go further," as Pablo had often said, probing their experience of migration or even their current lives in France. Representations of that past or this present would not constitute entertainment, as the seniors understood it. Instead, their collective diversion derived from storytelling practices that summoned apolitical spatio-temporal realms clearly severed from the here and now – blithe manifestations of a shared past, palatable forms of historical performance. With so many tales left untold, the possibility of critical reflection was accordingly constrained.

Polyvocal Representations of the Past

As a social and cultural institution the Centro promotes a form of community for the population that it serves. Through programming that highlights accessible forms of Spanish culture, such as an excursion to a Goya exhibition, or the Sunday dances where members can practise the bolero, the Centro enables identification with innocuous manifestations of the place that its members left behind. The seniors reveal their alignment with such cultural meaning-making through their own production of stereotypical forms of "Spanishness," not unlike the villagers in *¡Bienvenido, Mr. Marshall!*: they paint images of bullfighters in the painting workshop; they write paeans to their pueblos in the Escuela; they dance flamenco on feast days. For the Spaniards at the Centro the narrative of return – the decision and the consequences that it entails – functions in a similar way. Whether or not individuals attempted to go back, they are all in Paris now. The narrative thus serves them collectively as an accessible point of reference about the past – an invokable "chunk of history" that may be called into the present for social-semiotic ends (Blommaert 2015, 111).

Yet it is a particular version of the return narrative that most suits this project. As my analysis of *Back to Spain?* shows, the narrative is most felicitous when organized around a modernist chronotope in which France is associated with progress and Spain is associated with provincialism. Although this chronotope is far from contemporary – that is, it frames time, place, and personae from the early years of Spanish migration – it is certainly not obsolete. This is perhaps what renders it apt for an event designed to foment collective participation, even if it fails to generate the kind of reflexivity that Pablo envisions. As Kristina Wirtz (2014) writes about historically inflected spectacle in Cuba, representations of a community's past are often primarily forms of diversion and entertainment. Nevertheless, they may still "shape historical consciousness and historical knowledge, in ways perhaps less available to conscious reflection than readings of a history textbook chapter but perhaps more powerful because entertaining and vivid" (33). Performances of return migration, however they are executed, affirm the place of this narrative trope within a repertoire of semiotic forms that entail the past and that signal belonging to the realm of diasporic Spaniards represented by the Centro and, by extension, to Spain itself.

When Lina enters as Luisa to recite her autobiographical poem at the end of *Back to Spain?*, she disrupts the narrative that has been established, invoking and then altering the chronotope that has dominated the preceding scenes. She brings to stage a mournful version of return that has been eclipsed by the comedic storyline of the play, thereby confounding dominant preferences for engaging (or not) with the past. Lina thus illustrates how chronotopes may be recruited and modified in different ways to organize the telling of a common narrative, depending in part on the social objective that narrative is meant to serve, on the perspective that it is meant to reflect. In an intimate, elegiac tone she responds to the question posited in the play's title; the answer that she gives is familiar to everyone present, but it is difficult for many to hear. She makes the decision *not* to return to Spain, thus staging the moment when temporary migration becomes permanent, when the failure to return marks the decision or resignation to stay abroad. Leaving for the city at the end of the play, Lina performs a moment of rupture in the conception of the migratory project. The possibility of return has dissolved, but it is never forgotten.

Expressions of historicity often materialize through the intervention into a realm of socio-cultural life by an individual or group with a particular investment in how that historicity takes shape. Historical meaning-making – that is, the various ways in which the past circulates in the conversational here and now – thus enfolds a politics of remembering. Local norms around storytelling may include what counts as a story and how that story should be anchored in space and time. As the French philosopher Paul Ricoeur (2000, 584) writes, "recounting one drama means forgetting another" (raconter un drame, c'est en oublier un autre). Alluding to narrative authority, he implicates the following question: Who may claim rights to the act of storytelling, to the revelations and omissions that it entails? Among individuals in later life, for whom engagement with the past constitutes a necessary "task" of aging, this negotiation forms part of their everyday lives, both enabling and constraining possibilities of reflexivity (Myerhoff 1978, 265). In a setting populated by older adults and younger interlocutors, such as the Centro, authority on the past may be generated through allusions to age and forms of knowledge that have been acquired through differently valued means, such as phenomenological experience or scholarly practice. In the next chapter the relationship between knowledge and authority takes centre stage, as I shift focus from personal accounts of past experience to its official representation in a museum exhibition.

4 History at the Museum

For six weeks in 2008 the Museum of Art and History of Saint-Denis, a municipal museum not far from the Centro, held an exhibition on the bidonvilles that had once existed nearby. Dense settlements of improvised housing, the bidonvilles represented some of the worst aspects of migration for those arriving in France after the Second World War. During that country's Thirty Glorious years of social and economic expansion (Trente glorieuses), a housing crisis materialized in urban centres unable to absorb a rapid influx of migrants, first from North Africa and later from southern Europe. In the northwest suburbs of Paris, where the museum sits, many such individuals settled in conditions as miserable as the ones they had left behind.

The exhibition aimed to tell this story. Sponsored by the region's administrative council, *Bidonvilles: History and Representations, Seine-Saint-Denis (1954–1974)* comprised a collection of photographs, films, and texts that reconstructed the history of the bidonvilles – the facts of how they emerged, and why – and displayed their various representations in journalistic media.[1] On the back of a glossy twelve-page brochure that accompanied the exhibition (see figure 4.1), a quote from Claude Bartolone, the council's president, explained the motivation for presenting it:

Découvrir et analyser l'histoire des bidonvilles au travers notamment des images et représentations permet de mieux en comprendre les réalités, les acteurs, et les enjeux. Dans une période de profonds changements, cette collection et, en particulier, ce numéro contribue à la connaissance de notre héritage	To discover and analyse the history of the bidonvilles, especially through images and representations, enables a better understanding of their realities, actors, and stakes. In a period of profound changes, this collection and, in particular, this brochure, contribute to the appreciation

culturel et vise à favoriser la réflex-	of our cultural heritage and aim
ion de chacun et l'appropriation de	to promote individual reflection
l'histoire de notre département.	and the appropriation of our de-
	partment's history.

In his enthusiastic assessment of the exhibition Bartolone highlights its literal and symbolic value. Viewers will not only acquire knowledge about the bidonvilles (a twentieth-century phenomenon of particular importance in the region where they live) but also affirm their appreciation of "cultural heritage" in general, affiliating themselves with their place of residence through the appropriation of its history.

Bartolone's words seem to target a particular public – those who lack the historical knowledge that the exhibition imparts but are capable of acquiring it through intellectual resources. Consumers of the exhibition's "images and representations" are meant to assimilate this knowledge through the scholarly acts of reading, analysis, and reflection. The brochure, circulated by a cultural institution, thus articulates a dominant understanding of the way in which history is constituted – that is, through a dispassionate display of selected "realities, actors, and stakes." Those with first-hand knowledge of the bidonvilles, however, are likely to access the region's history more readily through other modes of knowing than the scholarly one that Bartolone invokes. Such was the case among the seniors with whom I visited the exhibition during one of the Centro's monthly cultural excursions, organized and led by Josep. They had migrated at a moment when the *"scandale des bidonvilles"* (scandal of the bidonvilles) as stated in the brochure, was just coming into public consciousness. Indeed, some of them had lived in these settlements, and if not, then they certainly knew people who had.

As conversations that day revealed, history may circulate in everyday talk through narrative performances that draw on personal experience, generating authority in part through the position in later life from which they are articulated. In this chapter I reveal the social dynamics of such historicity by analysing interactions among Josep and members of the Centro during and after the museum excursion. Illuminating a range of linguistic and discursive resources, including lexical items, deictic particles, and discourse markers, I show how the seniors engage in and evaluate modes of historical knowing – here, the scholarly-historical and the personal-biographical (see Wirtz 2016). Social actors whose recollections of lived experience fuse the personal and the historical, such as those featured in this book, may recruit discrepant modes of knowing the past – not only what they know but also

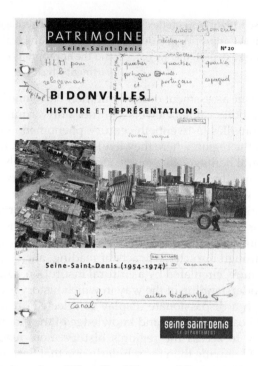

Figure 4.1. Brochure from *Bidonvilles: History and Representations, Seine-Saint-Denis (1954–1974)*.
Source: Conseil général de la Seine-Saint-Denis (2004). Courtesy of the Bureau du patrimoine contemporain, Conseil départemental de la Seine-Saint-Denis.

how they know it – to stake claims of authority and belonging in the present, as well as to enact processes of social distinction in the face of institutional discourse.

About the Bidonvilles

Bidonvilles, translated into English as "shantytowns," are settlements of precarious housing (shanties or shacks) typically found on the outskirts of an urban centre. As the exhibition brochure described them, such encampments are densely populated and lacking in basic public services, such as water, electricity, and sewage systems. The term was first used in French to describe the agglomeration of shanties that emerged outside of North African cities between the two world wars. In addition to the staple of materials with which people constructed them – wood, plastic, and cardboard – inhabitants of those shantytowns also made use of *bidons*, metal drums used to transport liquid.

The exhibition focused on a span of time (1954–74) that encompassed the emergence, proliferation, and containment of bidonvilles on the periphery of Paris. Their inhabitants were thus quite literally marginalized, comprising a mass of dark, poor, and foreign migrants whose labour drove France's post-war economy. These settlements were first populated by migrants from North Africa and, later, from elsewhere in Europe – notably Portugal and, to a lesser extent, Spain. In 1966 a national investigation estimated that 47,000 people, including 4,100 families, lived in the bidonvilles outside the French capital (Gastaut 2004). Around that time journalists and popular media sought to create awareness of what had come to be perceived as a housing crisis, circulating texts and images meant to expose the bidonvilles' deplorable conditions – many of which were featured in the museum exhibition. Their efforts ultimately triggered the creation of public policy that aimed to resorb the bidonvilles' inhabitants into more humane temporary settlements (*cités d'urgence*) and, later, into larger, permanent constructions of subsidized apartments (*habitations à loyer modéré*). Despite these attempts to address the situation, however, the bidonvilles of Seine-Saint-Denis, where some of the Centro's members had lived, existed until the 1974 inauguration of a public housing project in the nearby neighbourhood of Franc-Moisin, which today houses over 10,000 people.[2] As the exhibition's brochure acknowledged, housing conditions thereafter continued to impede trajectories of mobility for some immigrant groups, in particular those from North Africa. For the Spaniards with whom I visited the museum, however, this was not the case. After living in the bidonvilles for a couple of years, they had amassed enough money to seek alternative housing. Many of them eventually bought their own homes – modest apartments or individual houses (*pavillons*) in or near Paris.

Knowing about/with the Past

Through everyday discursive practices, such as conversational interaction and narrative performance, social actors animate historicities and articulate stances towards them.[3] Knowledge is thus paramount to historical meaning-making; its various forms may serve as resources for the production of intelligible talk about the past, along with the range of social-semiotic effects that such talk makes possible: authorization, differentiation, and affective resonance. In what follows, I perform close textual analysis on four interactions that occurred on the day of the museum visit to provide insight into the various modes of knowing, and the relationships among them, that expressions of historicity involve. Focusing on epistemological talk, I attend to the verbs and expressions that speakers use to indicate what and how they know about the past. In these Spanish data, two primary modes of knowing are encapsulated in a lexical contrast common to Romance languages: "*saber*" (from Latin *sapēre*) and "*conocer*" (from Latin *cognōscere*). Although they are both conventionally translated into English as "to know," the former verb tends to reference factual forms of knowledge learned through intellectual activity, while the latter verb references knowledge acquired through phenomenological experience.

In the introduction to his ethnography of a working-class neighbourhood in Naples, Thomas Belmonte (2005) discusses this lexical distinction in Italian: there is "knowing about" (*sapēre*), knowledge that is "objectively separable from the central core of one's subjectivity"; there is "knowing with" (*conōscere*), knowledge that "issues directly from the involvement of the person in the world" (xvii). In conversations about the past, then, knowing "about" and knowing "with" can function as epistemic stances that generate authority within a dynamic framework of values that emerges in interaction and that accommodates multiple voices – the institutional and the personal, the scholarly and the biographical, the old(er) and the young(er) (see Bucholtz and Hall 2005; Kuipers 2013).[4] In the exchanges that I analyse here, and indeed throughout my ethnographic data, the lexical contrast between "*saber*" (S) and "*conocer*" (C), and the modes of knowing that they index, are especially charged with social meaning when they emerge in talk about the past. Attending to their use during a mundane visit to a museum, I illuminate the various ways that historical knowledge may be marshalled in interaction to undergird claims of authority and moral personhood. Through their talk about the past, the seniors activate chronotopic frames that draw on different modes of knowing, thereby engaging in processes of social differentiation among those whose lives have been shaped in different ways by shared historical conditions.

Modes of Knowing: "*Saber*" (S) and "*Conocer*" (C)

The following four excerpts occurred on the day of the excursion. The first three have been extracted from an hour-long recording of conversations that took place at the museum, roughly the length of the visit. The final exchange happened a few hours later at the Centro between Marisol, who had attended the field trip, and Amalia, who had not.[5]

Establishing Who Knows What and How

On the morning of the excursion Josep met us at the museum. As participants arrived, he signalled for them to join him on the steps leading to the entrance, a large iron door built into a neoclassical façade. Once we were all present, he began to describe the content of the exhibition that we were about to see:

Excerpt 1: "You can't **know (S)** much because surely you didn't really **know (C)** it, eh?"

1	JOSEP: mirad, la exposición es pequeñita, ¿vale?	1	JOSEP: look, the exhibition is small, okay?
2	hay algunos documentos gráficos,	2	there are some written documents,
3	hay fotografías que son muy interesantes,	3	there are really interesting photographs,
4	hay algunos textos que explican	4	there are some texts that explain
5	también os dan un librito si queréis …	5	also they give you a little book if you want …
6	por lo tanto lo que yo os propongo es –	6	so what I propose to you is this –
7	como la gran mayoría **conocéis (C)** mejor que yo	7	since the majority of you **know (C)** better than I
8	qué es esto –	8	what this is –
9	es decir	9	that is
10	qué eran los *bidonvilles*	10	what the bidonvilles were
11	cómo surgen –	11	how they emerge –
12	cómo surgen no **sé (S)** si lo **sabéis (S)** o no	12	I don't **know (S)** if you **know (S)** how they emerge or not
13	o cómo –	13	or how –
14	pero bueno –	14	but anyway –
15	eso entre todos ya lo iremos hablando	15	we're all going to talk about this together
16	pero seguramente tenéis más experiencias	16	but surely you have more experiences
17	y **conocéis (C)** mejor vosotros que yo	17	and you **know (C)** better than I
18	((*laughter*))	18	((*laughter*))

((*Indecipherable voices erupt in reaction, then individuals discuss where they lived after migrating from Spain – some in the bidonvilles, some in northern Paris or suburbs to the northeast. Josep interrupts their chatter to restate his "proposal."*))

19	JOSEP: os hago – os hago un poco de introducción		19	JOSEP: I'll do – I'll do a little introduction for you
20	si queréis sentaros		20	if you want to sit down
21	porque luego entramos adentro		21	and then later we'll go inside
22	os hago un poco de introducción		22	I'll do a little introduction for you
23	y si hay algo que vosotros **sepáis (S)** que yo no **sé (S)**, ¿vale?		23	and if there's something that you **know (S)** that I don't **know (S)**, okay?
24	porque todo lo que **sé (S)** es lo que he estado leyendo –		24	because everything that I **know (S)** is what I've been reading –
25	CARLA: usted poco puede **saber (S)** porque seguramente no la **ha conocido (C)**, ¿eh?		25	CARLA: you can't **know (S)** much because surely you didn't really **know (C)** it, eh?
26	JOSEP: yo –		26	JOSEP: me –
27	bueno lo que yo he hecho es visitar la exposición		27	I mean what I did is visit the exhibition
28	y explicármelo un poco		28	and learn about it a bit on my own
29	pero yo lo **tengo de cabeza (S)**		29	but I **have it in my head (S)**
30	vosotros lo **tenéis allí (C)**		30	and you **have it there (C)**
31	((*Josep pats his forearm.*))		31	((*Josep pats his forearm.*))

After describing the exhibition's size and content – artefacts including photos, texts, and small books that "explain" the bidonvilles – Josep then offers to give us "a little introduction" to the social and political context in which the bidonvilles emerged. Various interactional strategies index his role as guide and instructor: he calls the group's attention with the discourse marker "look" (line 1); he interrupts the group's chatter to repeat what he intends to do (lines 1 and 19); he invites the group to sit down around him on the steps leading to the museum's entrance (line 20). Throughout the exchange, though, Josep also works to mitigate the authority associated with his institutional role by encouraging his interlocutors to participate in the collaborative project that he has laid out: reconstructing the history of the bidonvilles, of which he assumes they have first-hand experience. Twice he tells his audience that they know (*conocer*) the bidonvilles "better than he" because they have had more phenomenological experience ("more experiences," line 16); he acknowledges that they may have more factual knowledge (*saber*) as well. Indeed, in line 24 Josep implies that there are limits to what he has been able to glean through scholarly practices alone – as he states, "everything that I know (*saber*) is what I've been reading" – when compared to what the seniors have learned through their biographical trajectories. In his final turns, Josep exemplifies these two modes of knowing metonymically, contrasting acquisition through the head (*saber*) with acquisition through the body (*conocer*), which he illustrates nonverbally by patting his forearm as he uses a distal deictic – "there" (lines 30 and 31).

Josep's opening remarks incite participants to interject rapid and overlapping turns, only fragments of which are decipherable on the recording: "Did you all live in the bidonvilles?"; "There used to be a bar on that corner called El patilargo"; "The truth is I don't really know much about it." As they begin to enact the phenomenological mode of knowing that Josep has just associated with them, a surge of excitement imbues their interaction. When Carla claims that Josep *can't* know (*saber*) much about the bidonvilles because he did not experience them first hand (*conocer*) (line 25), she invokes an ideological framework that privileges a phenomenological perspective on historical meaning-making, enabled in part by her position in later life. Crucially, this does not exclude other forms of knowledge – namely, the scholarly-historical one that is manifested in the museum exhibition and its accompanying brochure. Rather, as Carla's comment shows, she understands such modes of knowing to be entangled in a constitutive relationship in which scholarly-historical forms of knowledge (*saber*) may derive from experiential ones (*conocer*).

Josep explained to me during a private walk to the subway after the museum visit that his recognition of the seniors' experiential knowledge was deliberate. As I recorded in field notes later that day, he believed that many people at the Centro "thought of history as something beyond them or outside them, when in fact their stories constitute[d] a significant part of twentieth-century Europe," and he wanted them to recognize this through their engagement with the exhibition. As I have discussed elsewhere, Josep often sought to legitimize the experience of the Centro's members, whom he understood to have endured unimaginable hardships in Francoist Spain and who, later in France, occupied a marginal position as aging transnational migrants (Divita 2012). The excursion to the bidonvilles exhibition was organized with this objective in mind. His deferential gestures, which epitomize the way he interacted with his older interlocutors, indirectly reveal the dominant forms of historical knowledge to which Josep alludes and with which they must contend when recollecting personal experiences of the past. It also enables and legitimizes a different kind of history-making among people whose access to such knowledge may be limited. Josep relies on knowledge generated through intellectual activity alone, while his older interlocutors, whose lived experience licenses claims to a phenomenological mode of knowing, may draw on other resources.

Fusing Scholarly-Historical and Personal-Biographical Modes of Knowing

The next excerpt begins nearly ten minutes later as Josep provides a historical overview of migration to Paris in the twentieth century. Here he is discussing the Algerian War (1954–62), which precipitated an influx of migration from North Africa in the late 1950s. This rapid surge of arrivals coincided with a wave of Spaniards that began in 1959, when Franco's government sanctioned emigration as part of an economic stabilization plan. As Josep explains, this created the conditions of a housing crisis:

Excerpt 2: "We Could Write a Book!"

1 JOSEP: llega esa gente – llega un gran movimiento de argelinos otra vez y gente que necesita reconstruir – ¿vale? – llegan, uh, llegan aquí, se instalan, y evidentemente falta – y allí es dónde en el año '54 dónde se explotan los bidonvilles – es decir, no hay espacio, la gente tiene que vivir en una parte, Francia reclama a gente obrera barata – ¡poom!
2 CARLA: y le pagaban a Franco por cada –

1 JOSEP: these people arrive – a big movement of Algerians arrive again and people who need to rebuild – okay? – they arrive, uh, they arrive here, settle in, and obviously there's a need – and that's when in 1954 when the bidonvilles explode – I mean, there's no space, the people have to live on the outskirts, France needs people, workers, manual labour – poom!
2 CARLA: and they paid Franco for every –

History at the Museum

3	JOSEP: y Franco – y Franco – a Franco le interesaba, es decir –		3	JOSEP: and Franco – and Franco – it interested Franco, I mean –
4	NICOLA: claro		4	NICOLA: of course
5	JOSEP: Franco empujó – para Francia pero sobre todo para Alemania también – empujó a gente ¿para qué? – porque Francia –		5	JOSEP: Franco encouraged – to France but especially also to Germany – encouraged people, why? – because France –
6	PEDRO: xx		6	PEDRO: xx
7	JOSEP: eran entradas de divisas, era dinero xx otra época, que la peseta estaba a cero, que les llegaba a las familias españolas el dinero		7	JOSEP: foreign currency was coming in, it was money xx another time, the peseta wasn't worth anything, the money was coming to Spanish families
8	EMILIA: lo primero que hicimos fue eso		8	EMILIA: that's the first thing that we did
9	JOSEP: el dinero le mandaban a la familia		9	JOSEP: they were sending money to their families
10	NICOLA: claro		10	NICOLA: of course
11	EMILIA: yo me vine [a París] antes – un mes antes porque él ((*indicating her husband*)) tenía una plaza muy buena de soldador – la plaza ya era muy buena allí [en España] – y yo tenía una cuñada y me vine, pero yo – me trajo otra chica de allí, me trajo y luego a mí mismamente me echó en la calles		11	EMILIA: I came [to Paris] first – one month earlier because he ((*indicating her husband*)) had a really good job as a welder – the job was really good there [in Spain] – and I had a sister-in-law and I came, but I – some other girl from home brought me and then she literally threw me into the street
12	((*laughter*))		12	((*laughter*))
13	EMILIA: me trajo y luego xx –		13	EMILIA: she brought me and then xx –
14	MARISOL: historias –		14	MARISOL: stories –
15	CARLA: *oh là là*		15	CARLA: *oh là là*
16	JOSEP: total –		16	JOSEP: so anyway –
17	MARISOL: – para hacer un libro		17	MARISOL: – to write a book
18	CARLA: sí, podrías hacer un libro		18	CARLA: yes, you could write a book
19	((*laughter*))		19	((*laughter*))
20	PEDRO: podría hacer un libro		20	PEDRO: she could write a book
21	EMILIA: podríamos hacer un libro – pero un libro, ¿eh?		21	EMILIA: we could write a book – but a book, eh?

Recounting the sequence of events that precipitated the emergence of the bidonvilles in Paris, Josep offers a narrative account imbued with the scholarly historicity that he references in the first excerpt. He also continues to encourage his interlocutors to participate in the act of historical representation that he is orchestrating – the collaborative process that he described explicitly when the museum visit began ten minutes earlier. In his first turn, for example, his use of the discourse marker "okay?" (line 1) invites their affirmation of the fact that he is presenting: an influx of immigrants came to France in 1954 at the start of the Algerian War. Moreover, his use of the adverb "obviously" indexes an epistemic stance of certainty on his remarks and implies that his audience already knows (*saber*) the events that he is recounting. A couple of turns later, he inserts a rhetorical question – "why?" (line 5) – that engages his interlocutors directly and signals that what follows is a salient element of the history being recalled. Through these various discourse strategies Josep draws attention to the mode of knowing that is shaping his talk about the past, and he invites his interlocutors' alignment with it.

During this scholarly-historical account two Centro members intervene, orienting themselves towards the past through this same epistemological frame. In line 2, Carla interrupts Josep to add that Franco – serving here again as a metonymic trope for Spain – benefited economically from the wave of Spanish migration that occurred shortly after the moment that Josep describes. In response Josep both acknowledges and expands on Carla's contribution, repeating "Franco" three times before elaborating on the economic dynamics that her comment invokes – that is, that Spaniards abroad sent remittances home and thus, he implies, propped up Spain's economy (line 7). Twice during this brief exchange Benita interjects "Of course," indicating her alignment with the scholarly-historical mode of knowing that dominates Josep's narrative. Her discourse marker here serves a similar purpose to Josep's, working both to insinuate her into the process of historical meaning-making in which the group is engaged and to validate the content of the narrative that this process is engendering.

But the reference to remittances triggers a different kind of intervention from Emilia (line 8), who draws on a mode of knowing the past (*conocer*) distinct from that which has shaped Josep's account until this moment. Using a first-person verb form – "that's the first thing that we did" (line 8) – she modifies the scholarly-historical narrative by contributing content generated by personal recollection. Emilia goes on to recount that she migrated to Paris a month before her husband, accompanying a young woman from her town in Extremadura who promptly threw her into the street when they arrived. This turn elicits an outburst of laughter among the Centro members (line 12), who perhaps recognize aspects of their own experience (*reconocer*) in the anecdote that she has told. In a quick succession of turns involving various manifestations of the "We could write a book!" refrain (lines 14–21), they project a speculative time-space in which they create an artefact comprising stories that tell their personal experiences of migration. Through their rapid shift in verb forms – "you could," "she could," "we could" (lines 18–21) – they create a rich moment of shared orientation not only towards the book that they imagine, but also towards the primary mode of knowing (*conocer*) by which this artefact would be constituted. In the here and now of this interaction, then, they conjure a possibility for the future that is contingent upon their recollection of the past in a particular – that is, experiential – way, which they share in part through their place in later life and the socio-historical conditions that have brought them there. The second outburst of laughter that punctuates this exchange (line 19) indexes their positive stance towards this speculative time-space. At this moment their engagement with one another is so intense that they ignore an attempt by Josep to redirect the conversation ("so anyway," line 16).

The "book that they could write" serves as a referent of inclusion for those who understand through personal experience (*conocer*) the stories that it contains. But a book also embodies scholarly historicity, and it confers authority on its creators and its content. The claim that they could write a book works to legitimize their biographical trajectories even if, due to their generally low levels of literacy and perhaps their limited access to scholarly-historical forms of knowledge, this is a task that would most likely prove difficult for them to accomplish. And yet, as I have discussed elsewhere, this remark emerged in various conversations while I was conducting fieldwork. Thus, participants in the museum excursion do not necessarily think of history as "beyond them or outside them," as Josep remarked to me; rather, they engage in historical meaning-making by negotiating tensions among "discrepant historicities" that are endowed with different kinds of authority and may not be equally accessed (Stewart 2016, 83). As Emilia does in the excerpt, social actors may fuse scholarly-historical accounts with recollections of personal experience, drawing authority through tales of what they have seen and felt – a phenomenological perspective on the past – rather than learned through secondary sources, such as books and exhibitions.

Authority on the Past through Chronotopic Calibration

Josep's introduction lasted nearly twenty minutes before he invited participants to follow him into the museum. As he suspected (and as he revealed to me later during our walk to the subway), the Centro's members were far more interested in the exhibition's photographs than in the text that accompanied them. Journalistic black-and-white representations of the bidonvilles that captured the miserable conditions in which their inhabitants lived, these photographs depicted, among other things, cramped shacks constructed of urban refuse (pieces of wood, metal, and cardboard), many of them with children idling in the foreground. (See figure 4.2.)

Among the visitors that day who had lived in the bidonvilles, the images provoked both resentment and nostalgia. Emilia, for example, remarked matter of factly that Spaniards at the time were not always generous with one another: "There was a lot of jealousy." Marisol, for her part, recalled with a smile how she and her family had kept the

Figure 4.2. At the *Bidonvilles* exhibition
Source: Image courtesy of the author.

Figure 4.3. Marville, Rue Rolland, Saint-Denis
Source: Douzenel (n.d.). Photograph by Pierre Douzenel; courtesy of Françoise Douzenel.

interior of their shack clean, wearing plastic bags on their shoes when it rained to prevent mud from getting inside. As she walked through the museum, she continued to share such anecdotal details until suddenly she called out to Josep; she had found a photograph of Marville, the very bidonville in Saint-Denis where she had lived after arriving in Paris in the 1960s (see figure 4.3). At this point the following narrative begins.

Excerpt 3: "We Used to Live Here When I Came from Spain, Do You Realize?"

1 MARISOL: Josep –	1 MARISOL: Josep –
2 **aquí** vine yo de España – **aquí** –	2 **here**'s where I came from Spain – **here** –
3 escúchame – escúchame Josep …	3 listen to me – listen to me Josep …
4 escúchame – escúchame Josep –	4 listen to me – listen to me Josep –
5 cuando yo vine de España	5 when I came from Spain

6	vino su hermano ((*indicating Nicola*)) –	6	her brother came ((*indicating Nicola*)) –
7	que estaba casado con mi hermana –	7	who was married to my sister –
8	a buscarme en la gare d'Austerlitz	8	to pick me up at the Austerlitz train station
9	y tenía una mobileta	9	and he had a moped
10	iba a trabajar en mobileta	10	he used to go to work on a moped
11	y me metió en un taxi	11	and he put me in a taxi
12	y le dijo al taxista	12	and he said to the taxi driver
13	"la lleva usted a Marville"	13	"take her to Marville"
14	yo cuando vine en el taxi	14	when I came in the taxi
15	yo no comprendí	15	I didn't understand anything
16	me dejó sola en el taxi …	16	he left me alone in the taxi …
17	y yo le dije al taxista que me llevara a la Courneuve	17	and I told the taxi driver to take me to la Courneuve
18	((*laughing*)) pero yo quería ir a Marville!	18	((*laughing*)) but I wanted to go to Marville!
19	y el taxista no lo encontraba – no lo encontraba	19	and the taxi driver couldn't find it – he couldn't find it
20	porque era muy pequeñito – ¿lo ves?	20	because it was really small – do you see it?
21	ahí éramos todos españoles, éramos una familia	21	there we were all Spaniards, we were a family
22	y cuando veo a mi hermana –	22	and when I saw my sister –
23	en la carretera veo a mi hermana –	23	I saw my sister in the road –
24	le digo al taxista	24	I say to the taxi driver
25	"¡**aquí aqui aquí**!"	25	"**here here here**!"
26	((*laughter*))	26	((*laughter*))
27	qué apuro,	27	what a mess,
28	pero sí vivíamos **aquí**	28	but yes we used to live **here**
29	cuando yo vine de España – ¿te das cuenta?	29	when I came from Spain – do you realize?
30	JOSEP: me han contado que esto	30	JOSEP: they told me that this
31	y que las escuelas –	31	and that the schools –
32	que se podía aprovechar las duchas las noches para poderse duchar	32	that one could use the shower facilities at night to take showers

33	MARISOL: íbamos a ducharnos **allí**,	33	MARISOL: we used to take showers **there**
34	sí sí	34	yes yes
35	íbamos a ducharnos –	35	we used to take showers –
36	y **ahora** todo esto es un hôpital	36	and **now** all this is a *hospital*
37	((*pointing to the photograph*)) éste es el *hôpital* – *Hôpital de la fontaine*	37	((*pointing to the photograph*)) this is the hospital – Hôpital de la fontaine
38	mis niñas nacieron **aquí**	38	my daughters were born **here**

In this excerpt Marisol recalls the difficulty of finding the bidonvilles in which her sister and brother-in-law lived when she arrived in Paris – an anecdote that is triggered by her discovery of a photograph of that very site. The image is an aerial shot of Marville, difficult to see from street level, as Marisol explained, because it was sandwiched between municipal buildings, and its façade was indistinguishable from the mundane urban architecture that surrounded it. Calling out to Josep (line 1) and imploring him four times to listen to the personal narrative that she is about to recount, Marisol seems moved by the unexpected discovery of a photograph of the bidonville that she came to know upon migrating from Spain.

As she engages with the photograph of the bidonville – a static, omniscient depiction of a place in the past – her narrative displays a collision of chronotopes in her recollection of the moment that she first attempted to find it, riding in a taxi through the streets of Saint-Denis forty years earlier. Whereas such semiotic activity is performed collectively in the second excerpt – "*we* could write a book!" – here it is enacted individually. Through Marisol's specific references to the Parisian suburbs, where she continues to live, and the positive evaluative claims that she makes about the bidonville ("we were a family," line 21), she calibrates the scholarly-historical chronotope of the museum exhibition, the personal-biographical chronotope of her recollection, and the here-and-now event chronotope of the interaction itself. Marisol achieves this alignment in part through her use of spatial and temporal deictics towards the end of the excerpt: she and her family showered "**there**" (line 33), in a school that is "**now**" (line 36) a hospital; "my daughters were born **here**" (line 38). Moreover, her use of discourse markers – "do you see it?" (line 20) and "do you realize?" (line 29) – target Josep as her primary interlocutor within the chronotopic envelope of the interaction itself, prodding his positive alignment towards the content of her anecdote and his ratification of her expertise, which he readily provides by way of nods and a smile. She addresses her narrative to Josep and, a few turns after this exchange, to me – the two younger individuals present who could not participate in her act of historical imagining through *our* primary mode of knowing (*saber*) and were thus unable to experience or interpret the exhibition in the same way.

Through her animated talk Marisol conveys a charge of excitement from the chronotopic fusion that she is experiencing: the place represented by this artefact is the same one that she animates in her narrative, acknowledging that it is *now* something else altogether. Talking explicitly about the photograph, Marisol displays an intimate mode of knowing it (*conocer*) and thus, in a sense, confirms its validity as part of the museum exhibition. She also embodies the exhibition's objective, as the brochure states, to "discover" history through the understanding of its actors and their lived realities. Josep acknowledges Marisol's expertise, seeking her confirmation of what he recollects hearing from a third party about common bathing practices in the bidonville, and she gives it (lines 33–5). Moreover, she conveys authority through the details of her story and the emotional resonance of her discourse, marked as it is by repetitions – "listen to me, listen to me"; "he couldn't find it, he couldn't find it"; "here here here"; "yes yes" – as well as laughter. But the positive affect generated through the coalescence of time-spaces in this exchange lasts no longer than a few moments, just as it did at the end of the last excerpt. Immediately after Marisol's monologue she turned away from the photograph with a shrug, matter of factly uttering the words "Well, that's that" (*Pues, nada*). The emotion produced by her act of personal recollection dissipated as she shifted footing back into the present, revealing a pragmatic stance on the past upon which she elaborated later that day.[6]

Claims to Moral Personhood and Social Differentiation

The visit to the museum exhibition lasted forty-five minutes, until participants dispersed, and Josep and I took our walk to the subway. That afternoon I headed back to the Centro to attend the weekly arts and crafts workshop, where the five women present sat around an oval table, cutting images out of magazines to create collages for an upcoming show. Shortly after I arrived, Marisol entered the room and announced with a burst of laughter that her hands had become dirty from her visit to the bidonvilles that morning: "Look my hands are dirty from the bidonvilles, right, David?" Amalia, with whom I was sitting at one end of the table, asked her to clarify what she meant. In response Marisol stated that Josep "did one of those things" – that is, an excursion – to see "the bidonvilles in Saint-Denis, where we Spaniards lived." Amalia, who had not known about the excursion, then asked Marisol where exactly the bidonvilles had existed. Marisol answered her before summarizing their conditions with a French word that she repeated twice: "*misère*" (poverty). At this point the following excerpt begins.

Excerpt 4: "The Person Who Hasn't Lived It Can't Understand It"

1	AMALIA: cuando se habla de eso hay gente que –	1	AMALIA: when you talk about this there are people –
2	DAVID: mm	2	DAVID: mm
3	AMALIA: – pero hay xx quienes – no lo quieren escuchar, tienen que **saber (S)**	3	AMALIA: – but there are xx who – they don't want to hear about it, they need to **know (S)**
4	MARISOL: no pero eso –	4	MARISOL: no but that –
5	AMALIA: espérate, espérate – no, *mais* espérate – hay uno que me dice "no le digas a nadie que hemos pasado miseria"	5	AMALIA: wait wait – no *but* wait – there's one guy who says to me "don't tell anyone that we experienced poverty"
6	MARISOL: pues –	6	MARISOL: then –
7	AMALIA: "no le digas a nadie"	7	AMALIA: "don't tell anyone"
8	MARISOL: *bah ça c'est la vie*	8	MARISOL: *well that's life*
9	AMALIA: no pero le gente se olvida – porque la gente –	9	AMALIA: no but people forget – because people –
10	MARISOL: es que la gente se olvida de que somos pobres	10	MARISOL: it's that people forget that we're poor
11	AMALIA: yo tengo una cuñada [en Madrid] – una cuñada que nos ve aquí, y todos – hemos hecho una vida, hemos trabajado, y todos tenemos para vivir – una casa, un piso – se olvida de todo, lo que hemos sufrido para poder conseguir eso – no nos han dado nada	11	AMALIA: I have a sister-in-law [in Madrid] – a sister-in-law who sees us here, and we all – we made a life for ourselves, we worked, and we all have enough to live – a house, an apartment – they forget everything that we went through to be able to get that – they didn't give us anything

12	MARISOL: bueno eso – y la persona que **no lo ha vivido (C)** no lo puede comprender		12	MARISOL: yea that – and the person **who hasn't lived it (C)** can't understand
13	AMALIA: pero bueno, es que los que están allí [en España] no se dan cuenta		13	AMALIA: but yea, it's that the ones who are there [in Spain] don't realize
14	MARISOL: pero no tienen la cultura – pero no tienen la cultura que tú –		14	MARISOL: but they don't have the culture – they don't have the culture that you –
15	AMALIA: no – ah eso no		15	AMALIA: no – ah, no way
16	MARISOL: ¿eh? porque a mí me dicen, "ah pero –" y digo "tú no tienes la cultura de yo, porque yo tengo dos – la francesa y la española – y tú no más que tienes una, así que **sé (S)** más que tú"		16	MARISOL: eh? because they say to me, "yea but –" and I say "you don't have the culture that I do, because I have two – French and Spanish – and you only have one, so I **know (S)** more than you"
17	AMALIA: y además –		17	AMALIA: and what's more –
18	MARISOL: mismo que tengan una carrera		18	MARISOL: even if they have an education
19	DAVID: mm		19	DAVID: mm
20	AMALIA: sí		20	AMALIA: yes
21	MARISOL: se lo digo así, ¿eh?		21	MARISOL: that's how I tell them, eh?
22	AMALIA: y el hecho de que ya nos defendemos en francés – en francés –		22	AMALIA: and the fact that we can get by in French – in French –
23	MARISOL: se callan		23	MARISOL: they shut up

After hearing Marisol's evocation of the bidonvilles, Amalia imagines different types of Spaniards familiar with the migratory history that the bidonvilles represent: those who do not know much (*saber*) about the bidonvilles and who do not want to hear about them (line 3); those who know (*conocer*) the bidonvilles but who prefer to forget them (line 10); and those who cannot understand the bidonvilles because they did not experience them first hand (line 12). Through fragments of reported speech (lines 5, 7, and 16), Marisol and Amalia animate the voices of these imagined people, activating an ideological framework that not only privileges their primary mode of knowing the past and thus their practices of historical meaning-making, but also establishes a moral order among the various figures of personhood that they ventriloquize. As Michele Koven (2015, 393) writes about the evocation of such figures among descendants of Portuguese immigrants to France, "narrators routinely summon up a range of socially recognizable types" with whom they then align or disalign (see also Wortham 2001). Here these types reflect individuals at the Centro in Saint-Denis who may or may not have lived in the bidonvilles, as well as Spaniards who migrated to other places in France and northern Europe in pursuit of social mobility or political refuge. Crucially, they also reflect those who remained in Spain – people with whom Marisol and Amalia interact when they return to their pueblos from Paris, which they have done annually since they first left. Within the ideological framework that the women invoke, evaluative contrasts enable them to position individuals who are affiliated in some way with the history in question. As they claim in this exchange, Marisol and Amalia value remembering over forgetting, openness over censorship, and modesty over pride. These qualities comprise what they perceive to be authentic acts of personal recollection; they preclude efforts to forget what may be construed as shameful, as well as exculpatory claims to ignorance about it. The women insist on recounting what is often left untold – that is, the poverty that motivated their migration – to affirm their moral superiority vis-à-vis their generational peers in Spain, who would rather they keep silent: "Don't tell anyone" (line 7).

Seniors at the Centro often distinguished different kinds of Spaniards, as Amalia and Marisol do here (and as the theatre workshop participants did in their production of *Back to Spain?*), to establish a social order by which they could make sense of their experience of migration. A few turns after the last exchange, for example, Amalia stated explicitly, "I like Spaniards in France better than I like Spanish Spaniards." Her comment, whispered to me and Marisol in a corner of the arts and crafts room, articulated a complex understanding of nationality – there are different ways of being Spanish – that challenged dominant interpretations of the concept. She thus risked offending other people present. These "Spanish Spaniards" often functioned as an object of critique in conversations among members at the Centro – Spaniards who, like them, had experienced the civil war and Franco's dictatorship but who chose to remain in Spain, Spaniards who may now be critical of those who left. Marisol refers to this population when she states that "the person who hasn't lived it can't understand" (line

12) – a statement with which Amalia concurs. What is not understood is implied in the preceding conversation: the hardships of migration and the value of recognizing them – that is, of making them visible to interlocutors through narrative acts that draw on knowledge acquired through phenomenological experience. Indeed, it is these very aspects of Spain's past that have been ignored in dominant accounts of twentieth-century Spanish history, the stories that remain untold.

Marisol both voices and defends herself against this group of "Spanish Spaniards," calling upon the cultural knowledge that she has acquired as a transnational migrant to legitimize her biographical trajectory in response to those who might in some way misconstrue it. As she states in line 16, "you don't have the culture that I do, because I have two of them – French and Spanish – and you only have one, so I know (*saber*) more than you." She goes on to qualify this oppositional group of people, acknowledging that they may even be educated (line 18). Interestingly, Marisol claims to have acquired knowledge (*saber*) associated with literary practices and institutional learning through her *experience* of migration – and Amalia, for her part, affirms Marisol's statement by adding that they have also become bilingual. The two women thus validate their experience by linking it to forms of scholarly knowledge – namely, cultural awareness and multilingualism – that they have gleaned through non-institutional means.

Their assertion reflects a perception of the constitutive relationship among modes of knowing. In other words, they understand that *saber* may derive from *conocer*. This echoes Carla's remark to Josep in the first excerpt ("you can't know (*saber*) much because surely you didn't know it (*conocer*), eh?"). It also recalls the text from the brochure cited in the introduction to this chapter, which describes the intended effect of the exhibition's scholarly-historical approach to the past – that of helping its readers develop *"connaissance,"* a term in French that derives from the same root as *"conocer"* and might be translated into English as "appreciation," "awareness," or even "knowledge." Here, though, the derivational sequence is reversed. What seems to matter then is not so much how one has acquired forms of knowledge about the past or how one understands the relationships among them, but rather the *claim* to knowing itself – a strategic move through which a speaker assumes an authoritative stance on the facts and feelings in question. Marisol's comment towards the end of this excerpt – "Even if they have an education" (line 18) – not only challenges conventional assumptions about the ways in which scholarly-historical knowledge is acquired; it also recognizes that this dominant mode of knowing may foreclose upon other valuable means of engaging with the past. Hers is a social-semiotic gesture so unexpected that it silences her dubious interlocutors. As she says in line 23, "they shut up."

History and Representations

A museum is a cultural institution, sustained by a "museumizing imagination" that objectifies concepts and phenomena, thereby constraining their semiotic potential (Anderson 1983).[7] Signs produced in this imaginary tend to remain signs *of* history rather than become signs *in* history (Parmentier 2007, 273) – that is, say, until a group of seniors enters an exhibition with a display of objects that reflect aspects of their lived experience, and their engagement with it transforms mere representations into active "players in the dynamics of social life." The title of the exhibition – *Bidonvilles: History and Representations* – reflects the spatio-temporal mechanisms at play during their visit. The use of singular "history" in reference to the bidonvilles suggests a dominant chronotopic frame that configures time and place according to scholarly historicity. "Representations," in the plural, suggests the myriad forms of narrating the past from a perspective of personal biography. For example, when Marisol engages with a photographic object in the exhibition – a material manifestation of history – she brings chronotopes into relation with one another, drawing on what she knows about the past through personal experience, as well as what she knows about the ontological here and now. This allows her to activate the historical imagination, generating a momentary charge of excitement and establishing authority on the past as she does so. As this example illustrates, such authority is not anchored in static institutions, such as the Museum of Art and History in Saint-Denis, or derived from institutional roles, such as director of the Centro, as dominant paradigms of historical knowledge might lead us to believe (see Ohnuki-Tierney 1990). Rather, it is produced through communicative acts that draw on institutional voices, along with other semiotic resources, but are by no means commensurate with them. Marisol and Amalia embody this process of authorization by claiming the legitimacy associated with scholarly historicity (*saber*) through their particular experience (*conocer*) of migration and displacement.

Much like the cultural performance of *Back to Spain?*, the museum reflects back to the Spaniards aspects of their experience, articulating a partial vision of their histories of migration and settlement in France – one that is filtered ideologically through negative associations of poverty and filth, which Marisol humorously invoked when we met back at the Centro on the afternoon of the excursion. Indeed, the Museum of Art and History, in all its neoclassical glory, embodies an evaluative framework that privileges the scholarly mode of knowing the objects that it displays. But this framework does not operate in isolation, as Josep revealed by inviting the seniors to offer insight into the exhibition through personal recollection. Their subsequent conversations illuminate how practices of historical meaning-making entail dialogical relationships among modes of knowing – modes of knowing that may contradict, coalesce with, or even constitute one another – that are differentially valued and can themselves be mobilized in the ideological processes through which social meanings are created. While two such modes are cued by contrasting verbs in Romance languages, these practices are not restricted to Romance-language speakers or Romance-language contexts – as recent scholarship on the anthropology of history has shown. There exist other ways of knowing the past, such as the supernatural or the kinaesthetic, that may not be lexically encoded in a particular language but are nevertheless indexed through various linguistic and discursive means.[8]

Whatever the source of knowledge about the past, practices of historical meaning-making necessarily involve frameworks of value through which individuals organize themselves in relation to others affected by the same historical, political, and social phenomena. In settings of transnational migration that are characterized by displacement and plurality, such ideological systems are often structured around questions of legitimacy and virtue, as individuals on both sides of a border make sense of their relationship to the past and situate themselves within a social landscape in the present: Who is more or less Spanish? Who is more or less cultured? Who is more or less moral? Answers to these questions are forged in part through the invocation of chronotopic frames and the narratives that they make possible. Such timespace configurations condition social identities, enabling individuals "to create a shared sense of cohort belonging with others" through their iteration (Blommaert and De Fina 2017, 2). Belonging – to the Centro, to the experience of migration and the nationwide community of expatriates that it represents – is entangled with what and how a "cohort" remembers, with the particular forms of historical knowledge that they alone can access. Among the older Spaniards who animate this book, expressions of historicity serve as a vital means of self-preservation, as their recollections of the past tend to be ignored or forgotten altogether by other (kinds of) Spaniards – or they become "museumized" in different ways through French efforts to impose a national narrative of assimilation. In the next chapter I continue this exploration of the relationships among knowledge, historicity, and authority in a very different setting – the Centro's internet workshop – and around a very different theme: popular music from the post-war period.

5 Search Terms and Sound Bites

"Adiós mi España preciosa,	"Goodbye my precious Spain,
la tierra donde nací,	the land where I was born,
bonita, alegre, y graciosa	beautiful, bright, and gracious
como una rosa de abril.	like a rose in April.
Ay, ay, ay,	Ay, ay, ay,
voy a morirme de pena	I'm going to die of pain
viviendo tan lejos de ti."	living so far from you."

– "Adiós a España" (1954), music and lyrics by Antonio Molina

On a brisk Monday afternoon Josep stood at a mobile dry-erase board while five seniors sat at attention before the turquoise iMacs that lined the back wall of the Centro's multi-purpose room. It was the first day of a popular ten-week course on how to use the internet, and the students struggled with a preliminary matter of practical importance: how to double-click a mouse. In a high-pitched, cartoonish voice Josep repeated "poom-poom" to represent the lightness and speed with which this mechanical gesture should be performed.

Hay que practicar el poom-poom … pero suave, si hacéis ((*knocks on desk, pauses, knocks on desk*)), [el ordenador] no entiende nada.	You have to practice the poom-poom … but gentle, if you go ((*knocks on desk, pauses, knocks on desk*)), it [the computer] doesn't understand anything.

All the seniors present that day mastered this skill within a matter of minutes, except for Amparo, a boisterous seventy-one-year-old novice, who, before reaching for the mouse, turned to Josep and asked wryly, "Will it bite me?" Before he could answer, Marta, who had taken the course before, interrupted by repeating the advice to keep the movement "*suave*" (gentle). At this point Josep burst into song:

JOSEP ((*singing*)): "suave, que me estás matando –"
ELENA ((*singing*)): "suave, que me estás matando –"
JOSEP ((*laughs*)): el ordenador si pudiera cantar lo diría: ((*singing*)) "suave, que me estás matando –" ((*laughter*)) vale ... aprendemos poco pero nos reímos mucho

JOSEP ((*singing*)): "gentle, because you're killing me –"
ELENA ((*singing*)): "gentle, because you're killing me –"
JOSEP ((*laughs*)): if the computer could sing, it would say: ((*singing*)) "gentle, because you're killing me –" ((*laughter*)) okay ... we learn little but we laugh a lot

Upon hearing the repeated use of "gentle," Josep broke through into the performance of "Espinita" (Little thorn), a well-known bolero from the 1940s.[1] Familiar with this tune from her childhood, Elena then echoed in her gravelly baritone the melodic plea that Josep had animated – "gentle, because you're killing me!" – prompting his laughter and some light-hearted teasing at the seniors' expense. At this point about halfway through the class they had not yet begun the day's lesson on Google because of their preoccupation with the computer's peripherals. Playfully transferring his frustration to the iMac, Josep imagined the machine voicing the verse that he and Elena had just sung – "you're killing me!" – thereby eliciting an outburst of laughter among the participants. Before turning back to the task at hand, he acknowledged with a smile that such diversions might preclude the seniors from mastering the course material: "We learn little but we laugh a lot!"

Contrary to Josep's remark, participants in the course did indeed learn a range of skills and concepts over the time that I observed it: how to turn on a computer and open a browser; how to search for content through Google and YouTube; how to send and open email. With Josep's prodding, they also came to see the internet as a medium for the acquisition of knowledge and the affirmation of their experience. This was no small feat for a population with scant exposure to technology. Of the nine people who took the course while I observed it, three of them had taken it once before, and only two of them had computers at home. The hour per week that they spent in front of a screen at the Centro was thus crucial for their learning and practice.

In the following pages I conduct close textual analysis on interactions that took place in the class as the seniors developed technological proficiency. I show how they engaged in a form of chronotopic meaning-making by accessing the familiar conceptual domain of "Spain" through a range of institutions associated with it – the pueblo, Iberia, *El País*, Zapatero. Calibrating various spatial and temporal coordinates mediated by the internet, they produced a sense of national belonging in their diasporic present. As I reiterate throughout this chapter, music was crucial to this enterprise. The seniors came to appreciate the internet most of all for the access that it provided to a seemingly infinite compendium of videos on YouTube that featured songs from their past. The website both facilitated their enjoyment of music that they recollected from the years before migration and furnished a platform for the circulation of their own creative projects. In a final section I present an instance in which Marisol, one of the most ardent devotees of YouTube in the class, wrote a rap song dedicated to Josep and recruited my help to put it on the site. My examination of this process illuminates the relationships among technology, age, and diasporic subjectivity. It also provides further insight into the variegated temporality of mnemonic practices, as Marisol makes use of the internet both to resurrect the past and to project herself into the future.

Diasporic Subjectivity and Musical Memory Online

Around twenty-five years ago Arjun Appadurai (1996) first articulated the term "diasporic public spheres" to name the imagined socio-cultural realms created by transnational groups through their use of new media. Since then, the internet has largely come to be understood by scholars of migration as a means of "constructing new transnational spaces of experience," as Li Wei and Zhu Hua (2013, 43) have argued with respect to the Chinese diaspora in Britain. Through various forms of technology, migrant groups may conjure a sense of national belonging by reconfiguring notions of home rather than merely recovering static representations of the past. The internet can affect perceptions of space and time, collapsing the temporal gap between past and present, as well as the geographical distance between, say, pueblo and Paris, as it facilitates a virtual experience of chronotopic calibration. Imagination makes all of this possible. The ruptures created by the coincidence of migration and new forms of media – ruptures embodied in the use of a turquoise iMac by a Spanish senior on the outskirts of Paris – open up vital possibilities "for the construction of imagined selves and imagined worlds" (Appadurai 1996, 3). Such imaginative work helps novice users of technology make sense not only of what the internet *is*, ascribing it human qualities and intentions, but also, and perhaps more importantly, of what the internet *affords* – that is, access to spatio-temporal worlds in which the self may be experienced in new ways, as Marisol's YouTube video illustrates.

Individuals in later life who are learning to use the internet might be thought of as "technological migrants" who have entered a sphere of communication that both requires new forms of knowledge and facilitates foreign experiences of intimacy (Marchetti-Mercer 2017, 12). While this may produce anxiety among some seniors, for others it fosters a sense of independence and agency, as Natalia Khvorostianov, Nelly Elias, and Galit Nimrod (2012) show in their study of migrants from the former Soviet Union who have settled in Israel. As they remark, to a large extent "memories of the past" shape the ways in which older informants make use of the internet as they draw on two main temporal perspectives in their engagement with it: that of personal history and that of national-cultural history (9). Such tendencies reflect a durative interest among older informants in fusing modes of knowledge about the past – the personal-biographical and the scholarly-historical, as I discuss in chapter 4 – thereby endowing their discursive practices with authority and affirming bounds of community in the present.

The imagined realms created through the use of technology thus enfold disparate temporalities into a reconfigured sense of place – that is, "home" – bringing familiar representations of the past and of elsewhere into a mediated present. As Karim H. Karim (2003) writes, "much of the cultural production of diasporas involves the (re-)creation of alternative imaginative space alongside existing mappings" (9). These established cartographies ensure the intelligibility of chronotopes that are animated virtually, enabling a sustained sense of belonging to spatio-temporal realms – "*mi pueblo*," Spain, Paris – that, though they may be reconfigured through the use of technology, nevertheless remain recognizable. Among transnational migrants in later life who participate in the kind of "diasporic public spheres" that Appadurai describes (see also Androutsopoulous 2006), the imagination enables them to bring a renewed sense of the local to bear on their everyday worlds, shaped through a dynamic coordination of there and here and, often, then and now (see Paz 2018; Quayson and Daswani 2013). One need look no further than the search histories of the Centro's computers to understand how the internet enables such spatio-temporal elasticity through various forms of content – namely, music videos.

According to José van Dijck (2006), the acts of listening to, talking about, and exchanging songs foment "a sense of belonging, and connect a person's sense of self to a larger community and generation" (357). This is particularly relevant to diasporic settings, where transnational migrants conjure the missing homeland through the music with which they associate it. Music remains embedded in mobile bodies; it shaped early memories and may resonate with acute emotion later on (Slobin 1994). As seniors navigate the present, music often generates or accompanies feelings of nostalgia for the past, an affective phenomenon particularly amplified among migrants in later life (see chapter 2). Carried from a place of origin across borders and over time, musical memories serve them as strands of attachment in diaspora – or, to use the words of Charles Hirschkind (2021), who examines flamenco in Andalucía, as "sonic connective tissue" (125). Musical forms from elsewhere, transported by global circuits such as YouTube, may thus be mobilized in local processes of community formation, helping to affirm claims of national belonging through the cultural and historical knowledge that their appreciation evidences (see Faudree 2012; Zheng 2010). Such was the case among seniors at the Centro, for whom the internet enabled access to traditional forms of music associated with their adolescence in 1950s Spain – the stretch of time just before the advent of Anglo-American pop and the regime's revised efforts at social control through the rapid modernization of Spanish society.

Age and the Internet

Much as in the Escuela, age surfaced in the internet course as a salient dimension of self-identification and social interaction, as the seniors made sense of technological skills often associated with a younger public. Josep's insistence on taking roll (in a course with just five students on any given day) and his repeated use of the vocative "youngsters" (*jóvenes*), pointed towards the seniors' status in the course as older, and sometimes childlike, beginners.[2] Moreover, on occasion he explicitly invoked their place in later life to situate pedagogical content that might have been perceived as patronizing. Describing potential hazards of internet use, for example, he explained that the course participants were easy prey for online criminals engaging in such practices as identity theft, precisely because they were "little old people"(*mayorcitos*) and therefore possessed a limited understanding of how computers functioned. For the most part, though, the seniors approached their lessons in the spirit of the rookie "youngsters" that Josep so frequently interpellated. More often than not, such posturing generated a ludic classroom ambiance, although on occasion it engendered frustration. While struggling to recall how to access his email account one afternoon, Enrique, a man in his mid-seventies who was eager to find a chatroom for Ferrari enthusiasts, muttered under his breath, "We're like kids."

Josep's sonic manifestation of a double-click – the "poom-poom" – epitomized the playful pedagogical tactics through which he rendered technology accessible to his roster of uninitiated students. With recourse to a repertoire of metaphors, he articulated and reinforced fundamental knowledge that most of the participants were encountering for the first time: Safari, Firefox, and Explorer, he explained, were the "Holy Trinity of navigators" (*la Santísima Trinidad de navegadores*). He referred to the computer itself as a "thingy" (*un bicho*) that takes time to "think" and might do something "very Spanish"(*muy español*) when not in use for a few minutes – that is, take a siesta. Such acts of personification helped to ground nebulous perceptions of the internet, which, as Josep explained early on, is both an entire universe and nowhere all at once.

Although seniors in the course came to value the internet for its many provisions – access to information, for example, and correspondence with far-away family members – their acquisition of technological skills was beleaguered by familiar burdens. As I discuss in chapter 1, many of them struggled to read and write with ease; the use of a keyboard and the perusal of content thus presented various pitfalls related to basic literacy. During one session, for example, Marta badgered Josep light-heartedly about the inconsistency of word boundaries online: Why, she wanted to know, did you have to put spaces between terms in a Google search (*El País*) but not in a URL address (elpais.com)? Many of the participants also complained that they found it difficult to remember what they had learned from one week to the next, invoking their position in later life to explain what they perceived as faulty memory. On one occasion, after repeatedly failing to enter the correct password for her email account, Marisol cried out: "Imagine that I want to learn how to use the internet at my age!" Josep, who generally dismissed such ageist proclamations, reminded Marisol that, during an earlier period in her life, she was quite capable of learning new skills: "Didn't you work for 35 or 40 hours a week for 40 years? Well, it's the same." Such a strategic allusion to their trajectories of labour provided evidence of the seniors' capacity and fortitude as they broached a new domain of knowledge in retirement. Ultimately the sense of discovery generated through technological aptitude overrode whatever frustration they felt in the slow process of its acquisition.

Search Terms and Sound Bites: Revelations from a Browser History

Conjuring Spain through Google

The three excerpts of data in this section occurred sequentially over the course of the ten-week session. In the following interaction, which took place on the first meeting, Josep explained to the seniors how to use Google:

Excerpt 1

1 JOSEP: vamos a hacer un ejemplo, vamos a buscar cada uno el **pueblo** donde nació –
2 MARTA: ¿cada uno?
3 JOSEP: – donde nacisteis. ((*Seniors look up their pueblos, chattering as they do so for a few minutes.*)) … yo os lo digo, ¿vale?, Google nos ayuda a buscar contenido, por ejemplo … si yo pongo "**conejo al horno**," ¿vale?, "**conejo al horno**" – no habrá ninguna página en el mundo que se llame "**conejo al horno**"; habrá páginas de recetas de cocina o restaurantes o de lo que sea que contengan recetas de **conejo al horno**, y allí me parecen un montón de resultados … si lo que quiero hacer es buscar, uh, el periódico *El País* y otra cosa muy concreta, es muy distinta es, um – buscar noticias sobre el debate del sábado de **Rajoy** y **Zapatero**, que me da igual quién me dé la noticia, quiero saber varias opiniones distintas ¿vale?
4 ARTURO: pero si pones "**El País** debate" te saldrá *El País*
5 JOSEP: sí sí

1 JOSEP: let's take an example, each one of us is going to look up the **pueblo** where they were born –
2 MARTA: each one of us?
3 JOSEP: – where you were born. ((*Seniors look up their pueblos, chattering as they do so for a few minutes.*)) … I'm telling you, okay?, Google helps us find content, for example … if I put "**baked rabbit**," okay?, "**baked rabbit**" – there's no page in the world that's called "**baked rabbit**"; there'll be pages of recipes or restaurants or whatever else that contain recipes of **baked rabbit**, and I'll get a bunch of results … if what I want to do is look for, uh, the newspaper *El País* or anything very concrete, it's very different it's, um – look for news on the debate from Saturday between **Rajoy** and **Zapatero**, if I don't care who gives me the news, I just want to know various opinions okay?
4 ARTURO: but if you put "**El País** debate," it'll come up *El País*
5 JOSEP: yes yes

Josep's calculated selection of search terms revealed how invocations of Spain remained vital to the processes through which members at the Centro made sense of their lives in the present. Although he referenced two possible entries more than any another throughout the course – El País and Iberia, the flag-carrier airline of Spain – Josep first encouraged the seniors to search for something personal: their pueblos (line 1). When Elena typed in "Santander," the capital of Cantabria in northern Spain where she was born, Google presented a string of links related to the multinational commercial bank that is based there, Banco Santander. Marta, however, found her pueblo immediately: Hontoria del Pinar, in the adjacent province of Burgos, has just under seven hundred inhabitants, and no one in the course had ever heard of it.[3] Josep used the occasion to inform seniors about specifying searches according to the type of information sought, adding that they should consider the various ways that the computer – "the thingy" – might interpret a term or expression.

In this introductory lesson on how to use Google effectively Josep went on to suggest a number of possibilities presumed to interest the population of seniors in the course: *conejo al horno*, a traditional Spanish recipe of baked rabbit that, on another occasion, Josep associated with his grandmother; *El País*, the widely read, centre-left daily newspaper founded during Spain's transition to democracy; Zapatero and Rajoy, Spain's socialist president and the conservative opposition leader, respectively – political rivals at the time.[4] This sequence of examples, drawing from both personal history and national-cultural history (Khvorostianov, Elias, and Nimrod 2012), reinforced a conception of Google as a way to summon mundane but meaningful forms of Spanish culture, fortifying the sense of national belonging that was generated through activities elsewhere at the Centro. Josep thus illustrated the recursive process of localization that often drives internet use in diaspora, whereby elements of a familiar elsewhere work to buttress claims of affiliation to the nation left behind, as well as crystallize formations of community in the here and now.[5] In this example, participation in such a "diasporic public sphere" occurs in the present tense – that is, through access to information and institutions, such as politics and *El País*, temporally tethered to the moment of navigation. In such instances, the chronotopic calibration facilitated by use of the internet is marked by spatial prominence; in other words, the seniors called upon contemporary Spanish content to transform, however slightly, their concurrent real-world experience in a suburb north of Paris (Agha 2007; see also Karimzad 2016). On other occasions, such as the seniors' preliminary use of YouTube, their engagement with the internet amplified the temporal dimension of chronotopic calibration as they accessed cultural forms associated with a shared past, which I discuss presently.

Musical Memory on YouTube

A few weeks later, once the seniors had become familiar with Google and the mechanics of email, Josep presented YouTube, a browser "just for videos" superior to any other that they could find online. In the following interaction, he began the class by explaining what the site offered:

Excerpt 2a

1 JOSEP: yo os lo digo igual que Google es el mejor buscador de contenidos que hay en internet, hay otro buscador que sirve sólo para videos, y se llama –
2 MARISOL: eso yo también tengo eso, sí –
3 JOSEP: YouTube –
4 MARISOL: video y música, ¿no?, toda la música
5 AMPARO: xx
6 MARTA: el YouTube, sí
7 JOSEP: tsh – ¡eh! para videos, ¿qué quiere decir? videos – evidentemente hay videos musicales, pero todos los videos no son musicales también
8 AMPARO ((*repeating slowly*)): YouTube, YouTube
9 MARISOL: eso porque yo con eso he buscado –
10 MARTA: xx videos –
11 MARISOL: y encuentro **Juanito Valderrama, Antonio Molina, Manolo Escobar** –
12 JOSEP: sí porque son videos musicales, pero sean o no sean musicales, allí están
13 MARISOL: eso sí
14 JOSEP: ¿vale?

1 JOSEP: I'm telling you the same way that Google is the best browser for content that there is on the internet, there's another browser that's just for videos, and it's called YouTube –
2 MARISOL: I have that, too, yes –
3 JOSEP: YouTube –
4 MARISOL: videos and music, no?, all the music
5 AMPARO: xx
6 MARTA: the YouTube, yes
7 JOSEP: tsh – eh! for videos, what does this mean? videos – obviously there are music videos, but also not all of the videos are musical
8 AMPARO ((*repeating slowly*)): YouTube, YouTube
9 MARISOL: right because with this I've looked for –
10 MARTA: xx videos –
11 MARISOL: and I find **Juanito Valderrama, Antonio Molina, Manolo Escobar** –
12 JOSEP: yes because they're music videos, but whether or not they're music, they're there
13 MARISOL: that's right
14 JOSEP: okay?

Josep's presentation of YouTube elicits different reactions from Amparo and Marisol. Amparo, who has never heard of the phenomenon, listens and then slowly vocalizes the name out loud, repeating it twice: "YouTube, YouTube" [dʒu-'tu-βe] (line 8). Marisol, familiar with the video-sharing service, interrupts Josep to announce that she already uses it to listen to music: "I have that, too" (line 2). As she explained in the previous class, her daughter showed her how to search YouTube on her desktop computer at home to find some of her favourite songs from the past. She evokes three musicians explicitly: Juanito Valderrama, Antonio Molina, and Manolo Escobar (line 11), all of whom became famous in Spain during the 1940s and 1950s for the traditional Spanish music – namely, *copla* – that they sang.[6] The form became popular at the time partly due to the regime's pointed appropriation of it as a symbol of national unity, reflecting the superiority of Spanish tradition and the cultural promise of Franco's New State (Ramos López 2013; see also Pérez Zalduondo and Gan Quesada 2013). Referencing this group of artists, Marisol reveals her esteem for YouTube as a provider of access to cultural phenomena from the past and appeals directly to the interests of her peers.

For seniors at the Centro, Valderrama, Molina, and Escobar conjure the Spain of the early post-war years – a stretch of time that enveloped not only the most repressive phase of Francoism but also their adolescence and the promise of adulthood. Recollections of music from this period manifest "the intersections of personal and collective memory," thereby limning the bounds of a collectivity forged in time through shared experience and cultural knowledge (Dijck 2006, 358). As interactions at the Centro reveal, the chronotopic fusion of musical memory may generate the kind of nostalgic affect associated with, say, certain recollections of the pueblo. The World Book Day event, for example, ended with Amparo's impassioned performance of a *copla* that was seen by members of the theatre workshop as a fitting culmination to their eclectic celebration of Spain. As Gayatri Gopinath (1995) writes about bhangra in the Indian diaspora, music may represent "a yearning and longing to recover and recuperate that which is also simultaneously and implicitly acknowledged to be irrecoverable and irrecuperable" (309–10). Members of the Centro value music as a form of communal and creative expression. Through explicit references such as Marisol's in excerpt 2a, as well as impromptu performance such as Josep's "*Suave, que me estás matando*," it emerges in everyday interactions, generating nostalgia along with amusement and pleasure. It comes as little surprise, then, that Marisol remains fixated on YouTube's musical potential.

Nevertheless, Josep endeavours to illuminate the full scope of the site's offerings – that is, videos of all kinds, "whether or not they're music" (line 12). A few turns later in the conversation, he offers a string of examples of YouTube content that might be of interest to the seniors.

Excerpt 2b

15 JOSEP: YouTube cuando le pida algo lo que me va a buscar es un video con referencia a – es decir, si yo allí le pongo "**los Morancos**" o le pongo "**entierro Franco**," "Francisco Franco" –
16 AMPARO: ¡qué va!
17 JOSEP: – o le pongo "**23F, el atentado de – el golpe de estado del 23 de F**," o le pongo "**discurso de Aznar**," o le pongo, um – ¿yo qué se?
18 MARTA: sí, lo que sea
19 JOSEP: vale me saldrán videos relacionados con –
20 MARISOL: por ejemplo si yo lo que quiero buscar es *Se llama copla*, tengo que venir a esto, a YouTube y escribir allí "**Se llama copla**," y me salen los videos
21 JOSEP: ¿qué es eso?
22 MARISOL: es un programa que ha hecho un famoso canal en Andalucía – súper, ha sido muy bonito el programa ése, 10 concursantes, todo de copla

15 JOSEP: when I ask for something from YouTube, what it's going to find me is a video about – I mean, if I put in "**los Morancos**" or if I put "**Franco's burial**," "Francisco Franco" –
16 AMPARO: no way!
17 JOSEP: – or if I put "**23F, the attack of – the coup d'état from the 23 of F**," or I put "**Aznar's speech**," or I put, um – whatever
18 MARTA: yes, whatever
19 JOSEP: okay I'll get videos related to –
20 MARISOL: for example if what I want to look for is *Se llama copla*, I have to come to this, to YouTube and write there "**Se llama copla**," and I get videos
21 JOSEP: what is that?
22 MARISOL: it's a program from a famous channel in Andalucía – super, that program has been great, 10 contestants, all about *copla*

Once again, Josep summons Spain by way of cultural, political, and historical references presumed to be familiar to his audience. His litany of non-musical search possibilities calls forth various temporal frames familiar to the course participants (lines 15 and 17). Los Morancos, a comedy duo of brothers from Andalucía, first became active in the mid-1980s and is widely appreciated today for its parodies of popular and political culture, which have garnered millions of views on YouTube.

From there, Josep turns towards a video of Franco's burial from 1975, triggering an unequivocal disavowal from Amparo that suggests her ideological proclivities: "no way!" (line 16). Josep then offers "23F," the popular name for an attempted coup d'état that occurred on 23 February 1981, during which an army officer led an eighteen-hour occupation of the Cortes Generales, Spain's congressional chambers, before abandoning his cause.[7] Finally, Josep proposes looking up a speech by the conservative politician José María Aznar, who had served as the prime minister of Spain from 1996 to 2004. The possibilities that Josep provides are tethered to the Spain that emerged in the transition to democracy – that is, in the years following the seniors' migration. His examples point to the enduring affiliation that characterizes the seniors' displaced present, demonstrated in part through their familiarity with the various forms of national-cultural knowledge that he calls forth. Such a concatenation of references underscores the value of technology for facilitating the formation of collectivities through temporal calibration, as anterior moments in time are brought to bear on the present.

Seemingly uninterested in Josep's non-musical search terms, Marisol asserts once again the value of YouTube for providing access to forms of music that conjure Spain, past and present. Adding to Josep's brief catalogue of suggestions, she offers, *It's Called Copla (Se llama copla)*, a singing competition that was broadcast from 2007 to 2016, in which contestants' performances were evaluated by audience members and a panel of expert judges (line 20).[8] As a web page from the network explains, the show aimed to renew interest among its viewers in the traditional musical form, endowing it with the widespread status that it once enjoyed.[9] On the heels of her invocation of Valderrama, Molina, and Escobar, Marisol's allusion to clips from *It's Called Copla* reaffirms the value of this music for her peers in the course, and indeed at the Centro more generally, including the joy that it provokes through whatever medium it is retrieved. This mundane example of a YouTube search illustrates the amplified form of chronotopic reckoning made possible by internet activity – a vital feature for diasporic subjects in later life – as various spatial and temporal resonances converge offline. From her computer in Paris today Marisol consumes a television program broadcast from southern Spain that celebrates a form of music associated with her adolescence in the 1950s. Moreover, the show's reality-television format works to contemporize *copla* and its admirers, while the technology that mediates its access confers modernity on both users and content. The mediated recuperation of musical forms thus animates the various temporalities that shape diasporic experience and the consumption of culture online.

Musical Knowledge and Inclusion

This next interaction occurred a couple of weeks later after Amparo asked Josep to help her find lyrics to her favourite songs. Her query generated a discussion of possible artists of interest, including Lola Flores, a singer, dancer, and actress who became popular in the 1950s, and once again Antonio Molina, whose renown had surged during the same period of time. As the seniors attempted to search for songs, Josep turned to me to ask if I had ever heard any of Molina's music:

Excerpt 3

1 JOSEP ((*to David*)): ¿conoces a Antonio Molina?
2 DAVID: no
3 JOSEP ((*laughs*)): ¿no sabes quién es? ((*to Marta*)) ¿me dejas – ¿me dejas enseñarle Antonio Molina? ... ((*to David*)) vas a alucinar, eso es la España profunda – Antonio Molina es – es uno de los productos –
4 MARTA: yo diría "la España negra" mejor
5 JOSEP: sí, es la España de Franco ...
6 AMPARO: yo he puesto "Antonio Molina" y no me ha salido
7 ((*A video of Antonio Molina singing "Cocinero, cocinero" begins to play from Marta's computer.*))
8 AMPARO ((*singing*)): "y prepara con esmero un arroz con habichuelas, cocinero, cocinero ..."
9 ((*The video continues to play.*))
10 ((*singing, laughter, chatter*))
11 JOSEP: es la España de los años '40 o '50
12 ((*chatter as participants try to search YouTube, then silence as Antonio Molina holds one of the final notes of the song, an impressive falsetto, for nearly 15 seconds before stopping*))

1 JOSEP ((*to David*)): do you know Antonio Molina?
2 DAVID: no
3 JOSEP ((*laughs*)): you don't know who that is? ((*to Marta*)) will you let me – will you let me show him Antonio Molina? ... ((*to David*)) you're going to flip out, that's deep Spain – Antonio Molina is – is one of the products –
4 MARTA: I'd say it's more like "black Spain"
5 JOSEP: yes, it's the Spain of Franco ...
6 AMPARO: I entered "Antonio Molina" and nothing came up
7 ((*A video of Antonio Molina singing "Cocinero, cocinero" begins to play from Marta's computer.*))
8 AMPARO ((*singing*)): "and he prepares with care some rice with green beans, chef, chef ..."
9 ((*The video continues to play.*))
10 ((*singing, laughter, chatter*))
11 JOSEP: it's Spain from the 1940s and '50s
12 ((*chatter as participants try to search YouTube, then silence as Antonio Molina holds one of the final notes of the song, an impressive falsetto, for nearly 15 seconds before stopping*))

13 JOSEP: ¡olé!	13 JOSEP: ¡olé!
14 ((laughter)) ...	14 ((laughter)) ...
15 JOSEP: vale, ahora os explico cómo le hago cantar	15 JOSEP: okay, now I'll explain to you how I make him sing

Throughout the internet course I sat in a chair at one end of the computer stations, plainly visible to Josep and the seniors, who acknowledged me regularly through direct address – "¿eh, David?" – or by summoning my participation in the conversation at hand. On one occasion Josep referred to me playfully as his "secretary" after asking me to verify what he had discussed the previous week; later in that same session he threatened to start charging me for the jokes that he made frequently in class, which I had been documenting on my digital recorder. The beginning of the exchange in excerpt 3 marks the most direct recognition not only of my presence but also of my subject position, as my national affiliation becomes the most salient dimension of my personhood. In other words, Josep reveals, then aims to redress, my lack of cultural knowledge about a popular Spanish figure intimately familiar to everyone else present: Antonio Molina. "You don't know who that is?" he asks me incredulously before reaching for Marta's keyboard to show me a video of him singing, certain that I will "flip out" (line 3).

Antonio Molina first drew national attention after winning a singing contest on public radio in 1949. Hailing from Málaga in southern Spain, he drove the demand for *copla* at the time and was celebrated for his crystalline voice and his florid technique. In a rapid sequence of turns (lines 3 to 5) Josep and Marta articulate the manifestation of Spain, both affectively and temporally qualified, that Molina represents: deep Spain, black Spain, the Spain of Franco.[10] Conflating his music with the spatio-temporal coordinates of its peak popularity, Josep states bluntly that it "*is* Spain from the 1940s and '50s" (line 11).[11] For the seniors at the Centro, Molina and his contemporaries conjure a chronotopic frame of the past that they experienced first hand and that continues to bear personal significance in the present, given its function as the soundtrack to a marked moment in their lives for which they often feel nostalgia – their adolescence, forged under the restrictive conditions of early Francoism. The music video that Josep selects, "Cocinero, cocinero," features the singer in a popular film from 1955, *Esa voz es una mina* (That voice is a mine), in which he plays a rural miner whose fortune changes when he is discovered by a music producer who takes him to Madrid. His performance in the video displays the hallmarks of his interpretation of *copla*, including the extended notes in falsetto that constitute its climax (line 12), triggering Josep's use of the quintessential Spanish

128   Untold Stories

interjection when it ends: "¡Olé!" (line 13). Amparo's exuberant accompaniment that begins in line 8, along with her peers' reactions (lines 10 and 12) during the song, evidence the enduring resonance of this music for the seniors. YouTube has mediated a form of musical memory, in which a song recollected from the past is brought to bear on the interactional here and now. Such a sonic calibration of chronotopes produces a sense of shared excitement, reflected in the participants' singing, chatter, and laughter. Josep's final assertion that he will now show them how he made Molina sing – that is, how he searched for and played a video of him performing (line 15) – reorients the class to the task at hand and recalls the pedagogical intent of his initial gesture: to impart cultural knowledge to me, opening up possibilities for my understanding of this music and its meaning in the lives of my research participants.

YouTube and Self-Memorialization

Marisol, perhaps more than any other person I encountered at the Centro, seemed keen on exploring possibilities of self-expression through the internet. During the final weeks of the course she approached me to ask if I would help her make a video and upload it to YouTube because she had written a rap song dedicated to Josep and wanted to broadcast it online. I willingly agreed, curious to know what her interpretation of the genre might reveal about her perceptions of the technology that she was learning how to use. An energetic sixty-five-year-old woman at the time, Marisol referred to herself as "*el terremoto*" (the earthquake) because she was constantly in motion: "I never stop." Indeed, when I asked for her performer's name to label the video that we would upload to YouTube, she replied without hesitation, "Navalcán terremoto," referring to her pueblo in the province of Castilla–La Mancha (which she describes in an assignment for the Escuela discussed in chapter 2). In the video, intended as a humorous token of gratitude to Josep, she played on the disjuncture between her age and the age-related practices in which she had engaged to produce it: recording original music to be consumed online.[12] Here is the text that she wrote and performed:

Excerpt 4: Navalcán terremoto on YouTube

1 Ahora yo me he metido en internet
2 dicen que eso no es para mí
3 que yo ya soy muy mayor

1 Now I've put myself on the internet
2 they say that this isn't for me
3 that I'm already very old

4	hay que vivir en la sociedad	4	we have to live in society
5	haciendo las cosas que la vida moderna nos da	5	doing things that modern life gives us
6	vente aprender internet	6	come learn how to use the internet
7	verás a tu pueblo y toda tu gente	7	you'll see your pueblo and all your people
8	dale que dale, dale al ratón	8	come on, come on, come on click the mouse
9	abre el correo, verás si tienes mensajes nuevos	9	open up your email, you'll see if you have any new messages
10	ay qué alegría, ay qué ilusión	10	isn't it fun, isn't it wonderful
11	viendo cantando a Antonio Molina "La hija de Juan Simón"	11	seeing Antonio Molina sing "La hija de Juan Simón"
12	es estupendo te lo digo yo	12	I'm telling you it's amazing
13	vente aprender con nuestro querido [Josep]	13	come learn with our dear [Josep]
14	aunque algún día la cabeza va a perder	14	even though he'll lose his mind someday
15	dale que dale, dale al ratón	15	come on, come on, come on click the mouse
16	si no comprendes, cierra la puerta y vámonos	16	if you don't get it, shut the door and let's get out of here

As seen in figure 5.1, in the video Marisol borrows signifiers – a baseball cap worn backwards and a baggy sweat jacket, physical gestures that include rhythmic bouncing and extended arm waves – that she associates with rap music and the male, urban youth who are its primary creators and consumers (see Alim, Ibrahim, and Pennycook 2009). Her exaggerated imitation of them alludes to her perception that she is violating age-related expectations about the people who typically participate in this medium. As she stated before I began filming the video, "Check it out – someone our age who knows what YouTube is!"[13] Marisol initiates her rap by animating ideologies about technology and its association with a younger public, setting up a preliminary tension in the opening verses between a first-person pronoun – "I" (line 1) – and an indeterminate "they" (line 2). The third-person form indexes an imagined group of individuals who subscribe to the ageist ideologies that Marisol's rap aims to challenge, and who believe that she should not use the internet precisely because she is older: "they say that this isn't for me / that I'm already very old" (lines 2–3).

The sentiment recalls the opening gambit of the poem that Lina read to her peers in the Escuela (analysed at length in chapter 1), in which she gives voice to a general, antithetical other who espouses negative

Figure 5.1. Marisol performs her rap on YouTube
Note: YouTube is a video-sharing service and this book is not endorsed by or affiliated with YouTube in any way.
Source: Divita (2008).

assumptions about the limitations of being "old": "They say, why go to school at our age?" Lina goes on to dismiss such a position as "empty words" before assuring her audience that returning to school as older adults carries no shame, despite dominant age-related ideologies about learning and the life course. Marisol alludes to similar notions about who should or should not "put themselves" online, referencing her status as "very old" (line 3) as possible grounds for her exclusion. As she raps "very old" in the video, Marisol brushes her cheeks with the palms of her hands as she bounces up and down to the beat. The gesture points again towards age by alluding to its physical manifestations; the only moment in the video that she makes such a movement, it establishes an interpretational ground for the content that follows. Age more than any other dimension of difference motivates the tension between those embodied in the voice of critique ("they say ...") and her performance's intended audience of seniors, whom she addresses directly, as well as consumers of YouTube in general.

Marisol then offers a counter-discourse to the marginalization of older adults, arguing for her peers to assimilate the technology that has become inextricable from modern life: "we have to live in society / doing things that modern life gives us" (lines 4–5). She invokes conventional notions about older people's estrangement from modernity and about their limited capacity for understanding the technological innovations that it brings. At this point Marisol's rap shifts from argument to invitation as she addresses an imagined interlocutor with an imperative in the second-person singular: "come learn how to use the internet / you'll see your pueblo and all your people" (lines 6–7). To persuade her audience to join her in the class she first appeals to their abiding attachment to Spain, invoking their places of origin – that is, their pueblos – and the network of kin who live there ("all your people"). This direct argument for acquiring technological skills points to Marisol's keen understanding of the possibilities for spatio-temporal mobility that the internet enables in the here and now. She thus reveals her conception of what most appeals to seniors among technology's affordances – that is, the renewed sense of the local that it fosters, enabling them to "see" their pueblos and "all" of their family, no matter where they may have dispersed.

After the first of two refrains – "come on, come on, come on click the mouse" (line 8) – Marisol goes on to specify the tools, such as email and YouTube, that an internet student will learn how to use. A reference to Antonio Molina, whom she and her peers had looked up on more than one occasion during the course, appeals again to her intended audience of Spanish seniors, who might enjoy using the internet to listen to musicians whom they appreciated in earlier years. "La hija de Juan Simón" (The daughter of Juan Simón) refers to the title song of a popular musical film from 1957 in which Molina played the leading role; his impassioned, mournful interpretation of this *copla* about love, death, and grief remains revered today.[14] Marisol thus bolsters her advocation of the internet by emphasizing the immediate access that it provides to valued spatio-temporal realms severed from the present – chronotopes instantiated in songs, videos, images, and texts. Perhaps anticipating resistance among her primary audience, Marisol intercuts such examples with positive evaluations of it: "Isn't it fun?" (line 10); "It's amazing!" (line 12). She goes on to give an affectionate nod to "our dear" Josep (line 13) – the performance was, after all, created to express gratitude for him – alluding to the patience that he demonstrated weekly while working with the seniors. Marisol's penultimate verse contains the refrain from line 8 – "come on, come on, come on click the mouse!" – before she caps her rap with a final remark. If at this point her audience fails to understand the value of the internet, they probably never will. As she sings somewhat disjointedly, "shut the door, and let's get out of here" (line 16).

Marisol begins her rap by animating ideologies about technology and its association with a younger public. The performance itself, though, challenges those very ideologies through the material and generic signifiers of youth that she exploits to create it, as well as the technological medium that she employs to diffuse it. Portraying a younger, male singer, she draws from her imagination to amplify the socially meaningful possibilities of disjuncture that are laid bare by her generation's use of modern technology. Marisol argues that the internet is valuable to older people because it mediates participation in a broader social aggregate – "society" – which she indicates with a sweeping gesture of both arms to her right, as though to indicate its separation from where she and her unconnected peers are standing; the examples that she gives, however, are decidedly local in orientation. Marisol thus underscores the internet's possibilities of access to personal interests, attempting to attract a population of seniors who, given their age and biographical trajectories, are likely to share her tastes. They may search for their pueblos and their kin, as well as popular songs from the past that stir up nostalgic feelings in the present. Representing the internet with these older audience members in mind, Marisol playfully challenges in her performance what they may perceive as the breach between their chronological age and the younger social types that they associate with the capacity to use technology.

Digital Remains

As Marisol's engagement with YouTube suggests, the seniors conceived of the internet as a portal to spatio-temporal realms that affirmed municipal and national affiliations, and as a platform for the imaginative manipulation of identity categories – old, female, rural – and their concomitant associations. Marisol's video demonstrates the age-related tension that emerges from logging on in later life: the internet provides possibilities for subversion of the ageist assumptions that inform its use and representation. Lasting just sixty seconds, Navalcán terremoto's performance reverberates with many of the themes that run throughout this book, illuminating the various ways in which Marisol and the seniors make sense of their position as transnational migrants in later life – individuals whose early lack of schooling may make them cautious about attempting to acquire new forms of knowledge in retirement. Through her verses she interpellates a public of generational peers whose biographical trajectories have been shaped by the vicissitudes of twentieth-century Spanish history – political violence, authoritarianism, migration. Still, Marisol identifies among this population an enduring affinity for their place of origin – the pueblo, Spain – while offering assurance that ways of life from the past need not be effaced by modern technology. Such longing may instead be tempered by new experiences of the local through the internet's elastic coordination of space and time – a process, as Appadurai (1996) claims and as Marisol shows, that unfolds through the imagination.

Bringing to life Navalcán terremoto, Marisol realizes the possibilities of self-transformation conditioned by the internet. Her recording might thus be considered a "cultural performance" of sorts, reflecting values of the population that she addresses (Bauman 2011). These include, of course, the pueblo and artefacts from a time before they left Spain – a time for which they may now feel nostalgic. They comprise an understanding of being "old" as a period of discovery and fulfilment, of participation in "society" through the modern technologies – both material and symbolic – that it has generated. Placing herself on YouTube, Marisol has also projected herself into the future, participating in the very process of memorialization that enabled her to enjoy her favourite songs from the past. For the fourteen years that it was online, her video served as a vehicle for how she might be remembered, facilitating possibilities of reflexivity among its consumers each of the 2,840 times that it was viewed.[15]

6 Conclusion

On 24 October 2019 the body of Francisco Franco was exhumed from a tomb at the Valley of the Fallen, an imposing monument near Madrid that the dictator began building after the war to commemorate those who had been sacrificed for "a better Spain" (Boletín Oficial del Estado 1940, 2240).[1] From the Valley's inauguration in 1959 until 1983, the remains of approximately 34,000 soldiers and civilians – Nationalist or Republican or with no affiliation at all – were brought to the memorial for interment, thereby fulfilling its purported function as a symbol of national reconciliation. Most of these remains were collected from mass graves created throughout Spain during the conflict and afterwards; some of them were transferred without permission from family members, and nearly one-third of them were never identified.[2]

Given the incongruous juxtaposition of Franco with victims of a war he is largely seen to have perpetrated, many Spaniards had come to view the Valley as little more than a celebration of military victory and a troubling tribute to fascism. In 2018, Pedro Sánchez, the newly installed, social democratic president, electrified ongoing debates about the mausoleum by setting the exhumation in motion through a calculated amendment to the Law of Historical Memory from 2007.[3] While some cheered this act as a sign of progress for a democratic state that had eschewed formal processes of transitional justice, others decried it as the shameless politicization of history and an unnecessary reopening of wounds.

On the day of the disinterment I woke up early in Los Angeles to witness the occasion as it happened.[4] The images that I saw were striking: solemn pallbearers, vintage Spanish flags, the Catholic rite of absolution. At some point a helicopter flew off with Franco's remains towards a modest municipal cemetery forty miles away. A few hours later I called Amalia in Paris, eager to hear her take on the event. Since I first left the field over ten years earlier, we had spoken to one another every month or so, and I visited her whenever I was in Europe. "Where are you?" she asked, as always, upon hearing my voice. Disappointed by my reply, she launched into an update on her health. Over a year earlier she had been diagnosed with pancreatic cancer. She was undergoing radiotherapy treatments a few times a week, and she was exhausted. After railing briefly against the French health-care system, she asked after my partner and wondered when I would next be in Paris.

We chatted for a few minutes longer, and then I inquired about the day's news: "Did you see what happened to Franco this morning?" Before I could finish my sentence, Amalia shot back: "Oh yes, yes, yes, yes! It's amazing that piece of shit was taken out of that place." I commented briefly on her fervour, and she went on: "He was a piece of shit, a piece of shit, a piece of shit! A murderer! And all the money that he stole from us was to build himself that thing that cost billions, do you get it? And now it's over. He's just like everyone else." As though to explain the fire of her indictment, Amalia then uttered a familiar refrain: "Franco's the one who made me leave."[5] Without equivocation, Amalia pinned her migration and its consequences directly to Franco – to the political figure and, metonymically, to the repressive dictatorship that he had led throughout her childhood and adolescence. I had heard this sentiment expressed in subtler ways by other Spaniards encountered in my fieldwork, whether in one-on-one interviews or fragments of everyday talk. Such momentary invocations served as semiotic shorthand for narratives of painful, personal experiences that Franco was believed in part to have caused. For labour migrants forced to flee Spain as young adults, "Franco" both pointed to untold stories and promised their relegation to silence. That morning during our call I remarked that people at the Centro had talked far less openly about life in Spain under the dictatorship than Amalia had to me. Clicking her tongue, she affirmed what I had learned in the field long before: "Of course not! It's forbidden."[6]

Such constraints have governed talk about the past among those who remained in Spain as well, although "Franco" for some may conjure other historicities altogether. When I visited the Valley of the Fallen as a tourist about a year before the exhumation, I stood at a distance from the dictator's tomb and watched while visitors took turns posing for cellphone snapshots. Emerging from the crowd, two short women with coiffed grey hair approached the grave and stopped a few feet from its edge. After observing their surroundings for a moment, one of them kissed her finger and leaned down to touch the stone. They seemed to be around the same age as the Spaniards I knew in Paris, although I could not envision any of those individuals performing the gesture that I had just witnessed, much less setting foot in the mausoleum. Like my research participants, the women must have been born around the time of the war and come of age during its aftermath. This probability fed my assumption about how their lives had been shaped in very different ways by the historical circumstances that labour migrants had endured. What else could explain their presence at this site, as well as their candid demonstration of reverence for its protagonist? What did "Franco" mean to them?

In Spain, coming to terms with the past has required the complicated task of assimilating such discrepant historicities in the present. In a political culture once characterized by wilful forgetting, consensus on what happened in the past – let alone on its meaning in the present – has remained a chimera. Writing about post-war societies in Europe, the political philosopher Jan-Werner Müller (2002) has argued that such disagreement reflects principles of healthy democratic engagement. As long as memories remain contested, he writes, "there will be no simple forgetting or repression *tout court*" (33; italics in the original). But memories must first be given voice before they can circulate in a discursive field of contention.

Since the early period of the dictatorship, the unspoken narratives of those who lived through it have crowded the fissure between repression and forgetting. Among younger generations of Spaniards today, efforts to remember their country's violent past have aimed to expose the material vestiges of Francoism that continue to exert influence on their everyday worlds. Concerted attention to street names, mass graves, and monuments – what Jonah S. Rubin (2018, 214) has called the "infrastructure of memory" – has revealed how the afterlife of an authoritarian regime does not depend on narrative consensus over how it is remembered. In the case of contemporary Spain, incongruous representations of the past reprise the social discord that was sublimated in the aftermath of war, serving the political interests of those who wield them.

Vox, for example, a far-right political party in Spain, rouses supporters by arguing for their freedom to espouse "opinions about [their] past ... however [they] so wish" (Abascal 2018; see also Divita 2023).[7] Its current leader, Santiago Abascal, has objected to what he perceives as the "obligatory interpretation" of history imposed by left-leaning politicians and scholars, who candidly discuss the suffering caused by Franco's regime in efforts to bolster the fragile foundations of Spain's democracy. Vox thus advocates a kind of insular relativism with regard to matters of historical interpretation, accusing its social democratic rivals of espousing a "sectarian vision" of Spain's past, while proffering accounts of its own that magnify Republican violence in the early years of the war and underscore the regime's economic reforms in the 1960s. The "freedom to opine" feeds a strategic conflation of historicity with history. Vox's partial perspective becomes reinterpreted among its supporters as a monolithic version of the past, resonant with truth because of its genesis from outside a domain of political correctness. As the historian Paul Preston (2020) has observed, such practices essentially "recycle the basic theses of Francoist propaganda" from decades earlier, as their advocates reject outright any form of critical historiography (548–9). And yet, an intransigent fact haunts this revisionist project: Spain's past resonates in living memory today.

With each passing year, however, the number of Spaniards who were born at the time of the war and came of age during its aftermath wanes considerably. Now in their eighties, those who survive must grapple with the physical and mental challenges of later life. They are also particularly vulnerable to public health crises, such as the coronavirus pandemic that first swept across the globe in early 2020.[8] As death tolls spiked among older populations, some in Spain began to view the emergency as a threat to processes of historical reckoning. *El Diario*, a progressive online newspaper, reported in April of that year that Covid-19 had "killed ... many people who were keeping alive the impulse against forgetting and impunity for Francoism."[9] The article quotes Emilio Silva, the founder of the Association for the Recovery of Historical Memory: "There's a generation that will soon no longer be with us, and that's the one that deserves help, the greatest recognition, and that has been abandoned by the State for the past forty years of democracy. We can't wait any longer."[10] These circumstances have lent urgency to arguments Silva has long put forth about the pressing responsibility of younger Spaniards to document the experience of their elders, who provide access to knowledge that conventional historiographies lack. As Pierre Nora (1989) has observed about memory in "our hopelessly forgetful" modern society, "there is so little of it left" (7–8). Featuring a diasporic community of this diminishing generation, *Untold Stories* contributes to the project of documentation that Silva calls forth. It has aimed to shed light on a bygone political regime by tracing its remnants in the discursive practices that its survivors enact today.

As I have shown throughout this book, seniors at the Centro seldom acknowledged painful dimensions of their past explicitly. On the rare occasion that they did, these conversations occurred with me in private, such as my call to Amalia, or on the margin of institutional activities, such as Carolina's recitation of a poem one afternoon at the end of the

Escuela (see chapter 2). Among older Spaniards such communicative activity reflects both the depth of trauma experienced long before and the enduring effects of authoritarian discourse that promoted a "conspiracy of silence" after the war to ensure the dictatorship's invincible future (Jerez-Farrán and Amago 2010, 1) – a conspiracy that was reinforced on a national scale by the amnesty law in 1977. Over time in the field I came to understand how this past circulates through discursive *forms* as much as content, through mnemonic *practices* as much as objects. The various texts disseminated by the seniors resonate with ideologies about language and literacy that were conferred through anaemic educational policies in the immediate post-war years. Tacit constraints among them about what can and cannot be said, which first emerged during the conflict decades earlier, continue to shape their social-semiotic activity in the present, including mundane projects of self-memorialization. Given the extremities of twentieth-century Spanish history – from civil war through dictatorship to democratic transition – the case of its citizens in later life exemplifies how the socio-political conditions in which individuals come of age shape the discursive practices that they carry across the life course.

The narratives that circulate among older individuals thus reveal the discursive effects of living in time. The opportunities and constraints, the learning and work settings, and the experience of relations of power that shape an individual's biographical trajectory necessarily condition the semiotic resources at her disposal to make sense of it.[11] Narratives both recount such circumstances and reflect them, deriving value in part from community and institutional norms around what constitutes a tellable story in the first place. Stories that are too painful or politically potent – those that are "forbidden," as Amalia said on the day of Franco's exhumation in 2019, and Josep over drinks at a bar in 2008 (chapter 2) – are often left unspoken to avoid the unpleasantness of self-disclosure and its attendant threats to social cohesion. Silence is less a lack of language than a condition for its pronouncement and intelligibility. Unspoken narratives point to historical subjectivity and the relations of power out of which it emerges. They bind collectivities at different scales – a literacy class, a senior centre, a diasporic cohort, a generation – that have come to share communicative practices in the present. As Stuart Hall (1994) wrote in his influential essay on cultural identity in diaspora, "identities are the names we give to the different ways we are positioned by, and position ourselves within, the narratives of the past" – including, I would add, those that we prefer not to tell (394).

Impoverished and uneducated when they left Spain in the 1960s, labour migrants have long comprised an untold story themselves, largely excluded from authoritative accounts of twentieth-century Spanish history that attempt to unearth its legacies today. The people at the heart of this book illuminate ignored aspects of Spain's past, as well as the complexities of belonging in diaspora and the navigation of later life. Summoning spatio-temporal realms from before, the seniors assimilate the transnational trajectories that have conditioned their here and now. Whether lived or imagined, such chronotopes are vital to their sense of being in relation to time and, thus, to the ongoing project of aging with which they must reckon in the present.

Reminiscence, the gerontologist Robert Butler (1968) once wrote, constitutes "a naturally occurring, universal mental process ... [among] the aged" (487). But remembering among older adults entails temporalities other than pastness alone. The narratives through which their memories materialize become available to social processes of uptake and intertextuality that extend into the future. Here is where *Untold Stories* has intervened. To understand how these seniors make sense of their lives, the book has documented their talk and texts while preserving them for the hereafter. It is an artefact both of and for remembering.

Afterword

In early February of 2020, I received a WhatsApp message in Los Angeles from Amalia's cousin, Jorge, telling me that her cancer had worsened. She had checked into a hospital near her apartment in Paris and was now waiting to move to a palliative care facility. Jorge was unsure how much longer Amalia would live. If I wanted to say goodbye, I should not hesitate to come.

In a haze of jetlag a week later I dropped off my suitcase at a rental apartment and hopped on the metro to La Pitié-Salpêtrière, a campus of incongruous medical buildings that has occupied a sizeable corner of the capital since the seventeenth century. A concierge directed me to the address that Jorge had given me, a wing for terminal cancer patients a short walk away.

The door to Amalia's room was slightly ajar. Peering into the darkened space, I could see a sliver of dusk through a tall casement window that overlooked an interior courtyard. On the bed Amalia's diminished frame caught flickers of light from an overhead television. I tapped lightly and waited a moment before entering. "Hello, my friend," I said. "Do you know who it is?"

"How could I *not* know? Come here, David."

I approached the chair beside her bed and asked how she was feeling. She responded with a slow shake of her head. It was late in the day, and the effort to talk seemed more than she could bear. I found myself commenting on mundane details in our immediate surroundings, like the magenta-coloured door that brought some vitality to an otherwise sterile room and the reality show that I recognized on TV. She reached for my hand, and we sat for a while in silence. I began to wonder if she had fallen asleep when suddenly she spoke up: "You know, I still think about California."

During the summer of 2009 Amalia came to visit me in San Francisco. Whenever we spoke by phone, she mentioned the album of photographs that she had created from that trip. Amalia flipped through its pages regularly, nostalgic for the moments that they brought to mind: a walk across the Golden Gate Bridge, a drive down the Pacific Coast Highway, a boat ride on the Bay.

"Do you remember what I loved most about the United States?" she asked, the hint of a smile edging into her weary voice. This had become one of her favourite jokes, and I knew the punchline well: "Safeway." Amalia had taken immense pleasure in wandering the aisles of the large supermarket a few blocks from my apartment, astounded by its size and the range of items that it sold. "Safeway was incredible." I concurred, and Amalia sighed, "We had such a magnificent time."

At some point during that trip – or perhaps before it began, while I sipped sherry with Amalia in Paris or visited her for a few weeks in Córdoba – an improbable friendship began to displace our diminishing roles as researcher and subject. Still, I called her regularly with questions that emerged while I was writing, and I often jotted down notes after we talked. Amalia never forgot that I was working on this book and made me promise on occasion to "tell the truth" about Franco.

Over the next couple of days I sat quietly at her bedside. Amalia was never short on words, and I couldn't resist teasing her: "For once in your life you have nothing to say?"[1] In response she managed a feeble laugh. Every now and then she became lucid and began to talk as she had before. I heard again about the long-standing grudge that she held against her brother, who had not once come to visit her in the hospital – not once! – and familiar stories about other people in her past set somewhere in Paris or Spain. At this point in our relationship I knew most of the narratives in Amalia's repertoire, the tales that, all together, comprised her sense of self.

When it came time to say goodbye the evening before my return home, Amalia was in a deep, opiate-induced sleep. She had struggled to eat her dinner, consuming no more than a few bites of *fromage blanc* before calling for the nurse to request another dose of morphine. For a while I sat there thinking about the unpredictability of her life's trajectory, which had begun in war-time Córdoba and was now ending in the thirteenth arrondissement of Paris. I thought about the fortuitous sequence of decisions and detours that had caused our paths to intersect. When it was clear that she would not wake up, I thanked Amalia one last time and closed the door softly behind me. The next day she was transferred to a hospice facility. Two weeks later Amalia's cousin texted me to say that she had passed away.

Out of our encounters in the field we construct narratives to convey the complexities of what we observe. In the creation of ethnographic knowledge we recount some stories while leaving others untold. Amalia helped make visible this process as it operates across socio-cultural realms, from the everyday lives of aging Spaniards to the production of this very book. Delighting in the defiance of norms, Amalia attuned my ear to the stories that remained unspoken among her peers, teaching me how silence shapes our narrative practices and the material traces that they leave behind.

Notes

Epigraphs

1 "On ne parle tant de mémoire que parce qu'il n'y en a plus."
2 "Para comprender algo humano, personal o colectivo, es preciso contar una historia."

Introduction

1 With the exception of public figures, all the names in this book are pseudonyms.
2 The book, *La Pompadour*, was written by René de la Croix de Castries and published in 1983.
3 "A Serge. En sympathique hommage de l'auteur."
4 Spanish domestic servants at the time were popularly called *bonnes-à-tout faire*, translated literally into English as "maids-who-do-everything" (see Fasquelle 1968).
5 "Je pourrais écrire un livre!"
6 The Centro was named after a soldier in the Spanish Republican Army who later participated in the French Resistance during the Second World War. Manuel Girón, a noted soldier from this time period, is used here as a pseudonym.
7 Lillo (2004) and Tur (2007), among others, point out that the categories *political refugee* and *economic migrant* overlap in more complex ways than much of the scholarship on Spanish immigration has implied. From the perspective of my research participants, however, this distinction remains significant.
8 See Albert, Ferring, and Lang 2016; Bolzman, Fibbi, and Vial 2006; Ciobanu and Hunter 2017; Dossa and Coe 2017; Horn and Schweppe 2017; Torres and Karl 2016; Näre, Walsh, and Baldassar 2017; Walsh and Näre 2016; Warnes et al. 2004; Warnes and Williams 2006.

9 Research on transnationalism and migration in applied linguistics and linguistic anthropology has often overlooked older populations. *The Routledge Handbook of Migration and Language*, for example, an otherwise impressive volume for its comprehensive account of the "interface between language and mobility," makes virtually no mention of later life (Canagarajah 2017, 1).

10 Much scholarship on later life has discussed the prevalence of narrative reflection among its subjects (Danely 2014; Degnen 2012; Hazan 1980; Lamb 2009; among others).

11 An extensive area of study in linguistic anthropology, language ideology refers in a broad sense to beliefs about language, its speakers, and their discursive practices – beliefs that are often morally loaded and politically charged (see Schieffelin, Woolard, and Kroskrity 1998; Kroskrity 2000). Among my research participants the most potent language ideologies revolved around conceptions of literacy, literacy practices, and literate subjectivity, as I discuss in chapter 1.

12 Of course, history is not neutral. Instead, its claims to a kind of neutrality operate as a form of historicity in itself.

13 See Behar 1991; Cole 2001; Eisenlohr 2004, 2006, 2018; Lambek 2002, 2016; Palmié and Stewart 2016; Quijada 2019; Swinehart and Browne Ribeiro 2019; Wirtz 2014, 2016.

14 See Agha 2007; Blommaert and De Fina 2017; De Fina and Georgakopoulou 2015; Georgakopoulou 2007; Schiffrin 2009; Woolard 2011, 2016.

15 "Pueblo," in this sense, means "village" or "town." Given the term's prevalence in the Spaniards' everyday discourse, I leave it untranslated throughout the book.

16 See Dick 2011a, 2011b; Divita 2014, 2019; Eisenlohr 2004; Karimzad 2016; Karimzad and Catedral 2018a, 2018b, 2021; Koven 2013a, 2013b; Lempert and Perrino 2007; Perrino 2007, 2015, 2020; Wirtz 2014.

17 See Hirschkind (2021) for thoughtful consideration of the epistemic value of "emotional attunements and sensibilities" to historical enquiry, in particular with regard to the case of Andalucía that he examines (20).

18 See also De Fina and Georgakopoulou 2015; Falconi and Graber 2019; Ochs and Capps 2001; Perrino 2020; Wirtz 2007, 2014.

19 See Bauman (1983) for a related account of silence among seventeenth-century Quakers.

20 For examples of related scholarship see the following: Bamberg and Georgakopoulou (2008) and Georgakopoulou (2007) on "small stories"; Norrick (2005) on the "dark side" of tellability; Medeiros and Rubinstein (2015) on "shadow stories."

21 Among other semiotic complexities, the term "historical memory" conflates the domains of history and memory, throwing into question

the foundational dichotomy in definitions of *collective* memory. To make sense of the relationships to the past that sustain social formations in the present, scholars of collective memory – namely, the sociologist Maurice Halbwachs (1980) and the historian Pierre Nora (1989) – have insisted, in different ways, on the distinction between these two domains. Sociocultural and linguistic anthropologists have long troubled such a distinction through various ethnographic engagements (Cole 2001; Comaroff and Comaroff 1992; Connerton 1989; French 2012; A. Smith 2004; Wertsch 2002, 2008, 2012; Wirtz 2016).

22 The small body of scholarship on the experience of economic migrants has tended to focus on those who have returned permanently to Spain, as opposed to those who remain in diaspora (Lillo 2004; Rogozen-Soltar 2016).

23 Preston (2012, xvi) rightfully notes that the Nationalists were not the only perpetrators of violence. Republican forces tortured and killed army officers, conservative party members, and Catholic clergy, totalling approximately one-fourth of the 200,000 victims of direct warfare. Nevertheless, their acts were more impelled by outrage than determined by deliberate policy, and they waned considerably as the war raged on.

24 Vincent cites this statistic from the National Institute of Emigration.

25 In a sense, they had been conditioned by a generational habitus, a set of dispositions towards historicity and what it should – or should not – entail (Bourdieu 1991).

26 See Faber (2018) for a provocative critique of Juliá Díaz's work, in which he problematizes the historian's strict distinction between history and memory, as well as his reluctance to consider historiography as "a socially embedded practice" (64).

27 The Ley de los Niños de la Guerra (2005) stipulated economic compensation for Spanish citizens who had been exiled abroad as children during the war, primarily by Republican authorities aiming to protect them from its ravages. Most, but not all, of these children were repatriated in the 1940s. Until 2020 the Ley de Memoria Histórica (2007) provoked the most vociferous debates in Spain, given its recognition of victims on *both* sides of the war, as well as its formal condemnation of the Franco regime. It did not bring about social or political action so much as serve as a symbolic gesture towards historical reckoning on the part of left-leaning politicians. Jo Labanyi (2007, 95) has defined "historical memory" pointedly as "the term used in Spain to refer to the memory of the Republic and Francoist repression." In a later paper she links its genesis to the absence of transitional justice in Spain's process of democratization (2008, 122). See Tremlett (2010) for a discussion of the social and political processes through which this law came into being.

28 In October 2022, Spain's Congreso de diputados ratified the Law of Democratic Memory (Ley de Memoria Democrática), which aimed to concretize and expand the provisions set out in 2007 (Boletín Oficial del Estado 2007). An official government website described the law's overarching objective as follows: "the recognition of those who suffered persecution or violence for reasons having to do with politics, ideology, religious beliefs, sexual orientation and identity during the period comprising the coup d'état of 1936, the Civil War, and the Francoist Dictatorship until the promulgation of the Spanish Constitution of 1978." (Last retrieved on 1 January 2023 from this official government website: https://www.lamoncloa.gob.es/consejodeministros/Paginas/enlaces/150920-enlace-memoria.aspx.) Also, see the chapter titled "History on trial" in Comaroff and Comaroff (2011) for discussion of the juridification of processes of historical reckoning.

29 Such centres also exist primarily in Germany, Switzerland, Luxembourg, Belgium, and the Netherlands (Tur and Marmol 2009).

30 In late 2016 the national federation that oversaw the network of Spanish ethnic associations throughout France announced its imminent liquidation. According to a statement released by the organization, its annual funding from the Spanish state had been abruptly and inexplicably stopped due to "the policy of brutal restrictions and cutbacks by Mr. Rajoy's government," referring to the conservative leader in power from 2011 to 2018. The Centro, given a small store of finances held in reserve, was able to continue serving its members indefinitely with a reduced roster of the organized activities that it had long offered. In the fall of 2017 its chairman and the Spanish ambassador to France reached an agreement that officially postponed cession of the building that housed the centre, allowing it to remain open for at least another four years. The Centro, and indeed many others like it throughout France, now operates in a state of precarity much like the one it was meant to redress in the lives of aging Spaniards.

31 In 2008 this ministry, the Ministerio de Trabajo y Asuntos Sociales, was restructured and divided into three separate entities: the Ministerio de Trabajo e Inmigración (Ministry of Labour and Immigration); the Ministerio de Educación, Política Social, y Deporte (Ministry of Education, Social Policy, and Sports); and the Ministerio de Igualdad (Ministry of Equality).

32 In accordance with the constitution of 1978, the territory of Castilla la Nueva was reconfigured and renamed Castilla–La Mancha.

33 To be sure, there are other social centres throughout France that cater to specific regional populations, such as those from Galicia or Valencia. For example, a short walk from the Centro leads to the Hogar extremeño de París in nearby Aubervilliers – a centre for migrants from Extremadura. See Rogozen-Soltar (2017) for an enlightening discussion of the potency of regional identity in Spain.

34 "¡Porque aquí estamos en España!"
35 Compare this to Aomar Boum's (2013) exclusive focus on male respondents in his research on the memory of Jews among Muslims in Morocco, given his desire to respect "the strong cultural restrictions surrounding male-female encounters" across his field settings (5).
36 See Wynn and Israel (2018) for a provocative discussion of written consent forms in anthropological research and the various ways in which they trouble the ethnographic enterprise. Such forms, they write, reflect "culturally specific views of paper, writing, signatures, and contracts grounded in a Western legalistic culture and particular historical imaginations of the authenticity of the signature" (797). My experience with the seniors at the Centro corroborated the problematic nature of this practice. Although I complied with my university's IRB requirement of written consent, I also incorporated a more situational approach to the ethical issues that these forms are assumed to address, talking with the seniors in intelligible terms about the aims and stakes of my project and reiterating their right to participate in it – or not – however they so wished.
37 Amalia's exclusive use of French in this introduction's opening vignette is something of an anomaly. Unlike most of the other women at the Centro, who settled down with endogamous partners, she married a Frenchman who spoke no Spanish. Early on in my fieldwork she confessed to me that she preferred to speak French, given the affective associations that it held for her. French thus became the language that she and I spoke outside the Centro.
38 To be sure, a life story is merely one mode of self-representation among others, and it is informed by the conditions of its elicitation. In line with critical considerations of the interview that began with Briggs (1986), I analysed these conversations as socio-culturally situated encounters, rife with pertinent narrative content. See also Atkinson and Delamont 2006; De Fina and Georgakopoulou 2012; Koven 2014.
39 Connerton's observation brings to mind the quotation from Ortega y Gasset (1961) that appears as an epigraph to this book. The personal and the collective are inextricable from one another in an individual's narrative practices.
40 These methods and objectives thus intersect with those of oral historians, who use interviews to bring to light "the stories of people whose histories have been marginalized or even excluded from the existing historical record" (G. Smith 2010, 3; see also Hamilton and Shopes 2008; Portelli 1997).
41 This information was taken from the official government websites of Spain (http://www.seg-social.es/wps/portal/wss/internet/Trabajadores/PrestacionesPensionesTrabajadores/10963/28393/28396/28472) and France (https://www.cleiss.fr/docs/regimes/regime_france3.html), last accessed on 1 January 2023.

1. Literacy in Later Life

1 Here is the original: Women, "una gran mayoría silenciosa y silenciada," were considered "siervas abnegadas a las que no les convenía destacar en inteligencia sobre el hombre so pena de perder su feminidad."
2 As an anonymous reviewer points out, the noun *"analfabeto/analfabeta"* (illiterate person) is used in Spain as a highly pejorative epithet. Josep's avoidance of the related term *"alfabetización"* points to the significance of literate subjectivity for this group of seniors, as well as the shame that they associate with their lack of it.
3 In Spanish the orthographic symbols *b* and *v* correspond to the same sound. The use of one or the other depends largely on phonetic context.
4 "Usamos la letra *jota* en los tiempos verbales llamados 'pretéritos fuertes': 'dije'; 'conduje'; 'traje.'"
5 While I was writing a first draft of this chapter, a headline in the daily newspaper *El País* coincidentally illustrated the negative stereotypes about Andalucía that circulate in Spain today, in particular with regard to education and worldliness. The article was reporting on a controversial comment made by an administrative member of Spain's conservative political party, Partido Popular, and was titled "Tejerina: 'What a 10-Year-Old Child in Andalucía Knows Is What an 8-Year-Old Knows in Castilla and León'" (Saiz 2018).
6 "No entiendo na'. ¡Na'!"
7 See Faudree (2013, 21), in which the author discusses a similar interest in textual artefacts among people who may not be able to read them.
8 For the most part, interactions in the arts and crafts workshop took place in Spanish. Given the patterns of code-switching that occurred at the Centro, it is probable that this interaction took place in French because the language was triggered by my reading of the text in that language. Moreover, as I have stated elsewhere, Amalia and I tended to use French with one another in our conversations outside the Centro.
9 Her inscription, in which *"acuerdes"* was rendered *"a cuerdes,"* demonstrated once again a prevalent lack of familiarity with word boundaries.
10 Niko Besnier (1989), writing about a small, newly literate community in Western Polynesia, analyses how literacy is interwoven with local definitions of personhood that involve affect and gender.
11 "Creo que has contestado por muchas de nosotras."

2. Nostalgia for Pueblos Past

1 Unfortunately I do not have written copies of all of the students' compositions. In some cases (such as Marisol's) I must rely on audio recordings

that I made of the Lengua castellana class. I have represented excerpts from these compositions in standard orthographic and written form, using diacritics and punctuation that students may have omitted.
2 Pointing to the importance of literate subjectivity for the women in the Escuela, Marisol also includes within her composition the claim to an affinity for reading: "I used to collect espadrilles and iron, and in exchange, they would give me comic strips, which I liked to read a lot" (line 9). See chapter 1.
3 Jane Hill (1998) has referred to this in general terms as "oppositional discourse," which counters nostalgia "by exposing its formulas to contradiction and even to parody" (69).
4 "Recuerdos malos. *Mais oui*. Cálmate, cálmate. No sigas más, y lo dirás otro día."
5 The poem, in fact, was not written by Carolina's father. In a collection of "prisoner poetry" published in 1940 (*Musa redimida*, Talleres penitenciarios Alcalá), the text is attributed to a writer from Galicia, Antonio Muelas Orejón.
6 Ribert (2015b) discusses how heterogeneous memories coexist among Spanish migrants in France in this article that features a close look at the FACEEF, the national federation that oversaw the operation of institutions like the Centro until it dissolved in 2018.

3. Return Migration on Stage

1 The unrest in May 1968 was characterized by widespread student demonstrations and worker strikes that ultimately led to a dissolution of government; much of this political activity took place in Paris and the surrounding area. This moment is widely regarded as a turning point in French society that upended long-standing social norms and brought about cultural change.
2 To ensure a steady inflow of money, the Spanish government helped its citizens abroad to set up bank accounts, thereby promoting a functional and transitory approach to migration (Oso Casas 2005, 114).
3 "C'est nous qui avons remonté ce pays! Et eux, ils oublient!"
4 Victor Turner (1986) goes so far as to link performance to possibilities of self-transformation, writing that actors may "come to know [themselves] better" through the process of enactment, and that a group of people may "come to know [itself] better" through their observation of the actors' performance (81).
5 This staging on a bench brings to mind Maria Vesperi's (1985) ethnographic study of retirement and later life in St Petersburg, Florida: *City of Green Benches: Growing Old in a New Downtown*.

6 *"Pueblecito"* is the diminutive form of "pueblo," meaning "little" or "precious" pueblo.
7 "C'est vrai. Je l'ai vécu."

4. History at the Museum

1 The exhibition, *Bidonvilles: Histoire et représentations en Seine-Saint-Denis (1954–1974)*, was first organized by the Museum of History and Immigration in Paris in 2006. Here in Saint-Denis it was sponsored by the Conseil départemental, the regional council that oversees the administrative department of Seine-Saint-Denis, an agglomeration of cities northeast of Paris, where many Spaniards settled after migrating to France.
2 See Tetreault (2015) for a concise discussion of the history of public housing in France.
3 See Sahlins (1985) for a detailed discussion of the culturally contingent nature of history and practices of historical meaning-making.
4 Certainly, these verbs of knowing may be used in Romance languages in ways that complicate this categorical distinction. When used with an infinitive form, for example, *"saber"* denotes knowledge about how to do something – knowledge that may indeed have been acquired through some kind of phenomenological experience. There may also be dialectal differences with regard to how these verbs are used. Matei Candea (2010), for example, writes about the nonstandard, intransitive use of French *"connaître"* in Corsica, which he understands to reflect an open-ended form of knowledge among its users that entails "question[s] of belonging or mutual possession" (80). In a phrase such as *"ici, il faut connaître"* (here, you have to know), the verb, lacking a direct object, carries what he describes as a property of "pseudo-intransitivity," by which speakers express a notion of knowing a "multiplicity of interconnected" and unspecified objects (153).
5 In conversations 1 and 3, which contain monologic turns, each line represents a rhythmic unit. In conversations 2 and 4, which are more interactional, each line represents an individual turn at talk.
6 It also recalled the dismissive reflexivity that materialized among participants in the theatre workshop when they were called upon to articulate the value of their performance at a cultural institution such as the Centro.
7 Benedict Anderson's (2006) discussion of museums appears in a chapter ("Census, Map, Museum") that was added to the revised edition of his 1983 book *Imagined communities*. As he states in a preface, this new contribution entailed a consideration of "changing apprehensions of space" in the colonial state, complementing his original consideration of "changing apprehensions of time" (xiv). I am grateful to an anonymous reviewer for pointing this out.

Notes to pages 112–25   153

8 See Lambek (2002), Palmié (2014), and Wirtz (2007, 2014), for example, for extensive discussions of the role of spirit possession in the production of historical affect.

5. Search Terms and Sound Bites

1 The bolero, a popular form of music with a slow tempo and associated dance steps, originated in Cuba in the late nineteenth century before spreading throughout Latin America and Spain. "Espinita" was originally recorded by Los Panchos, a musical trio from Latin America that became popular in Spain in the early post-war years.
2 In addition, the computers had been inadvertently set up with parental control software by a previous administrator, and Josep insisted that participants use the same password for their email accounts to ensure that they would not forget it: *patata* (potato).
3 Marta's search for Hontoria del Pinar revealed that it had nearly twice as many inhabitants, just under fifteen hundred, when she emigrated in the 1960s. This shift epitomizes a gradual and widespread abandonment of rural areas that is of great concern to Spanish demographers and politicians. An article (Conde 2018) in the daily newspaper El Mundo, for example, addresses this phenomenon: "Half of the pueblos in Spain are at risk of disappearing."
4 During the first stretch of my fieldwork in 2007–8, José Luis Rodríguez Zapatero, a member of the Partido Socialista Obrero Español (PSOE), served as Spain's prime minister, while Marino Rajoy led the Partido Popular (PP), the main opposition party. Josep may be referring here to a televised debate that was about to occur, given that a national election was held in March 2008, shortly after this conversation took place.
5 See Martín Rojo and Márquez Reiter's (2017) edited volume for discussion about the spatial and temporal dimensions of deterritorialization and reterritorialization, processes associated with the experience of diaspora.
6 Also known as *copla andaluza* or *copla folklórica*, *copla* explores dramatic themes of fatality, love, and jealousy in plaintive melodies through which singers display their virtuosity via vocal ornamentation and improvisation. Although classifications vary, *copla* is generally understood to intersect with flamenco – that is, the term refers to the verses of a *cante* (song) *flamenco*. Typically, flamenco not only entails singing but also guitar, dance, *jaleo* (words of encouragement called out from a chorus), and *palmas* (hand-clapping).
7 On 23 February 1981, Lieutenant-Colonel Antonio Tejero Molina, along with nearly two hundred law enforcement agents, staged a coup d'état in Congress for eighteen hours, a manifestation of dissatisfaction with

Spain's transition to democracy. During the time that Spanish politicians were held hostage, King Juan Carlos denounced the coup on national television; the rebels ceded shortly thereafter.

8 The show aired on Canal Sur, a television channel that is part of the public broadcasting company Radio y Televisión de Andalucía.

9 Canal Sur Radio y Televisión (n.d.) maintains a web page dedicated to the program, on which it discusses its success and purpose: "El programa *'Se llama copla'* se ha convertido en los últimos años en un referente de CanalSur Televisión de indudable éxito de audiencia y que intenta poner de nuevo en el lugar que se merece a *'la copla.'*" (The program *Se llama copla* has become in the past few years an inarguably successful point of reference for CanalSur Televisión, which intends to give back to "*la copla*" the status that it deserves.)

10 There are different ways of interpreting "*España negra.*" Marta may be referring generally to the period of time enveloped by the war's repressive aftermath or to the poor, uneducated figures who populate many *copla* narratives. Whatever the case, Josep interprets her remark to mean "the Spain of Franco," as his response shows.

11 Jose's remark exemplifies the ideological process by which an index transforms into an icon (Gal and Irvine 2019, 19).

12 The video that we produced remained on YouTube until early January 2023, when I last accessed it. Changes to the platform shortly afterwards caused the unexpected deletion of my account. I include this still shot of the video with Marisol's permission (figure 5.1).

13 "¡Fíjate – alguien con nuestra edad que conozca YouTube!"

14 This is a remake of a film from 1935 directed by José Luis Sáenz de Heredia, which itself was based on a musical play by Nemesio Sobrevila.

15 By 1 January 2023, Marisol's video had been viewed 2,840 times.

6. Conclusion

1 In current efforts to "resignify" the Valley of the Fallen, the monument's name was officially changed to the Valley of Cuelgamuros when the Law of Democratic Memory was ratified in late 2022. At the time I am writing, the monument is still largely known by its former name, and so I use that here.

2 Since around 2000, civic groups led primarily by the Association for the Recovery of Historical Memory have worked to exhume the remains of victims of the war and dictatorship from unmarked graves throughout Spain. According to Francisco Ferrándiz (2020), over the last twenty years 9,000 bodies have been recovered from 750 excavations (46). *The Silence of Others* (Carracedo and Bahar 2019), a stirring documentary film, explores

the social and political dimensions of these exhumations in present-day Spain. In the wake of the Law of Democratic Memory, which was ratified in 2022, forensic experts began to exhume and identify remains at the Valley of the Fallen during summer 2023.
3 This amendment asserted that the Valley of the Fallen was a site of "commemoration, memory, and homage" befitting those who had died "as a *consequence* of the Civil War" (Boletín Oficial del Estado 2018, 10; italics added). It thereby excludes Franco.
4 Only a small group of people, including a few government and religious officials and approximately twenty descendants of Franco, were allowed inside the basilica to witness the actual disinterment. Members of the press reported on the event from outside on the wide esplanade in front of the Valley's entrance.
5 DAVID: "Tu as vu ce qui s'est passé à Franco ce matin?"
ARACELI: "Oh oui, oui, oui, oui! C'est une merveille que cette ordure, elle sorte de cet endroit ... C'était une ordure, une ordure, une ordure! Un assassin! Et tout l'argent qu'il nous volait, c'était pour se construire lui un truc qui coûtait des milliards, tu me comprends? Et maintenant c'est fini. Il est comme tout le monde ... C'est Franco qui m'a fait partir."
6 "Mais non! C'est défendu."
7 This quotation comes from a campaign speech given by Santiago Abascal, the leader of Vox, in April 2018.
8 An article from El País in June 2020 reported that 86 per cent of the almost thiry thousand people who had thus far died from Covid-19 in Spain were over the age of seventy (Llano 2020).
9 Covid-19 "ha matado ... a muchas personas que sostenían el impulso contra el olvido y la impunidad del franquismo" (Baquero 2020).
10 "Hay una generación que dejará pronto absolutamente de estar entre nosotros que es la que merece ayuda, el máximo reconocimiento, y ha sido desamparada por el Estado durante 40 años de democracia. No se puede esperar más."
11 See Blommaert and Backus (2013, 30) for discussion of such phenomena in relation to the development of linguistic repertoires.

Afterword

1 DAVID: "Bonsoir, ma copine. Tu sais qui c'est?"
ARACELI: "Comment je ne pourrais pas savoir? Viens, David ... Tu sais, je pense toujours à la Californie ... Tu te rappelles ce que j'ai aimé le plus des États-Unis? ... Safeway, c'était incroyable ... On a passé des moments magnifiques ..."
DAVID: "Pour une fois dans ta vie tu n'as rien à dire?"

References

Abascal, Santiago. 2018. "Qué piensa VOX de la Ley de Memoria Histórica y por qué quiere derogarla." VOX España, 30 April 2018. YouTube video, 1:48, https://youtu.be/st_oe9xzUKw?si=wNlUOjsDMsVTWcwc.

Agha, Asif. 2007. "Recombinant Selves in Mass Mediated Spacetime." *Language & Communication* 27, no. 3 (July): 320–35. https://doi.org/10.1016/j.langcom.2007.01.001.

– 2015. "Chronotopic Formulations and Kinship Behaviors in Social History." *Anthropological Quarterly* 88, no. 2 (Spring): 401–16. https://doi.org/10.1353/anq.2015.0016.

Aguilar, Paloma. 2002. *Memory and Amnesia: The Role of the Spanish Civil War in the Transition to Democracy*. New York: Berghahn Books. https://doi.org/10.1515/9781782384854.

Albert, Isabelle, Dieter Ferring, and Frieder Lang. 2016. "Introduction to the Special Issue on 'Aging and Migration in Europe.'" *Journal of Gerontopsychology and Geriatric Psychology* 29, no. 2 (June): 53–5. https://doi.org/10.1024/1662-9647/a000142.

Alim, H. Samy, Awad Ibrahim, and Alastair Pennycook, eds. 2009. *Global Linguistic Flows: Hip Hop Cultures, Youth Identities, and the Politics of Language*. New York: Routledge. https://doi.org/10.4324/9780203892787.

Anderson, Benedict. 1983. *Imagined Communities: Reflections on the Origin and Spread of Nationalism*. London: Verso.

Androutsopoulous, Jannis. 2006. "Multilingualism, Diaspora, and the Internet: Codes and Identities on German-Based Diaspora Websites." *Journal of Sociolinguistics* 10, no. 4 (September): 520–47. https://doi.org/10.1111/j.1467-9841.2006.00291.x.

Angé, Olivia, and David Berliner. 2015. "Introduction: Anthropology of Nostalgia – Anthropology as Nostalgia." In *Anthropology and Nostalgia*, edited by Olivia Angé and David Berliner, 1–15. New York: Berghahn. https://doi.org/10.1515/9781782384540-003.

Appadurai, Arjun. 1996. *Modernity at Large: Cultural Dimensions of Globalization*. Minneapolis: University of Minnesota Press.
Atkinson, Paul, and Sara Delamont. 2006. "Rescuing Narrative from Qualitative Research." *Narrative Inquiry* 16, no. 1: 164–72. https://doi.org/10.1075/ni.16.1.21atk.
Bakhtin, M.M. 1981. *The Dialogic Imagination*. Austin: University of Texas Press.
Bamberg, Michael, and Alexandra Georgakopoulou. 2008. "Small Stories as a New Perspective in Narrative and Identity Analysis." *Text & Talk* 28, no. 3: 377–96. https://doi.org/10.1515/TEXT.2008.018.
Baquero, Juan Miguel. 2020. "La pandemia amenaza a los impulsadores de la Memoria Histórica: 'Hay una generación que no puede esperar más.'" *El Diario*, 11 April 2020. https://www.eldiario.es/sociedad/Memoria-Historica-coronavirus-pandemia-franquismo_0_1013848947.html.
Basso, Keith. 1970. "'To Give up on Words': Silence in Western Apache Culture." *Southwestern Journal of Anthropology* 26, no. 3 (Autumn): 213–30. https://doi.org/10.1086/soutjanth.26.3.3629378.
Battaglia, Debbora. 1995. "On Practical Nostalgia: Self-Prospecting among Urban Trobrianders." In *Rhetorics of Self-making*, edited by Debbora Battagla, 77–96. Berkeley: University of California Press. https://doi.org/10.1525/9780520915251-006.
Bauman, Richard. 1983. *Let Your Words Be Few: Symbolism of Speaking and Silence among Seventeenth-Century Quakers*. New York: Cambridge University Press.
– 1992. "Performance." In *Folklore, Cultural Performances, and Popular Entertainments*, edited by Richard Bauman, 41–9. New York: Oxford University Press.
– 2011. "Commentary: Foundations in Performance." *Journal of Sociolinguistics* 15, no. 5 (November): 707–20. https://doi.org/10.1111/j.1467-9841.2011.00510.x.
Behar, Ruth. 1991. *The Presence of the Past in a Spanish Village: Santa María del Monte*. Princeton, NJ: Princeton University Press. https://doi.org/10.1515/9781400862399.
Belmonte, Thomas. 2005. *The Broken Fountain*. New York: Columbia University Press.
Besnier, Niko. 1989. "Literacy and Feelings: The Encoding of Affect in Nukulaelae Letters." *Text* 9, no. 1: 69–91. https://doi.org/10.1515/text.1.1989.9.1.69.
Bissell, William Cunningham. 2015. "Afterword: On Anthropology's Nostalgia – Looking Back / Seeing Ahead." In *Anthropology and Nostalgia*, edited by Olivia Angé and David Berliner, 213–24. New York: Berghahn Books. https://doi.org/10.1515/9781782384540-013.
Blommaert, Jan. 2015. "Chronotopes, Scales, and Complexity in the Study of Language in Society." *Annual Review of Anthropology* 44 (October): 105–16. https://doi.org/10.1146/annurev-anthro-102214-014035.

Blommaert, Jan, and Ad Backus. 2013. "Superdiverse Repertoires and the Individual." In *Multilingualism and Multimodality: Current Challenges for Educational Studies*, edited by Ingrid de Saint-Jacques and Jean-Jacques Weber, 11–32. Rotterdam: Sense Publishers. https://doi.org/10.1007/978-94-6209-266-2_2.

Blommaert, Jan, and Anna De Fina. 2017. "Chronotopic Identities: On the Timespace Organization of Who We Are." In *Diversity and Super-Diversity*, edited by Anna De Fina and Jeremy Wegner, 1–14. Washington, DC: Georgetown University Press.

Boletín Oficial del Estado. 1940. "Decreto, de 1 de abril de 1940 disponiendo se alcen Basílica, Monasterio y Cuartel de Juventudes, en la finca situada en las vertientes de la Sierra de Guadarrama (El Escorial), conocida por Cuelga-muros, para perpetuar la memoria de los caídos en nuestra Gloria Cruzada." *Boletín Oficial del Estado* 93 (2 April): 2240.

— 2006. "Ley 40/2006, de 14 de diciembre, del Estatuto de la ciudadanía española en el exterior." *Boletín Oficial del Estado* 299 (14 December): 44156–66.

— 2007. "Ley 52/2007, de 26 de diciembre, por la que se reconocen y amplían derechos y se establecen medidas en favor de quienes padecieron persecución o violencia durante la guerra civil y la dictadura." *Boletín Oficial del Estado* 310 (27 December): 53410–16.

— 2018. "Real decreto-ley 10/2018, de 24 de agosto, por el que se modifica la Ley 52/2007, de 26 de diciembre, por la que se reconocen y amplían derechos y se establecen medidas en favor de quienes padecieron persecución o violencia durante la Guerra Civil y la Dictadura." *Boletín Oficial del Estado* 206 (25 August): 84607–10.

Bolzman, Claudio, Rosite Fibbi, and Marie Vial. 2006. "What to Do after Retirement? Elderly Migrants and the Question of Return." *Journal of Ethnic and Migration Studies* 32, no. 8 (November): 1359–75. https://doi.org/10.1080/13691830600928748.

Boum, Aomar. 2013. *Memories of Absence: How Muslims Remember Jews in Morocco*. Stanford, CA: Stanford University Press. https://doi.org/10.1515/9780804788519.

Bourdieu, Pierre. 1991. *Language and Symbolic Power*. Cambridge, MA: Harvard University Press.

Boyer, Dominic. 2012. "From Algos to Autonomos: Nostalgic Eastern Europe as Postimperial Mania." In *Post-Communist Nostalgia*, edited by Maria Todorova and Zsuzsa Gille, 17–28. New York: Berghahn Books. https://doi.org/10.1515/9781845458348-003.

Boym, Svetlana. 2007. "Nostalgia and Its Discontents." *The Hedgehog Review* 9, no. 2 (Summer): 7–18.

Briggs, Charles. 1986. *Learning How to Ask*. New York: Cambridge University Press. https://doi.org/10.1017/CBO9781139165990.

Bucholtz, Mary, and Kira Hall. 2005. "Identity and Interaction: A Sociocultural Linguistic Approach." *Discourse Studies* 7, nos. 4–5 (October): 585–614. https://doi.org/10.1177/1461445605054407.

Butler, Robert N. 1968. "The Life Review: An Interpretation of Reminiscence in the Aged." In *Middle Age and Aging: A Reader in Social Psychology*, edited by Bernice L. Neugarten, 486–97. Chicago: University of Chicago Press.

Canagarajah, Suresh. 2017. "The Nexus of Migration: The Emergence of a Disciplinary Space." In *The Routledge Handbook of Migration and Language*, edited by Surseh Canagarajah, 1–28. New York: Routledge.

Canal Sur Radio y Televisión. n.d. *Se llama copla*. Accessed 1 January 2023. https://www.canalsur.es/television/programas/se-llama-copla/detalle/60.html.

Candea, Matei. 2010. *Corsican Fragments: Difference, Knowledge, and Fieldwork*. Bloomington: University of Indiana Press.

Carracedo, Almudena, and Robert Bahar, dirs. 2019. *The Silence of Others*. Madrid: Semilla Verde Productions.

Casanova, Julián. 2010. "The Faces of Terror: Violence during the Franco Dictatorship." In Jerez-Farrán and Amago 2010, 90–120.

Castries, René de la Croix de. 1983. *La pompadour*. Paris: Albin Michel.

Cavanaugh, Jillian R. 2004. "Remembering and Forgetting: Ideologies of Language Loss in a Northern Italian Town." *Journal of Linguistic Anthropology* 14, no. 1 (June): 24–38. https://doi.org/10.1525/jlin.2004.14.1.24.

– 2009. *Living Memory: The Social Aesthetics of Language in a Northern Italian Town*. Malden, MA: Wiley-Blackwell. https://doi.org/10.1002/9781444308273.

Chaput, Marie-Claude, Géraldine Galeote, Maria Llombart Huesca, Mercè Berché, and Bruno Tur, eds. 2015. *Migraciones e identidades en la España plural: Estudios sobre los procesos migratorios*. Madrid: Biblioteca nueva.

Ciobanu, Ruxandra Oana, and Alistair Hunter. 2017. "Older Migrants and (Im)mobilities of Ageing: An Introduction." *Population, Space and Place* 23, no. 5 (July): 1–10. https://doi.org/10.1002/psp.2075.

Cole, Jennifer. 2001. *Forget Colonialism? Sacrifice and the Art of Memory in Madagascar*. Berkeley: University of California Press.

Comaroff, John, and Jean Comaroff. 1992. *Ethnography and the Historical Imagination*. Boulder, CO: Westview Press.

–, eds. 2011. *Theory from the South: Or, How Euro-America Is Evolving toward Africa*. New York: Routledge. https://doi.org/10.4324/9781315631639.

Conde, Raúl. 2018. "La mitad de los pueblos de España está en riesgo de desaparición," *El Mundo*, 27 January 2018. https://www.elmundo.es/espana/2018/01/27/5a6b9793468aebc5468b4696.html.

Connerton, Paul. 1989. *How Societies Remember*. New York: Cambridge University Press. https://doi.org/10.1017/CBO9780511628061.

Conseil général de la Seine-Saint-Denis. 2004. Bidonvilles : Histoire et représentations, Seine-Saint-Denis (1954–1974). *Patrimoine en Seine-Saint-Denis*, no. 20. Bobigny, France: Conseil général de la Seine-Saint-Denis. https://patrimoine.seinesaintdenis.fr/IMG/pdf/patrimoine_en_ssd_20.pdf.

Corwin, Anna I. 2021. *Embracing Age: How Catholic Nuns Became Models of Aging Well*. New Brunswick, NJ: Rutgers University Press. https://doi.org/10.36019/9781978822313.

Coutin, Susan Bibler. 2016. *Exiled Home: Salvadoran Transnational Youth in the Aftermath of Violence*. Durham, NC: Duke University Press. https://doi.org/10.1215/9780822374176.

Danely, Jason. 2014. *Aging and Loss: Mourning and Maturity in Contemporary Japan*. New Brunswick, NJ: Rutgers University Press. https://doi.org/10.36019/9780813565187.

Das, Sonia. 2016. *Linguistic Rivalries: Tamil Migrants and Anglo-Franco Conflicts*. New York: Oxford University Press. https://doi.org/10.1093/acprof:oso/9780190461775.001.0001.

Davis, Madeleine. 2005. "Is Spain Recovering Its Memory?: Breaking the *Pacto del Olvido*." *Human Rights Quarterly* 27, no. 3 (August): 858–80. https://doi.org/10.1353/hrq.2005.0034.

De Fina, Anna, and Alexandra Georgakopoulou. 2012. *Analyzing Narrative: Discourse and Sociolinguistic Perspectives*. New York: Cambridge University Press. https://doi.org/10.1017/CBO9781139051255.

–, eds. 2015. *The Handbook of Narrative Analysis*. Malden, MA: John Wiley & Sons. https://doi.org/10.1002/9781118458204.ch0.

De Fina, Anna, and Amelia Tseng. 2017. "Narrative in the Study of Migrants." In *The Routledge Handbook of Migration and Language*, edited by Suresh Canagarajah, 381–96. New York: Routledge. https://doi.org/10.4324/9781315754512.

Degnen, Cathrine. 2012. *Ageing Selves and Everyday Life in the North of England*. Manchester, UK: Manchester University Press. https://doi.org/10.2307/j.ctt21216jf.

Dick, Hilary Parsons. 2010. "Imagined Lives and Modernist Chronotopes in Mexican Nonmigrant Discourse." *American Ethnologist* 37, no. 2 (May): 275–90. https://doi.org/10.1111/j.1548-1425.2010.01255.x.

– 2011a. "Language and Migration to the United States." *Annual Review of Anthropology* 40 (October): 227–40. https://doi.org/10.1146/annurev-anthro-081309-145634.

– 2011b. "Making Immigrants Illegal in Small-Town USA." *Journal of Linguistic Anthropology* 21, no. S1 (August): E35–E55. https://doi.org/10.1111/j.1548-1395.2011.01096.x.

– 2018. *Words of Passage: National Belonging and the Imagined Lives of Mexican Migrants*. Austin: University of Texas Press. https://doi.org/10.7560/314012.

Dijck, José van. 2006. "Record and Hold: Popular Music between Personal and Collective Memory." *Critical Studies in Media Communication* 23, no. 5 (December): 357–74. https://doi.org/10.1080/07393180601046121.

Divita, David. 2008. *Navalcán terremoto!!!!!* Personal video recording, uploaded in June 2008. YouTube, 00:59.
- 2012. "Online in Later Life: Age as a Chronological Fact and a Dynamic Social Category in an Internet Class for Retirees." *Journal of Sociolinguistics* 16, no. 5: 585–612. https://doi.org/10.1111/josl.12000.
- 2014. "From Paris to *Pueblo* and Back: (Re-)Emigration and the Modernist Chronotope in Cultural Performance." *Journal of Linguistic Anthropology* 24, no. 1: 1–18. https://doi.org/10.1111/jola.12034.
- 2019. "Recalling the Bidonvilles of Paris: Historicity and Authority among Transnational Migrants in Later Life." *Journal of Linguistic Anthropology* 29, no. 1: 50–68. https://doi.org/10.1111/jola.12211.
- 2023. "Radical-Right Populism in Spain and the Strategy of Chronopolitics." *Language in Society* 52, no. 5 (November): 757–81. https://doi.org/10.1017/S0047404522000227.
Dodman, Thomas. 2018. *What Nostalgia Was: War, Empire, and the Time of a Deadly Emotion.* Chicago: University of Chicago Press. https://doi.org/10.7208/chicago/9780226493138.001.0001.
Dossa, Parin, and Cati Coe. 2017. "Introduction: Transnational Aging and Reconfigurations of Kin Work." In *Transnational Aging and Reconfigurations of Kin Work*, edited by Parrin Dossa and Cati Coe, 1–21. Rutgers, NJ: Rutgers University Press. https://doi.org/10.36019/9780813588100-001.
Douzenel, Pierre. n.d. *Bidonville R. Rolland.* Photograph, c. 1950s. In Conseil général de la Seine-Saint-Denis 2004, 6.
Eisenlohr, Patrick. 2004. "Temporalities of Community: Ancestral Language, Pilgrimage, and Diasporic Belonging in Mauritius." *Journal of Linguistic Anthropology* 14, no. 1: 81–98. https://doi.org/10.1525/jlin.2004.14.1.81.
- 2006. *Little India: Diaspora, Time, and Ethnolinguistic Belonging in Hindu Mauritius.* Berkeley: University of California Press. https://doi.org/10.1525/9780520939967.
- 2018. "Diaspora, Temporality, and Politics: Promises and Dangers of Rotational Time." *Sikh Formations: Religions, Culture, Theory,* 1–6.
Encarnación, Omar G. 2014. *Democracy without Justice in Spain: The Politics of Forgetting.* Philadelphia: University of Pennsylvania Press. https://doi.org/10.9783/9780812209051.
Faber, Sebastiaan. 2018. *Memory Battles of the Spanish Civil War: History, Fiction, Photography.* Nashville, TN: Vanderbilt University Press. https://doi.org/10.2307/j.ctv16759c1.
Falconi, Elizabeth, and Kathryn E. Graber. 2019. "Ethnographic Approaches to Storytelling as Narrative Practice." In *Storytelling as Narrative Practice: Ethnographic Approaches to the Tales We Tell*, edited by Elizabeth Falconi and Kathryn E. Graber, 1–24. Leiden: Brill. https://doi.org/10.1163/9789004393936.

Fasquelle, Solange. 1968. *Conchita et vous: Manuel pratique à l'usage des personnes employant des domestiques espagnoles*. Paris: Éditions Albin Michel.

Faudree, Paja. 2012. "Music, Language, and Text: Sound and Semiotic Ethnography." *Annual Review of Anthropology* 41 (October): 519–36. https://doi.org/10.1146/annurev-anthro-092611-145851.

– 2013. *Singing for the Dead: The Politics of Indigenous Revival in Mexico*. Durham, NC: Duke University Press. https://doi.org/10.1215/9780822391890.

Ferrándiz, Francisco. 2008. "Cries and Whispers: Exhuming and Narrating Defeat in Spain Today." *Journal of Spanish Cultural Studies* 9, no. 2 (July): 177–92. https://doi.org/10.1080/14636200802283704.

– 2013. "Exhuming the Defeated: Civil War Mass Graves in 21st-century Spain." *American Ethnologist* 40, no. 1 (February): 38–54. https://doi.org/10.1111/amet.12004.

– 2014. *El pasado bajo tierra: Exhumaciones contemporáneas de la Guerra Civil*. Barcelona: Anthropos.

– 2018. "Death on the Move: Pantheons and Reburials in Spanish Civil War Exhumations." In *A Companion to the Anthropology of Death*, edited by Antonius C.G.M. Robben, 189–204. Oxford: John Wiley & Sons. https://doi.org/10.1002/9781119222422.ch14.

– 2020. *Contemporary Ethnographies: Moorings, Methods, and Keys for the Future*. New York: Routledge. https://doi.org/10.4324/9781003039631.

Fleischmann, Suzanne. 1995. "Imperfective and Irrealis." In *Modality in Grammar and Discourse*, edited by Joan L. Bybee and Suzanne Fleischmann, 519–51. Amsterdam: John Benjamins. https://doi.org/10.1075/tsl.32.

French, Brigittine. 2012. "The Semiotics of Collective Memories." *Annual Review of Anthropology* 41 (October): 337–53. https://doi.org/10.1146/annurev-anthro-081309-145936.

Fritzsche, Peter. 2001. "On Nostalgia, Exile, and Modernity." *The American Historical Review* 106, no. 5 (December): 1587–618. https://doi.org/10.2307/2692740.

Gal, Susan, and Judith T. Irvine. 2019. *Signs of Difference: Language and Ideology in Social Life*. New York: Cambridge University Press. https://doi.org/10.1017/9781108649209.

García Berlanga, Luis, dir. 1953. *¡Bienvenido, Mister Marshall!* New York: Janus Films.

Gastaut, Yvan. 2004. "Les bidonvilles, lieux d'exclusion et de marginalité en France durant les trente glorieuses." *Cahiers de la Méditerranée* 69: 233–50. https://doi.org/10.4000/cdlm.829.

Georgakopoulou, Alexandra. 2007. *Small Stories, Interaction and Identities*. Philadelphia: John Benjamins Publishing. https://doi.org/10.1075/sin.8.

Golob, Stephanie R. 2008. "Volver: The Return of/to Transitional Justice Politics in Spain." *Journal of Spanish Cultural Studies* 9, no. 2 (July): 127–41. https://doi.org/10.1080/14636200802283647.

Gopinath, Gayatri. 1995. "'Bombay, U.K., Yuba City': Bhangra Music and the Engendering of Diaspora." *Diaspora: A Journal of Transnational Studies* 4, no. 3 (Winter): 303–31. https://doi.org/10.1353/dsp.1995.0011.

Graber, Kathryn E. 2015. "On the Disassembly Line: Linguistic Anthropology in 2014." *American Anthropologist* 117, no. 2 (July): 350–63. https://doi.org/10.1111/aman.12232.

Graham, Helen. 2005. *The Spanish Civil War: A Very Short Introduction*. New York: Oxford University Press. https://doi.org/10.1093/actrade/9780192803771.001.0001.

— 2012. *The War and Its Shadow: Spain's Civil War in Europe's Long Twentieth Century*. Eastbourne, UK: Sussex Academic Press.

Greenberg, Jessica, and Andrea Muehlebach. 2007. "The Old World and Its New Economy: Notes on the 'Third Age' in Western Europe Today." In *Generations and Globalization: Youth, Age, and Family in the New World Economy*, edited by Jennifer Cole and Deborah Durham, 190–213. Bloomington: Indiana University Press.

Grugel, Jean, and Tim Rees. 1997. *Franco's Spain*. London: Arnold.

Gumperz, John J. 1982. *Discourse Strategies*. New York: Cambridge University Press. https://doi.org/10.1017/CBO9780511611834.

Halbwachs, Maurice. 1980. *The Collective Memory*. New York: Harper & Row.

Hall, Stuart. 1994. "Cultural Identity and Diaspora." In *Colonial Discourse and Post-Colonial Theory: A Reader*, edited by Patrick Williams and Laura Chrisman, 392–403. New York: Columbia University Press.

Hamilton, Paula, and Linda Shopes. 2008. "Introduction: Building Partnerships Between Oral History and Memory Studies." In *Oral History and Public Memories*, edited by Paula Hamilton and Linda Shopes, vii–xvii. Philadelphia: Temple University Press.

Hartog, François. 2016. *Regimes of Historicity: Presentism and Experiences of Time*. New York: Columbia University Press.

Hazan, Haim. 1980. *The Limbo People: A Study of the Constitution of the Time Universe among the Aged*. London: Routledge.

Heath, Shirley Brice. 1983. *Ways with Words: Language, Life, and Work in Communities and Classrooms*. New York: Cambridge University Press. https://doi.org/10.1017/CBO9780511841057.

Hill, Jane H. 1995. "The Voices of Don Gabriel: Responsibility and Self in a Modern Mexicano Narrative." In *The Dialogic Emergence of Culture*, edited by Dennis Tedlock and Bruce Mannheim, 97–147. Urbana: University of Illinois Press.

— 1998. "'Today There Is No Respect': Nostalgia, 'Respect,' and Oppositional Discourse in Mexicano (Nahuatl) Language Ideology." In *Language Ideologies: Practice and Theory*, edited by Bambi Schieffelin, Kathryn A. Woolard, and Paul V. Kroskrity, 68–86. New York: Oxford University Press.

Hirsch, Eric, and Charles Stewart. 2005. "Introduction: Ethnographies of Historicity." *History and Anthropology* 16, no. 3 (September): 261–74. https://doi.org/10.1080/02757200500219289.

Hirschkind, Charles. 2021. *The Feeling of History: Islam, Romanticism, and Andalusia*. Chicago: University of Chicago Press. https://doi.org/10.7208/chicago/9780226747002.001.0001.

Horn, Vincent, and Cornelia Schweppe. 2017. "Transnational Aging: Toward a Transnational Perspective in Old Age Research." *European Journal of Ageing* 14, no. 4 (December): 335–39. https://doi.org/10.1007/s10433-017-0446-z.

Horn, Vincent, Cornelia Schweppe, and Seong-gee Um. 2013. "Transnational Aging: A Young Field of Research." *Transnational Social Review* 3, no. 1 (January): 7–10. https://doi.org/10.1080/21931674.2013.10820744.

Jaffe, Alexandra, ed. 2009. *Stance: Sociolinguistic Perspectives*. New York: Oxford University Press. https://doi.org/10.1093/acprof:oso/9780195331646.001.0001.

Jaworski, Adam, ed. 1997. *Silence: Interdisciplinary Perspectives*. Berlin: Walter de Gruyter.

Jerez-Farrán, Carlos, and Samuel Amago, eds. 2010. *Unearthing Franco's Legacy: Mass Graves and the Recovery of Historical Memory in Spain*. Notre Dame, IN: University of Notre Dame Press.

Juliá Díaz, Santos, ed. 1999. *Víctimas de la guerra civil*. Madrid: Temas de hoy.

Karim, Karim H. 2003. "Mapping Diasporic Mediascapes." In *The Media of Diaspora*, edited by Karim H. Karim, 1–18. New York: Routledge. https://doi.org/10.4324/9780203380642.

Karimzad, Farzad. 2016. "Life Here beyond Now: Chronotopes of the Ideal Life among Iranian Transnationals." *Journal of Sociolinguistics* 20, no. 5 (November): 607–30. https://doi.org/10.1111/josl.12211.

Karimzad, Farzad, and Lydia Catedral. 2018a. "Mobile (Dis)connection: New Technology and Rechronotopized Images of Homeland." *Journal of Linguistic Anthropology* 28, no. 3 (December): 293–312. https://doi.org/10.1111/jola.12198.

— 2018b. "'No, We Don't Mix Languages': Ideological Power and the Chronotopic Organization of Ethnolinguistic Identities." *Language in Society* 47, no. 1 (February): 89–113. https://doi.org/10.1017/S0047404517000781.

— 2021. *Chronotopes and Migration: Language, Social Imagination, and Behavior*. New York: Routledge. https://doi.org/10.4324/9781351000635.

Keane, Webb. 2011. "Indexing Choice: A Morality Tale." *Journal of Linguistic Anthropology* 21, no. 2 (December): 166–78. https://doi.org/10.1111/j.1548-1395.2011.01104.x.

Khvorostianov, Natalia, Nelly Elias, and Galit Nimrod. 2012. "'Without It I Am Nothing': The Internet in the Lives of Older Immigrants." *New Media & Society* 14, no. 4 (June): 1–17. https://doi.org/10.1177/1461444811421599.

Kidron, Carol A. 2009. "Toward an Ethnography of Silence: The Lived Presence of the Past in the Everyday Life of Holocaust Trauma Survivors and Their Descendants in Israel." *Current Anthropology* 50, no. 1 (Februrary): 5–27. https://doi.org/10.1086/595623.

Kneas, David. 2018. "Emergence and Aftermath: The (Un)becoming of Resources and Identities in Northwestern Ecuador." *American Anthropologist* 120, no. 4 (December): 752–64. https://doi.org/10.1111/aman.13150.

Koven, Michele. 2013a. "Antiracist, Modern Selves and Racist, Unmodern Others: Chronotopes of Modernity in Luso-Descendants' Race Talk." *Language & Communication* 33, no. 4, part B (October): 544–58. https://doi.org/10.1016/j.langcom.2013.04.001.

— 2013b. "Speaking French in Portugal: An Analysis of Contested Models of Emigrant Personhood in Narratives about Return Migration and Language Use." *Journal of Sociolinguistics* 17, no. 3 (June): 324–54. https://doi.org/10.1111/josl.12036.

— 2014. "Interviewing: Practice, Ideology, Genre, and Intertextuality." *Annual Review of Anthropology* 43 (October): 499–520. https://doi.org/10.1146/annurev-anthro-092412-155533.

— 2015. "Narrative and Cultural Identities: Performing and Aligning with Figures of Personhood." In De Fina and Georgakopoulou 2015, 388–407. https://doi.org/10.1002/9781118458204.ch20.

Kroskrity, Paul V., ed. 2000. *Regimes of Language: Ideologies, Polities, and Identities*. Santa Fe, NM: School for Advanced Social Research.

Kuipers, Joel. 2013. "Evidence and Authority in Ethnographic and Linguistic Perspective." *Annual Review of Anthropology* 42 (October): 399–413. https://doi.org/10.1146/annurev-anthro-081309-145615.

Labanyi, Jo. 2007. "Memory and Modernity in Democratic Spain: The Difficulty of Coming to Terms with the Spanish Civil War." *Poetics* 28, no. 1 (March): 89–116. https://doi.org/10.1215/03335372-2006-016.

— 2008. "The Politics of Memory in Contemporary Spain." *Journal of Spanish Cultural Studies* 9, no. 2 (July): 119–25. https://doi.org/10.1080/14636200802283621.

— 2010. "Testimonies of Repression: Methodological and Political Issues." In Jerez-Farrán and Amago 2010, 192–205.

Labov, William, and Joshua Waletzky. 1967. "Narrative Analysis: Oral Versions of Personal Experience." In *Essays on the Verbal and Visual Arts*, edited by June Helm, 12–44. Seattle: University of Washington Press.

Lamb, Sarah. 2009. *Aging and the Indian Diaspora: Cosmopolitan Families in India and Abroad*. Bloomington: University of Indiana Press.

— 2014. "Permanent Personhood or Meaningful Decline? Toward a Critical Anthropology of Successful Aging." *Journal of Aging Studies* 29 (April): 41–52. https://doi.org/10.1016/j.jaging.2013.12.006.

- 2017. "Introduction: Successful Aging as a Twenty-First-Century Obsession." In *Successful Aging as a Contemporary Obsession*, edited by Sarah Lamb, 1–23. New Brunswick, NJ: Rutgers University Press. https://doi.org/10.36019/9780813585369-003.
Lambek, Michael. 2002. *The Weight of the Past: Living with History in Mahajanga, Madagascar*. New York: Palgrave Macmillan. https://doi.org/10.1007/978-1-349-73080-3.
- 2010. Introduction to *Ordinary Ethics: Anthropology, Language, and Action*, edited by Michael Lambek, 1–36. New York: Fordham University Press. https://doi.org/10.1515/9780823292318.
- 2016. "On Being Present to History: Historicity and Brigand Spirits in Madagascar." *HAU: Journal of Ethnographic Theory* 6, no. 1 (Summer): 317–41. https://doi.org/10.14318/hau6.1.018.
Laslett, Peter. 1991. *A Fresh Map of Life: The Emergence of the Third Age*. Cambridge, MA: Harvard University Press.
Lempert, Michael, and Sabina Perrino. 2007. "Entextualization and the Ends of Temporality." *Language & Communication* 27, no. 3 (July): 205–11. https://doi.org/10.1016/j.langcom.2007.01.005.
Levitt, Peggy, and Nina Glick Schiller. 2004. "Conceptualizing Simultaneity: A Transnational Social Field Perspective on Society." *International Migration Review* 38, no. 3 (September): 1001–39. https://doi.org/10.1111/j.1747-7379.2004.tb00227.x.
Li Wei, and Zhu Hua. 2013. "Diaspora: Multilingual and Intercultural Communication across Time and Space." *AILA Review* 26, no. 1 (January): 42–56. https://doi.org/10.1075/aila.26.04wei.
Lillo, Natacha. 2004. *La Petite Espagne de la Plaine-Saint-Denis : 1900–1980*. Paris: Éditions Autrement.
- 2007. "Histoire et mémoire des espagnols de la Plaine Saint-Denis." *Migrance : Un siècle d'immigration espagnole en France* (Hors série): 9–18.
Llano, Pablo de. 2020. "Así perdimos a la generación que cambió España," *El País*, 27 June 2020. https://elpais.com/sociedad/2020-06-27/asi-perdimos-a-la-generacion-que-cambio-espana.html.
Llavador, Francisco Beltrán, and José Beltrán Llavador. 1996. *Política y prácticas de la educación de personas adultas*. Valencia, Spain: Universidad de València.
Maison d'Espagne de la Région Parisienne. 2008. *Celebración del Día Internacional del Libro*. Saint-Denis, France: Maison d'Espagne.
Marchetti-Mercer, Maria C. 2017. "'The Screen Has Such Sharp Edges to Hug': The Relational Consequences of Emigration in Transnational South African Emigrant Families." *Transnational Social Review* 7, no. 1 (January): 1–18. https://doi.org/10.1080/21931674.2016.1277650.
Martín Rojo, Luisa, and Rosine Márquez Reiter, eds. 2017. *A Sociolinguistics of Diaspora: Latino Practices, Identities, and Ideologies*. New York: Routledge. https://doi.org/10.4324/9781315883571.

Martínez Veiga, Ubaldo, ed. 2000. *Situaciones de exclusión de los emigrantes españoles ancianos en Europa*. Paris: FACEEF.
McAdams, Dan P. 2001. "The Psychology of Life Stories." *Review of General Psychology* 5, no. 2 (June): 100–22. https://doi.org/10.1037/1089-2680.5.2.100.
Medeiros, Kate de, and Robert L. Rubinstein. 2015. "'Shadow Stories' in Oral Interviews: Narrative Care through Careful Listening." *Journal of Aging Studies* 34 (August): 162–8. https://doi.org/10.1016/j.jaging.2015.02.009.
Müller, Jan-Werner. 2002. "Introduction: The Power of Memory, the Memory of Power and the Power over Memory." In *Memory and Power in Post-War Europe*, edited by Jan-Werner Müller, 1–35. New York: Cambridge University Press. https://doi.org/10.1017/CBO9780511491580.
Myerhoff, Barbara. 1978. *Number Our Days*. New York: Simon & Schuster.
– 1984. "Rites and Signs of Ripening: The Intertwining of Ritual, Time, and Growing Older." In *Age and Anthropological Theory*, edited by David Kertzer and Jennie Keith, 305–30. Ithaca, NY: Cornell University Press.
Näre, Lena, Katie Walsh, and Loretta Baldassar. 2017. "Ageing in Transnational Contexts: Transforming Everyday Practices and Identities in Later Life." *Identities: Global Studies in Culture and Power* 24, no. 5 (September): 515–23. https://doi.org/10.1080/1070289X.2017.1346986.
Neugarten, Bernice L. 1974. "Age Groups in American Society and the Rise of the Young-Old." *The Annals of the American Academy of Political and Social Science* 415, no. 1 (September): 187–98. https://doi.org/10.1177/000271627441500114.
Nora, Pierre. 1984. *Les lieux de mémoire, tome 1 : La République*. Paris: Gallimard.
Norrick, Neal R. 2005. "The Dark Side of Tellability." *Narrative Inquiry* 15, no. 2: 323–43. https://doi.org/10.1075/ni.15.2.07nor.
Ochs, Elinor, and Lisa Capps. 2001. *Living Narrative: Creating Lives in Everyday Storytelling*. Cambridge, MA: Harvard University Press. https://doi.org/10.4159/9780674041592.
Ohnuki-Tierney, Emiko, ed. 1990. *Culture through Time: Anthropological Approaches*. Stanford, CA: Stanford University Press. https://doi.org/10.1515/9781503621817.
Ortega y Gasset, José. 1961. *Historia como sistema y del imperio romano*. Madrid: Ediciones Castilla.
Oso Casas, Lara. 2004. *Españolas en París: Estrategias de ahorro y consumo en las migraciones internacionales*. Barcelona: Edicions Bellaterra.
– 2005. "La réussite paradoxale des bonnes espagnoles de Paris : Stratégies de mobilité sociale et trajectoires biographiques." *Revue Européenne des Migrations Internationales* 21, no. 1: 107–29. https://doi.org/10.4000/remi.4222.
Palmié, Stephan. 2014. "The Ejamba of North Fairmount Avenue, the Wizard of Menlo Park, and the Dialectics of Ensoniment: An Episode in the History

of an Acoustic Mask." In *Spirited Things: The Work of "Possession" in Afro-Atlantic Religion*, edited by Paul Christopher Johnson, 47–78. Chicago: University of Chicago Press. https://doi.org/10.7208/chicago/9780226122939.001.0001.

Palmié, Stephan, and Charles Stewart. 2016. "Introduction: For an Anthropology of History." *HAU: Journal of Ethnographic Theory* 6, no. 1 (Summer): 207–36. https://doi.org/10.14318/hau6.1.014.

Parmentier, Richard J. 2007. "It's about Time: On the Semiotics of Temporality." *Language & Communication* 27, no. 3 (July): 272–7. https://doi.org/10.1016/j.langcom.2007.01.006.

Paz, Alejandro. 2018. *Latinos in Israel: Language and Unexpected Citizenship*. Bloomington: Indiana University Press.

Pérez Zalduondo, Gemma, and Germán Gan Quesada, eds. 2013. *Music and Francoism*. Turnhout, Belgium: Brepols Publishers.

Perrino, Sabina. 2007. "Cross-Chronotope Alignment in Senegalese Oral Narrative." *Language & Communication* 27, no. 3 (July): 227–44. https://doi.org/10.1016/j.langcom.2007.01.007.

— 2011. "Chronotopes of Story and Storytelling Event in Interviews." *Language in Society* 49, no. 1 (February): 91–103. https://doi.org/10.1017/S0047404510000916.

— 2015. "Chronotopes: Time and Space in Oral Narrative." In De Fina and Georgakopoulou 2015, 140–59. https://doi.org/10.1002/9781118458204.ch7.

— 2020. *Narrating Migration: Intimacies of Exclusion in Northern Italy*. New York: Routledge. https://doi.org/10.4324/9780429505836.

Piazza, Roberta, ed. 2019. *Discourses of Identity in Liminal Places and Spaces*. New York: Routledge. https://doi.org/10.4324/9781351183383.

Pickering, Michael, and Emily Keightley. 2006. "The Modalities of Nostalgia." *Current Sociology* 54, no. 6 (November): 919–41. https://doi.org/10.1177/0011392106068458.

Portelli, Alessandro. 1997. *The Battle of Valle Giulia: Oral History and the Art of Dialogue*. Madison: University of Wisconsin Press.

Preston, Paul. 2012. *The Spanish Holocaust: Inquisition and Extermination in Twentieth-Century Spain*. New York: W.W. Norton.

— 2020. *A People Betrayed: A History of Corruption, Political Incompetence and Social Division in Modern Spain*. New York: Liveright Publishing.

Quayson, Ato, and Girish Daswani. 2013. "Diaspora and Transnationalism: Scapes, Scales, and Scopes." In *A Companion to Diaspora and Transnationalism*, edited by Ato Quayson and Girish Daswani, 1–26. Malden, MA: Blackwell. https://doi.org/10.1002/9781118320792.

Quijada, Justine Buck. 2019. *Buddhists, Shamans, and Soviets: Rituals of History in Post-Soviet Buryatia*. New York: Oxford University Press. https://doi.org/10.1093/oso/9780190916794.001.0001.

Ramos López, Pilar 2013. Beyond Francoist Propaganda and Current Nostalgia: Some Remarks on Coplas. In *Music and Francoism*, edited by Gemma Pérez Zalduondo and Germán Gan Quesada, 235–52. Turnhout, Belgium: Brepols.

Ribeiro de Menezes, Alison. 2010. "From Recuperating Spanish Historical Memory to a Semantic Dissection of Cultural Memory: *La malamemoria* by Isaac Rosa." *Journal of Iberian and Latin American Research* 16, no. 1: 1–12. https://doi.org/10.1080/13260219.2010.487509.

Ribert, Évelyne. 2015a. "Between Silences and Rewritings: Two Approaches to Memory Construction by Spanish Refugees and Economic Immigrants in France." In *Diaspora, Memory, Intimacy*, edited by Sarah Barbour, David Howard, Thomas Lacroix, and Judith Misrahi-Barak, 63–80. Montpellier, France: Presses universitaires de la Méditerranée.

— 2015b. "La patrimonialización de las migraciones españolas en Francia en el seno de la FACEEF." In Chaput et al. 2015, 29–38.

Richards, Michael. 2006. "Between Memory and History: Social Relationships and Ways of Remembering the Spanish Civil War." *International Journal of Iberian Studies* 19, no. 1 (August): 85–94. https://doi.org/10.1386/ijis.19.1.85/3.

— 2010. "Grand Narratives, Collective Memory, and Social History: Public Uses of the Past in Post-War Spain." In Jerez-Farrán and Amago 2010, 121–45.

— 2013. *After the Civil War: Making Memory and Re-making Spain since 1936*. New York: Cambridge University Press. https://doi.org/10.1017/CBO9781139021746.

Ricoeur, Paul. 2000. *La mémoire, l'histoire, l'oubli*. Paris: Seuil.

Robbins, Jessica C. 2021. *Aging Nationally in Contemporary Poland: Memory, Kinship, and Personhood*. New Brunswick, NJ: Rutgers University Press. https://doi.org/10.36019/9781978814004.

Rogozen-Soltar, Mikaela H. 2016. "'We Suffered Just Like Them': Comparing Migrations at the Margins of Europe." *Comparative Studies in Society and History* 58, no. 4 (August): 880–907. https://doi.org/10.1017/S0010417516000463.

— 2017. *Spain Unmoored: Migration, Conversion, and the Politics of Islam*. Bloomington: Indiana University Press.

Rubin, Jonah S. 2018. "How Francisco Franco Governs from Beyond the Grave: An Infrastructural Approach to Memory Politics in Contemporary Spain." *American Ethnologist* 45, no. 2 (May): 214–27. https://doi.org/10.1111/amet.12633.

— 2020. "Exhuming Dead Persons: Forensic Science and the Making of Post-Fascist Publics in Spain." *Cultural Anthropology* 35, no. 3: 345–73. https://doi.org/10.14506/ca35.3.01.

Sahlins, Marshall. 1985. *Islands of History*. Chicago: University of Chicago Press.

Saiz, Eva. 2018. "Tejerina: 'En Andalucía lo que sabe un niño de 10 años es lo que sabe uno de ocho en Castilla y León,'" *El País*, 18 October 2018. https://elpais.com/politica/2018/10/18/actualidad/1539859781_258823.html.

Schieffelin, Bambi B., Kathryn A. Woolard, and Paul V. Kroskrity, eds. 1998. *Language Ideologies: Practice and Theory*. Oxford: Oxford University Press.

Schiffrin, Deborah. 2009. "Crossing Boundaries: The Nexus of Time, Space, Person, and Place in Narrative." *Language in Society* 38, no. 4 (September): 421–45. https://doi.org/10.1017/S0047404509990212.

Shaw, Rosalind. 2002. *Memories of the Slave Trade: Ritual and the Historical Imagination in Sierra Leone*. Chicago: University of Chicago Press. https://doi.org/10.7208/chicago/9780226764467.001.0001.

Silverstein, Paul. 2004. *Algeria in France: Transpolitics, Race, and Nation*. Bloomington: Indiana University Press.

Slobin, Mark. 1994. "Music in Diaspora: The View from Euro-America." *Diaspora: A Journal of Transnational Studies* 3, no. 3 (Winter): 243–51. https://doi.org/10.1353/dsp.1994.0012.

Smith, Andrea L. 2004. "Heteroglossia, 'Common Sense,' and Social Memory." *American Ethnologist* 31, no. 2 (May): 251–69. https://doi.org/10.1525/ae.2004.31.2.251.

Smith, Graham. 2010. "Toward a Public Oral History." In *The Oxford Handbook of Oral History*, edited by Donald A. Ritchie, 1–22. New York: Oxford University Press. https://doi.org/10.1093/oxfordhb/9780195339550.013.0030.

Starobinski, Jean. 1966. "The Idea of Nostalgia." *Diogenes* 14, no. 54 (June): 81–103. https://doi.org/10.1177/039219216601405405.

Stewart, Charles. 2016. "Historicity and Anthropology." *Annual Review of Anthropology* 45 (October): 79–94. https://doi.org/10.1146/annurev-anthro-102215-100249.

Swinehart, Karl, and Anna Browne Ribeiro. 2019. "When Time Matters." *Signs and Society* 7, no. 1 (Winter): 1–5. https://doi.org/10.1086/701150.

Tannen, Deborah and Muriel Saville-Troike, eds. 1985. *Perspectives on Silence*. Norwood, NJ: Ablex Publishing.

Tetreault, Chantal. 2015. *Transcultural Teens: Performing Youth Identities in French Cités*. Malden, MA: Wiley-Blackwell.

Torres, Sandra, and Ute Karl. 2016. "A Migration Lens on Inquiries into Ageing, Old Age and Elderly Care: Carving a Space While Assessing the State of Affairs." In *Ageing in Contexts of Migration*, edited by Sandra Torres and Ute Karl, 1–12. New York: Routledge. https://doi.org/10.4324/9781315817606.

Tremlett, Giles. 2010. "The Grandsons of Their Grandfathers: An Afterword." In Jerez-Farrán and Amago 2010, 327–44.

Trouillot, Michel-Rolph. 2015. *Silencing the Past: Power and the Production of History*. Boston: Beacon Press.

Tur, Bruno. 2007. "Stéréotypes et représentations sur l'immigration espagnole en France." *Migrance : Un siècle d'immigration espagnole en France* (Hors série): 69–78.
– 2015. "Del olvido al homenaje: Exiliados políticos y emigrantes económicos en las leyes memoriales españolas (2005–2007)." In Chaput et al. 2015, 63–71.
Tur, Bruno, and Maite Molina Marmol. 2009. *El mundo asociativo de la emigración española en Europa: Situaciones actuales y perspectivas del futuro.* Paris: FACEEF.
Turner, Victor. 1986. *The Anthropology of Performance.* New York: PAJ Publications.
Tusting, Karin, Roz Ivanic, and Anita Wilson. 2000. "New Literacy Studies at the Interchange." In *Situated Literacies: Reading and Writing in Context,* edited by David Barton, Mary Hamilton, and Roz Ivanic, 207–15. New York: Routledge. https://doi.org/10.4324/9780203984963.
Twigg, Julia, and Wendy Martin. 2015. "The Field of Cultural Gerontology: An Introduction." In *Routledge Handbook of Cultural Gerontology,* edited by Julia Twigg and Wendy Martin, 1–16. New York: Routledge. https://doi.org/10.4324/9780203097090.
Vertovec, Steven. 2009. *Transnationalism.* New York: Routledge. https://doi.org/10.4324/9780203927083.
Vesperi, Maria D. 1985. *City of Green Benches: Growing Old in a New Downtown.* Ithaca, NY: Cornell University Press. https://doi.org/10.7591/9781501717277.
Vincent, Mary. 2007. *Spain, 1833–2002: People and State.* New York: Oxford University Press.
Walsh, Katie, and Lena Näre, eds. 2016. *Transnational Migration and Home in Older Age.* New York: Routledge. https://doi.org/10.4324/9781315713564.
Warnes, Anthony M., Klaus Friedrich, Leonie Kellaher, and Sandra Torres. 2004. "The Diversity and Welfare of Older Migrants in Europe." *Ageing & Society* 24, no. 3 (May): 307–26. https://doi.org/10.1017/S0144686X04002296.
Warnes, Anthony M., and Allan Williams. 2006. "Older Migrants in Europe: A New Focus for Migration Studies." *Journal of Ethnic and Migration Studies* 32, no. 8 (November): 1257–81. https://doi.org/10.1080/13691830600927617.
Wertsch, James V. 2002. *Voices of Collective Remembering.* New York: Cambridge University Press. https://doi.org/10.1017/CBO9780511613715.
– 2008. "The Narrative Organization of Collective Memory." *Ethos* 36, no. 1 (March): 120–35. https://doi.org/10.1111/j.1548-1352.2008.00007.x.
– 2012. "Texts of Memory and Texts of History." *L2* 4, no. 1: 9–20. https://doi.org/10.5070/L24110007.
Wirtz, Kristina. 2007. *Ritual, Discourse, and Community in Cuban Santería: Speaking a Sacred World.* Gainesville: University Press of Florida.

- 2014. *Performing Afro-Cuba: Image, Voice, Spectacle in the Making of Race and History*. Chicago: University of Chicago Press. https://doi.org/10.7208/chicago/9780226119199.001.0001.
- 2016. "The Living, the Dead, and the Immanent: Dialogue across Chronotopes." *HAU: Journal of Ethnographic Theory* 6, no. 1 (Summer): 343–69. https://doi.org/10.14318/hau6.1.019.

Woolard, Kathryn. 2011. "Is There Linguistic Life after High School? Longitudinal Changes in the Bilingual Repertoire in Metropolitan Barcelona." *Language in Society* 40, no. 5 (November): 617–48. https://doi.org/10.1017/S0047404511000704.

- 2016. *Singular and Plural: Ideologies of Linguistic Authority in 21st Century Catalonia*. New York: Oxford University Press. https://doi.org/10.1093/acprof:oso/9780190258610.001.0001.

Wortham, Stanton. 2001. *Narratives in Action: A Strategy for Research and Analysis*. New York: Teachers College Press.

Wynn, L.L., and Mark Israel. 2018. "The Fetishes of Consent: Signatures, Paper, and Writing in Research Ethics Review." *American Anthropologist* 120, no. 4 (December): 795–806. https://doi.org/10.1111/aman.13148.

Zheng, Su. 2010. *Claiming Diaspora: Music, Transnationalism, and Cultural Politics in Asian/Chinese America*. New York: Oxford University Press.

Index

Note: The letter *f* following a page number denotes a figure.

Abascal, Santiago, 136
affect: as attachment among transnational migrants in later life, 6; through chronotopic calibration, 10, 102–6; experienced as sorrow, 57; generated by talk of pueblos, 45; and historical meaning-making, 93, 95–8, 98–101; legacy of shame, 29, 33; and memory, 64; and performance, 61, 103–6
aftermath, 14, 16, 17, 57, 136
agency: and historicity, 42; and literacy, 40, 44; moral, 24
aging: and *Back to Spain?*, 76–7; and diaspora, 6–7; dominant notions about, 42, 130; feeling young in Spanish Language class, 34, 36; ideas about "successful" aging, 24; and internet class, 118–19, 130–2; and later life, 23; and marginality, 98; as ongoing project, 9, 139; and social exclusion, 20, 129–31; and storytelling, 88–9; transnational aging, 6. *See also* generation(s); later life; migrants, Spanish labour
alfabetización (literacy), 29, 150n2
Algerian War, 98

Amalia (research participant), 3–4, 67–8; attempts to return to Spain, 67; conversations with author, 134–5, 141–2; and Córdoba, 4, 67, 142; on Franco and his regime, 68, 135, 138; "I could write a book!," 4, 10, 26; interactions with Marisol, 38–9, 107–11 (on bidonvilles).
Amparo (research participant), 3, 114, 122–6, 128
Ana (theatre teacher): compared with Pablo, 86
Andalucía, 20, 30, 32, 50, 118, 124, 146n17, 150n5
Anderson, Benedict, 111, 152n7
anti-nostalgia, 51, 65, 151n3; and social differentiation, 51–4. *See also* nostalgia
Appadurai, Arjun, 117, 118, 133
Aragón, 51
artefact(s), 11, 23, 25, 47, 96, 101, 106, 133, 139; books as, 37, 38; brochure as, 90–1, 92*f*, 100; and community formation, 26; consent forms as, 22; dictionaries as, 37, 40; in museum exhibition, 96; photocopies as, 37; photographs

artefact(s) (*continued*)
  as, 102, 111; *Untold Stories* as, 26, 139. *See also* music; poems; song(s)
Association for the Recovery of Historical Memory (ARMH), 18, 137, 154–5n2
authority: associated with written artefacts, 21, 41; claims to, through dictionary, 38; conferred through scholarly-history, 101; and institutional role, 97, 111; and institutions, 111; and modes of knowing, 25; through narratives of history, 91–2; on the past, 12, 102–6; recognized in Pablo, 37; as social meaning generated by untold stories, 11
authorship: claims to, 40–1, 56; valued by research participants, 26, 33–6, 54–8
Aznar, José María, 124–5
Azorín, José Martínez Ruiz: *El paisaje de España visto por los españoles*, 37

Back to Spain? (one-act play), 25, 68–81, 87–9; audience receptions of, 83–6, reflections on, 81–3. *See also* Lina; Pablo
Bakhtin, Mikhail: on chronotopes, 8–10, 12
Barcelona, 21, 63
Bartolone, Claude: on bidonvilles in Paris post–Second World War, 90–1
Battaglia, Debbora, 65
Bauman, Richard, 69–70, 85, 133
Belmonte, Thomas, 94
belonging: through historical knowledge, 91–2; through internet, 116–18, 121; legitimized through chronotopes, 8, 70; through narrative of return migration, 88; and nostalgia, 46; and practices of remembering, 112–13; sense at senior centre, 19; through silence, 11; through songs, 117–18; among transnational migrants in later life, 6; through use of standard language, 44
Benita (research participant), 30–1, 60, 61; and anti-nostalgia, 52–3; on impossible talk at the Centro Manuel Girón, 64; interaction with Marisol, 40; role in *Back to Spain?*, 74–5; unique literacy of, 40, 74
bidonvilles, 25, 50; history of, 92–3; museum exhibition on, 90–113, 92*f*, 102*f*, 103*f*; research participant reflections on, 103–6; "*scandale*," 91
Bienvenido, Mister Marshall! (film): scenes enacted at Centro, 86–7
Blommaert, Jan, 70, 87, 112, 155n11
bolero, 87, 115, 153n1. See also *copla*; music; song(s)
bonnes-à-tout-faire (maids-who-do-everything), 145n4. *See also* domestic service
books: as emblems of literacy, 3–4, 22, 37–9, 151n2; as embodiment of scholarly knowledge, 42; recovered from trash, 38–9; transcending time, 42–4; valued because old, 39. *See also* "I could write a book!"; literacy; poems
Boym, Svetlana, 47
Briggs, Charles, 149n38
Butler, Robert, 139

Candea, Matei, 152n4
Capp, Lisa, 11, 84
Carla (research participant): on Franco, 100; on Josep's lack of access to personal-biographical forms of knowledge, 98–101

Carmen (research participant), 30, 32, 33, 60, 61
Carolina (research participant), 33, 41; criticizes privileged classmate, 53; nostalgic essay about Valencia, 54; recites poem from father in prison, 54–7, 137–8
Casanova, Julián, 13, 60
Castilla-La Mancha, 20, 33, 128, 148n32
Castilla y León, 86, 150n5
Cataluña, 37, 63
Catholic Church: in aftermath of civil war, 13–14, 16; education system in the early years of dictatorship, 28; exhumation of Franco, 134
Cavanaugh, Jillian, 46, 84
Centro Manuel Girón, 3, 4; accommodating chronotopic tension, 36; accommodation of French speakers, 22; arts and crafts workshop, 106; benefits Spanish migrants in France, 20–2, 87; core members, 20; gendered participation, 21; internet class at, 25, 114–33; museum excursions, 25, 90–101; requirements for membership, 20; and social cohesion, 62, 64, 151n6; Spanish Language class, 24, 30–3; staff members, 21; theatre workshop, 25, 68–89. See also *Back to Spain?*; education; internet; literacy; Spanish Language class
children, 68, 81. See also grandchildren
chronotope(s), 8–9; age and aging, 9, 36; in *Back to Spain?*, 69–71, 88; Bakhtin on, 8–10; calibration through internet, 116–17, 121, 123, 127–8, 131; calibration in performance, 69; calibration in poem, 36; fusion, 10, 105–6; and identity, 112; and internet, 116–17, 121, 123, 125–8, 131; as invokable histories, 70, 87; of kinship, 44; literacy practices and, 42; migration and diaspora, 9; modernist, 70–1, 76–9, 82; of nostalgia, 47, 49, 50; present vs. past, 74, 139; and semiotic activity, 9–10, 105–6, 111; "the war," 60; workplace as, 39. See also pueblo; historicity/historicities
code-switching, 22, 51
Concepción (research participant): on reactions to play, 84–5; role in *Back to Spain?*, 76–7
concierge: work as, after migration to Paris, 38–9
Connerton, Paul, 7, 23
conocer/saber distinction: and research participants' "knowledge" of bidonvilles, 94–113, 117, 152n4. See also knowing; modes of knowing
consensus politics, 17–18, 136
consent forms, 22; as potentially troublesome for ethnographic enterprise, 149n26
copla, 125, 127–8, 131, 153n6. See also music; song(s)
Córdoba, 4, 67, 142
Covid-19, 137, 155n8
cultural performance, 69–71, 85–6, 133. See also performance

David (author): classroom interactions, 38–9, 126–7, 128; and code-switching, 22; ethnographic fieldwork, 20–2; return to field site, 86–7; revisits Amalia, 134–5, 141–2; subject position, 21–2

Degnen, Cathrine, 23
democracy: pre-Franco, 13; post-Franco, 17–18, 63, 65, 68, 121, 134, 136–7, 138
diaspora: aging and memory in 6–7; diasporic public spheres, 116; importance of return narrative in, 71; invoking pueblo in, 45; and Jews, 6–7; and later life, 7; and regimes of remembering, 46; and songs, 118; from Spain 4, 15–17. *See also* migrants, Spanish labour; transnationalism
dictatorship: agreement about, 64; dominant ideas about how to discuss, 63; economic migration officially related to, 19; educational policies, 28, 29, 35, 36; ensured through silence, 138. *See also* Franco, Francisco
Díaz, Santos Julía, 18
Dijck, José van, 117–18
domestic service, 4, 15, 145n4

education, 24; gendered attitudes towards, at Centro, 28; and limitations, 110; offerings at Centro, 27; public, under Franco, 14, 28; women's pursuit of literacy (at Centro), 29–30. *See also* Centro Manuel Girón; Franco, Francisco; literacy; Spanish Language class
Elena (research participant): advises silence on past, 57; autobiographical essay and follow-up, 58–62, 62f, 65; interaction with Josep in internet class, 115
Emilia (research participant), 102; personal knowledge of immigration, 99, 100–1
Encarnación, Omar, 14, 17

Escuela, 27, 33–4. *See also* Spanish Language class
Extremadura, 20, 101, 148n33

Faber, Sebastiaan, 12, 147n26
Falange, 13; Falangists, 60–1
Federation of Associations and Centres for Spanish Emigrants in France (FACEEF), 20
Ferrándiz, Francisco, 155n2
fieldwork, 22–3
forgetting: *pacto del olvido*, 17–18; as psychological response, 16; willful, 136. *See also* silence
flamenco, 20, 87, 118, 126, 153n6
Flores, Lola, 126
France: associated with modernity, 76–9; as destination for Spanish labour migrants, 15, 17; and difficulty for Spaniards, 35–6; 54; economic downturn in 1970s, 15; and migrants' sense of independence, 67; needs manual labour after Second World War, 15–16, 98–9; and resemblance to pueblo, 81–2; and retirement, 6, 23; and senior centres, 19, 20–1. *See also* Paris; Trente glorieuses
Franco, Francisco: benefited from emigration, 15–16, 98–9, 100; "black Spain," 126–7, 154n10; "censorship" by, 59–60, 61; death of, 17, 68; disparate memories of, 135–6; and economic stagnation, 14; education inadequate under, 28, 35, 42, 50; exhumed from memorial, 134, 135, 155n4; "gentler" post-war policies under, 14; National Catholicism under, 13–14, 16; regime of, 13–15, 18; role in civil war, 13; as taboo subject, 64–5, 124–5, 142;

Index   179

and Valley of the Fallen, 134. *See also* silence; Spanish Civil War

Gal, Susan, 20, 154n11
Galicia, 33, 74, 148n33
generation(s): communicative practices, 138; diminishing, 12, 26, 137, 155n10; identity, 11, 138, 147n25; intergenerational perspectives, 18, 62–4, 89; invoked by research participants, 33, 44; membership demonstrated through knowledge, 60–1; and music, 117–18; and narrative, 10; parenthetical generation, 5; peers, 4, 11, 29, 33, 36, 41, 44, 60, 109; younger Spaniards, 136. *See also* aging
Gil y Carrasco, Enrique: *El señor de Bembibre*, 74–5
Glick Schiller, Nina, 6
Google: taught in internet class, 120–2. *See also* internet; YouTube
Gopinath, Gayatri, 123
Graham, Helen, 5, 12, 16, 63
Granada, 28, 86
grandchildren, 24; great-grandchildren, 56; as speakers of French, 22. *See also* children

Halbwachs, Maurice, 146–7n21
Hall, Stuart, 138
Hirschkind, Charles, 118
historical memory (*memoria histórica*), 12–13, 136–7, 146–7n21, 147n27
historicity/historicities: acts of writing and, 42; Centro participants and (regarding bidonvilles), 90–113; conflated with history, 137; defined, 7–8; discrepant, 101, 135–6; ideological frameworks of, 97; juxtaposition of conflicting, 70–1; models of, 8; nostalgia and, 8, 46; personal-biographical vs. scholarly-historical modes of knowing, 93–113 passim; storytelling and, 88–9. *See also* chronotope(s); history; memory; narrative(s); remembering; storytelling
history: according to scholarly-history, 111–13; and anthropology 7–8, 12, 112; as distinct from historicity, 8; dominant accounts, 5, 17, 26; and historiography, 11; from perspective of labour migrants, 13–19; and representation, 111–13; of twentieth-century Spain, 12–19, 68, 109–10, 135–9. *See also* Franco, Francisco; historicity/historicities; Spanish Civil War

Iberia Airlines, 116, 121
"I could write a book!": Amalia's quote, 4, 10, 26, 38, 42–3, 44; Elena paraphrases, 61, 65; participants in museum excursion paraphrase, 98–101
imagination: and book about one's life, 4, 26; and museums, 111; recreates "home" from abroad through internet, 116–17, 132; and self-transformation through YouTube, 25; and types of Spaniards, 108; as way to understand history, 106
institutional review board, 22
internet: class at Centro, 114–33; and cultural inclusion, 126–8; and diasporic public spheres, 116–18; and experience of age, 118–19, 130–2; and frustration, 115, 119, 132;

internet (*continued*)
and imagination, 116–17, 132–3; and Josep's teaching methods, 118–19; and literacy, 119; and Marisol, 128–32; and memorialization, 128–33; and musical memory, 117–18, 122–5; and music videos, 116, 122–5; and pueblo, 116–17, 121, 133; and reflexivity, 132–3; searches for Spanish public figures and things, 120–1; spontaneous singing, 115, 126–8; and temporality, 121–2, 125; and use among seniors, 117–18. *See also* Molina, Antonio; Josep; technology
Irvine, Judith, 20, 154n11
It's Called Copla (televised singing competition), 125

Jews, elderly immigrants, 6–7, 23
Josep (activities director; teacher of internet class), 25, 29, 41; discourse markers used during tour, 100; leading museum excursion, 91, 94–106; Marisol dedicates song to, 128–32, 130*f*; on seniors' knowledge of history, 97–8, 101, 106; on Spaniards' silence about war, 62–3, 138; teaching internet class, 114–33; teaching methods, 119
Juliá Díaz, Santos, 18, 147n26
Julieta (research participant): role in *Back to Spain?*, 75–6

knitting, 38–9, 77
knowing: Belmonte on, 94; Candea on, 152n4. *See also* modes of knowing
Koven, Michele, 109

Labanyi, Jo, 17–18, 147n27
language ideology/ideologies, 7, 30, 32–3, 41–4, 146n11; challenging monolingual norms, 52; standard language, 43
Laslett, Peter, 23
later life, 23–4; and the acquisition of knowledge, 42; and literacy, 33–6. *See also* aging; migrants, Spanish labour
Law of Children of the War, 18, 147n27
Law of Democratic Memory, 148n28, 154–5n2
Law of Historical Memory, 17–18, 134, 147n27, 154n2
Law of Political Responsibilities, 16
Lengua castellana (class), 27. *See also* Escuela; Spanish Language class
Levitt, Peggy, 6
life stories, 22–3, 149n38
Lillo, Natacha, 21, 38
Lina (research participant): autobiographical role in *Back to Spain?*, 79, 81–3, 88; comedic sketches in *Back to Spain?*, 76–9, 83; poem and poetry recitation, 33–6, 40–1, 129–30
literacy: acquired in later life, 33–6, 114–33; and agency, 40; avoidance of term in Spanish, 29; "basics" of, 30–1, 35; books symbolize, 37–9; class, at Centro, 27–44; gender and, 28; and moral rectitude, 40; national affiliation and, 42; stigmatization, 150n2; and time, 30, 42; valued by women, 37–41. *See also* education; literate subjectivity; Spanish Language class
literacy events, 46
literate subjectivity, 24, 29–30, 33, 42, 44, 53; explicit claims to, 40–1, 151n2; as language ideology, 146n11; and material artefacts 38;

stigma of illiteracy, 150n2. *See also* education; literacy; Spanish Language class

machismo, 28
Madrid, 48, 107
Manuel (research participant), 72; reaction to *Back to Spain?* performance, 83–4
María (research participant), 37
Marisol (research participant): account of pueblo, 48–51; brings ribald joke book to class, 38–9; claims to read in French, 40; dedicates rap song to Josep, 128–32; difficulty with spelling, 40; knowledge of YouTube, 122–3, 124, 125; on learning internet skills, 119; and memories of bidonville, 102–13, 103f; as Navalcán terremoto, 128, 130f; as student of Spanish Language class, 27–8, 31, 32, 37
Marshall, George C., 86
Marta (research participant), 114–15, 119, 121, 126, 127
mass graves, 18, 134, 136, 154–5n2
memorialization, 26, 37–9, 44; through *Untold Stories*, 139; on YouTube, 128–33
memory: collective, 123, 146–7n21; laws, 18; as personal recollection, 8. *See also* historical memory; nostalgia; remembering; silence
men: machismo, 28; resistant to education/conversation, 21, 28
metaphors/personification: used in teaching technology to seniors, 119
Mexico City, 21, 31
migrants, Spanish labour (seniors): absent from official historiographies, 5, 26, 52; and aging 6–7; contrasted with political exiles, 5, 19, 52, 145n7; and exogamous relationships, 3, 22; and French language, 16, 20, 51; heading to northern Europe, 15; mentality of impermanence, 16; mobility in France (1945–75), 15–16; in Paris (1959–73), 15; preference for speaking Spanish, 22; reasons for leaving Spain, 135; remaining in France, 16–17, 68; return from France to Spain, 7, 17, 67–89; return narratives of, 70–1; and social distinction, 51–4; and social status after migrating, 16, 67–8, 79; state support for, 18–19, 68; temporariness, 15, 72; "third wave" in Paris, 15, 19; as untold story, 5, 138. *See also Back to Spain?*; literacy; remembering; *and individual research participant names*
milagro español (Spanish miracle), 16–17, 68
mi pueblo, 45–6, 48. *See also* pueblo
modernization, 14, 16, 118; desire for "hypermodernity," 17; lack of recognition of labour migrants' participation in, 68; as national project, 5
modes of knowing 25, 91, 93–101; and chronotopes, 9–10; claims to moral personhood and, 108–11; *saber* vs. *conocer*, 93–4, 97–100; scholarly-historical vs. personal-biographical, 9, 93–4. *See also* chronotope(s); historicity/historicities; literacy; remembering; storytelling
Molina, Antonio, 114, 123, 126–8, 131
moral personhood, 9, 24, 46, 86, 94, 109; and linguistic proficiency, 40;

moral personhood (*continued*)
  and literate subjectivity, 38–40;
  and social differentiation, 106–11
Morancos, Los, 124–5
Müller, Jan-Werner, 136
multilingualism: at Centro, 22;
  of Benita, 31; of Paula, 51; as
  scholarly knowledge, 110
Murcia, 37
museum(s) 3; claims to appreciation,
  52–3; as cultural institution,
  91; excursions to, 20–1; pueblo
  lacks, 48
Museum of Art and History of Saint-
  Denis: exhibition on bidonvilles,
  90, 92*f*
music: as embodied memory,
  117–18; Marisol's YouTube rap
  song, 129–33; recreates homelands
  in Spain, 117–18, 122–3, 133;
  spontaneous singing, 115, 126–7;
  and temporality, 121–2, 125. *See
  also* bolero; *copla*; internet; song(s)
Myerhoff, Barbara: on elderly Jewish
  immigrants to US, 6–7, 23, 45

narrative(s): and authenticity, 85;
  and chronotopes, 10; constructed
  in field work, 143; of elderly on
  Spanish history, 137–8; and figures
  of personhood, 109; "forbidden,"
  63, 138; and history, 91–2; as
  interactional performances, 10,
  95–6, 98–9, 103–5; as linchpin
  between individual and
  communities, 10; and memory,
  11; and official representations,
  111–13; and phenomenological
  experience, 89, 110; and polyvocal
  perspectives, 87–9; and return
  migration, 68–9, 71–2; revealed
  through friendship, 142; revealing
  discursive effects of living in
  time, 138; and silence, 10–11; as
  textual resources, 10; and untold
  stories, 10–12, 55, 61–2. *See also*
  chronotope(s); historicity/
  historicities; storytelling; tellability
National Catholicism, 13–14, 16
National Economic Stabilization
  Plan, 15, 98
National Institute of Emigration, 15
Nationalists, 7, 13, 14, 147n23; ideal
  of autonomy, 14
Navalcán terremoto, 128, 130*f*.
  See also Marisol
Neugarten, Bernice, 23
Nora, Pierre, 137, 146–7n21
nostalgia: in *Back to Spain?*, 75–6,
  79–81; as chronotope, 47; defined,
  46; internet nurtures, 120–33;
  music evokes in seniors, 118,
  122–3; perceived as problem, 53;
  for place of origin, 75; as regime
  of historicity, 46; replaced by
  pragmatism, 51–4; and rupture,
  47; veils war memories, 63–5.
  See also anti-nostalgia; narrative(s);
  pueblo; remembering; silence;
  Spain
Nuria (research participant): reasons
  for attending Spanish Language
  class, 43–4

Ochs, Elinor, 11, 84
older adults. *See* aging; later life

Pablo (teacher of Spanish Language
  class and theatre workshop), 24,
  27–8, 31; assigns writings about
  pueblos, 45; devises and directs
  play, 72–89 passim; encourages
  narratives about memories of war,
  58–60, 63–4, 84–5; encourages

students to "go further," 71–2, 85, 87; and reflexivity, 61, 72, 74, 84, 85; teaching methods, 31–2, 37, 44, 58–60, 71, 84–5; on women's yearning, 43. *See also* Ana; *Back to Spain?*
pacto del olvido (pact of forgetting): and democratic transition, 17; as "institutionalized amnesia," 19
País, El, 116, 119, 120–1, 150n5, 155n8
Paquita (research participant), 31, 32–3
parenthetical generation, 5
Paris, 19, 67, 148n33, 151n1, 152n1; advantages and disadvantages for labour migrants, 15; and bidonvilles 92–3, 100; desired destination for Spanish migrants, 15; events of 1968, 67–8, 151n1; navigating public transportation in, 30; perceptions of cosmopolitanism and, 49, 52; resembling pueblo, 81–2; return to, in *Back to Spain?*, 81. *See also* France
Parmentier, Richard, 111
Paula (research participant): anti-nostalgia, 51–2
performance: of essays in Spanish Language class, 46, 58–60; of monologue in *Back to Spain?*, 79; of poems, 33–4, 54; rap by Marisol, 128–32; and reflexivity, 70; and stancetaking, 70; in theatre workshop, 72–81. See also *Back to Spain?*; cultural performance; music; poems; song(s)
Petite Espagne, La: book, 21; neighborhood, 20
Pitié-Salpêtrière, La, 141
poems, 33–4, 55–6, 79–80; gift from research participant, 41

political exiles, 5, 19, 52, 145n7
poverty: and Andalucía, 32; associated with bidonvilles, 107, 111–12; associated with labour migrants as opposed to political exiles, 52; and denial by Spaniards who did not migrate, 107–8; and expressions of nostalgia, 53; Franco's neglect of, 14; migration to escape from, 15; personal recollection of, 107–9, 111–12. *See also* bidonvilles
Preston, Paul, 13, 137, 147n23
pueblo: chronotopic contrast with city, 48–9; connotations of, 47, 48, 116; depictions of eccentric villagers in *Back to Spain?*, 76–9; essays about, 48, 54, 85; on Google, 121; and internet class, 116; "mi pueblo," 45–6, 48; nostalgia for, 47–51, 130–1; represented for public display, 47; and rurality, 47, 49; writing assignment about (in Spanish Language class), 45. *See also* nostalgia; Spain; Spanish Language class

Rajoy, Mariano, 120–1, 148n30, 153n4
red (colour), 59–61
reflexivity: among audience, 83–6; cultural performance and, 69–71; Pablo encourages, 61, 72, 74, 84, 85; in performance, 71–83, 133; regimes of, 83–6; resistance to, 85
rehearsal(s), 72–81. *See also* performance
remembering, 26, 109, 136, 139; difficult for senior students, 119; and emotion, 10, 101; and ideologies about the past, 64; modes of (for seniors), 7; politics of, 88; as productive for victims

remembering (*continued*)
  of war, 66; and seniors' use of internet, 117. *See also* narrative; nostalgia; silence; storytelling; untold stories
remittances, 16, 67, 99, 100, 151n2
Republicans, 13, 147n23
resignification, 154n1
retirement, 6, 23–4, 82; acquiring technological skills in, 119
return migration: failed attempt at, 67–8, 81–3; meaningful trope among labour migrants, 68; and the modernist chronotope, 70–1, 76–9, 87–8; personal reflections on, 81–3; polyvocal representation of, 97–9; reactions to performance of, 83–6; staged in *Back to Spain?*, 68–89, 69f, 72–81. See also *Back to Spain?*; chronotope(s); migrants, Spanish labour; narrative(s)
return visits to Spain, 15, 40, 45, 50, 54, 109
Richards, Michael, 12, 14, 65
Ricoeur, Paul, 88
Rosa (research participant): in *Back to Spain?*, 72–4
Rosario (research participant): on educational background, 28–9; nostalgic about pueblo, 50
Rubin, Johan S., 136

saber/conocer distinction: and research participants' "knowledge" of bidonvilles, 94–113, 117, 152n4. *See also* knowing; modes of knowing
Safeway, 142
Sánchez, Pedro, 134
Santander 20, 57–8, 121
seamstress(es), 4, 33
Second Republic, 13

Second World War, 15, 86, 90, 145n6
Seine-Saint-Denis, 92–3, 152n1
Señor de Bembibre, El (Gil y Carrasco), 74–5
seniors. *See* aging; migrants, Spanish labour
shame: described in poem, 33–6; for lack of literacy, 29, 33, 35, 40, 41, 42, 150n2
sherry, 3, 4, 22
silence, 10–11, 14, 17–18, 19, 24, 57, 135, 137–8, 143; to avoid reflexivity, 57, 84, 85; Benita on, 64–5; as condition for the intelligibility of language, 138; "conspiracy of," 138; as destructive, 65; distinct from forgetting, 65; Elena and, 59–62, 65; as mode of engagement with the past, 46; nostalgia veils, 64–5; "obstinate," 57–62; Pablo advises breaking, 61–2; recollection replaces (1999–), 18. *See also* forgetting; Franco, Francisco; narrative(s); Spanish Civil War; untold stories
Silence of Others, The (film), 154–5n2
Silva, Emilio, 137
Silverstein, Paul, 19
social differentiation: and anti-nostalgia, 51–4; and chronotopic variation, 71; through discrepant narratives about the past, 69; through the invocation of particular chronotopes, 9; literacy as a point of reference, 32; through modes of knowing, 93–4; and moral personhood, 106–11
song(s): "Adiós a España," 114; "Cocinero, cocinero," 126–8; as cultural performance, 133; "Espinita," 115; "La hija de Juan Simón," 128–9, 131; public

performance at Centro, 45; rap by Marisol, 128–9. *See also* bolero; *copla*; music
Spain: benefits from contributions of labour migrants, 15–16, 67–8, 99, 100; conjured through Google/YouTube, 120–33; government funds senior centres, 4, 18–19; hierarchy among citizens, 32; history of, 12–19, 109–10, 135–9; internet/music recreates for diasporic subjects, 116–18; migrants' return to (in play), 67–89. *See also* Franco, Francisco; migrants, Spanish labour; Spanish Civil War
Spaniards: categorized by attitudes, 107–10; mentality of impermanence among migrants, 16; practices of consumption in 1960s, 16; regional stereotypes, 20; and relationship to language, 20, 38, 41–3; Spaniards in France vs. Spanish Spaniards, 109. *See also* migrants, Spanish labour; Spain
Spanish Civil War, 3, 4, 13–14; avoidance of topic through silence, 64–6; legacies of, 12; memory of revived, 18; repressive aftermath, 13–15, 28, 35, 57; seniors' recollections of, 59–62; and Valley of the Fallen / Valley of Cuelgamuros, 134; and victimhood, 18. *See also* Franco, Francisco; historicity/historicities; silence
Spanish Holocaust, The, 13
Spanish Language class, 27; the "basics" of, 28, 35; and essay assignment, 45–6; and gendered participation, 28; and hierarchy among students, 33; perceptions of difficulty, 27–8, 29, 31, 35–6, 48; and praise for "merit" of peers, 32, 35, 40; and preoccupation with spelling, 32; and sense of lack, 29, 35, 42–3; and sense of shame, 29, 35; standard language ideology, 43. *See also* Escuela; nostalgia
Statute of Spanish Citizenry Abroad, 18–19
storytelling, 22–3; as apolitical practice, 87; claiming rights to, 88; "forbidden," 138; historicity and, 88–9; as legitimizing, 26; "memory talk" among seniors, 23; and "untold stories," 11, 109–10, 137–9. *See also* narrative(s); silence; untold stories

technology: limited experience among seniors, 115; peripherals, 114–16. *See also* Google; internet; literacy; YouTube
Tejero Molina, Antonio, 124–5, 153n7–8
tellability, 11, 25, 84
tercera edad (third age), 23–4, 33–6
theatre workshop. See *Back to Spain?*
Toledo, 40, 48, 50
transition, 7, 17, 65, 138, 153–4n7
transnationalism, 6; and ideological systems, 112; and perceptions of marginality, 98; migration sanctioned, 15, 98; research overlooks older populations, 146n9. *See also* diaspora; migrants, Spanish labour
Trente glorieuses (Thirty Glorious Years), 15, 90
Trouillot, Michel-Rolph, 9
Turner, Victor, 151n4

untold stories, 5, 58–62, 86–7, 137–9, 143; and "Franco," 135; and social meaning, 11
Valencia 32, 54–6, 148n33

Valley of the Fallen / Valley of
 Cuelgamuros, 134, 135, 154n1, 155n3
Verónica (research participant): in
 Back to Spain?, 76–9
Vox (political party), 136–7

Wirtz, Kristina, 87–8, 91
women: receptive toward education/
 conversation at Centro, 21, 24, 28;
 value literacy, 37–41. *See also* men;
 Spanish Language class

World Book Day, 71, 123; play
 presented at, 68–89, 69f; senior
 writings to honour, 45–6

YouTube: and Marisol's self-
 expression, 128–33; taught in
 internet class, 122–5; valued for
 access to music, 116

Zapatero, José Luís Rodríguez, 116,
 120–1, 153n4

Anthropological Horizons

Editor: Michael Lambek, University of Toronto

The Varieties of Sensory Experience: A Sourcebook in the Anthropology of the Senses/Edited by David Howes (1991)
Arctic Homeland: Kinship, Community, and Development in Northwest Greenland/Mark Nuttall (1992)
Knowledge and Practice in Mayotte: Local Discourses of Islam, Sorcery, and Spirit Possession/Michael Lambek (1993)
Deathly Waters and Hungry Mountains: Agrarian Ritual and Class Formation in an Andean Town/Peter Gose (1994)
Paradise: Class, Commuters, and Ethnicity in Rural Ontario/Stanley R. Barrett (1994)
The Cultural World in Beowulf/John M. Hill (1995)
Making It Their Own: Severn Ojibwe Communicative Practices/Lisa Philips Valentine (1995)
Merchants and Shopkeepers: A Historical Anthropology of an Irish Market Town, 1200–1991/P.H. Gulliver and Marilyn Silverman (1995)
Tournaments of Value: Sociability and Hierarchy in a Yemeni Town/Ann Meneley (1996)
Mal'uocchiu: Ambiguity, Evil Eye, and the Language of Distress/Sam Migliore (1997)
Between History and Histories: The Making of Silences and Commemorations/Edited by Gerald Sider and Gavin Smith (1997)
Eh, Paesan! Being Italian in Toronto/Nicholas DeMaria Harney (1998)
Theorizing the Americanist Tradition/Edited by Lisa Philips Valentine and Regna Darnell (1999)
Colonial "Reformation" in the Highlands of Central Sulawesi, Indonesia, 1892–1995/Albert Schrauwers (2000)
The Rock Where We Stand: An Ethnography of Women's Activism in Newfoundland/Glynis George (2000)

"Being Alive Well": Health and the Politics of Cree Well-Being/Naomi Adelson (2000)
Irish Travellers: Racism and the Politics of Culture/Jane Helleiner (2001)
Of Property and Propriety: The Role of Gender and Class in Imperialism and Nationalism/Edited by Himani Bannerji, Shahrzad Mojab, and Judith Whitehead (2001)
An Irish Working Class: Explorations in Political Economy and Hegemony, 1800–1950/Marilyn Silverman (2001)
The Double Twist: From Ethnography to Morphodynamics/Edited by Pierre Maranda (2001)
The House of Difference: Cultural Politics and National Identity in Canada/Eva Mackey (2002)
Writing and Colonialism in Northern Ghana: The Encounter between the LoDagaa and "the World on Paper," 1892–1991/Sean Hawkins (2002)
Guardians of the Transcendent: An Ethnography of a Jain Ascetic Community/Anne Vallely (2002)
The Hot and the Cold: Ills of Humans and Maize in Native Mexico/Jacques M. Chevalier and Andrés Sánchez Bain (2003)
Figured Worlds: Ontological Obstacles in Intercultural Relations/Edited by John Clammer, Sylvie Poirier, and Eric Schwimmer (2004)
Revenge of the Windigo: The Construction of the Mind and Mental Health of North American Aboriginal Peoples/James B. Waldram (2004)
The Cultural Politics of Markets: Economic Liberalization and Social Change in Nepal/Katharine Neilson Rankin (2004)
A World of Relationships: Itineraries, Dreams, and Events in the Australian Western Desert/Sylvie Poirier (2005)
The Politics of the Past in an Argentine Working-Class Neighbourhood/Lindsay DuBois (2005)
Youth and Identity Politics in South Africa, 1990–1994/Sibusisiwe Nombuso Dlamini (2005)
Maps of Experience: The Anchoring of Land to Story in Secwepemc Discourse/Andie Diane Palmer (2005)
We Are Now a Nation: Croats between "Home" and "Homeland"/Daphne N. Winland (2007)
Beyond Bodies: Rainmaking and Sense Making in Tanzania/Todd Sanders (2008)
Kaleidoscopic Odessa: History and Place in Contemporary Ukraine/Tanya Richardson (2008)
Invaders as Ancestors: On the Intercultural Making and Unmaking of Spanish Colonialism in the Andes/Peter Gose (2008)
From Equality to Inequality: Social Change among Newly Sedentary Lanoh Hunter-Gatherer Traders of Peninsular Malaysia/Csilla Dallos (2011)
Rural Nostalgias and Transnational Dreams: Identity and Modernity among Jat Sikhs/Nicola Mooney (2011)

Dimensions of Development: History, Community, and Change in Allpachico, Peru/Susan Vincent (2012)

People of Substance: An Ethnography of Morality in the Colombian Amazon/Carlos David Londoño Sulkin (2012)

"We Are Still Didene": Stories of Hunting and History from Northern British Columbia/Thomas McIlwraith (2012)

Being Māori in the City: Indigenous Everyday Life in Auckland/Natacha Gagné (2013)

The Hakkas of Sarawak: Sacrificial Gifts in Cold War Era Malaysia/Kee Howe Yong (2013)

Remembering Nayeche and the Gray Bull Engiro: African Storytellers of the Karamoja Plateau and the Plains of Turkana/Mustafa Kemal Mirzeler (2014)

In Light of Africa: Globalizing Blackness in Northeast Brazil/Allan Charles Dawson (2014)

The Land of Weddings and Rain: Nation and Modernity in Post-Socialist Lithuania/Gediminas Lankauskas (2015)

Milanese Encounters: Public Space and Vision in Contemporary Urban Italy/Cristina Moretti (2015)

Legacies of Violence: History, Society, and the State in Sardinia/Antonio Sorge (2015)

Looking Back, Moving Forward: Transformation and Ethical Practice in the Ghanaian Church of Pentecost/Girish Daswani (2015)

Why the Porcupine Is Not a Bird: Explorations in the Folk Zoology of an Eastern Indonesian People/Gregory Forth (2016)

The Heart of Helambu: Ethnography and Entanglement in Nepal/Tom O'Neill (2016)

Tournaments of Value: Sociability and Hierarchy in a Yemeni Town, 20th Anniversary Edition/Ann Meneley (2016)

Europe Un-Imagined: Nation and Culture at a French-German Television Channel/Damien Stankiewicz (2017)

Transforming Indigeneity: Urbanization and Language Revitalization in the Brazilian Amazon/Sarah Shulist (2018)

Wrapping Authority: Women Islamic Leaders in a Sufi Movement in Dakar, Senegal/Joseph Hill (2018)

Island in the Stream: An Ethnographic History of Mayotte/Michael Lambek (2018)

Materializing Difference: Consumer Culture, Politics, and Ethnicity among Romanian Roma/Péter Berta (2019)

Virtual Activism: Sexuality, the Internet, and a Social Movement in Singapore/Robert Phillips (2020)

Shadow Play: Information Politics in Urban Indonesia/Sheri Lynn Gibbins (2021)

Suspect Others: Spirit Mediums, Self-Knowledge, and Race in Multiethnic Suriname/Stuart Earle Strange (2021)

Exemplary Life: Modelling Sainthood in Christian Syria/Andreas Bandak (2022)
Without the State: Self-Organization and Political Activism in Ukraine/Emily Channell-Justice (2022)
Moral Figures: Making Reproduction Public in Vanuatu/Alexandra Widmer (2023)
Truly Human: Indigeneity and Indigenous Resurgence on Formosa/Scott E. Simon (2023)
Moving Words: Literature, Memory, and Migration in Berlin/Andrew Brandel (2023)
Untold Stories: Legacies of Authoritarianism among Spanish Labour Migrants in Later Life/David Divita (2024)

Printed and bound by CPI Group (UK) Ltd, Croydon, CR0 4YY

31/08/2025

14727201-0002